TERRORISM IN AMERICAN MEMORY

Terrorism in American Memory

*Memorials, Museums, and Architecture
in the Post-9/11 Era*

Marita Sturken

NEW YORK UNIVERSITY PRESS
New York

NEW YORK UNIVERSITY PRESS
New York
www.nyupress.org

© 2022 by New York University
All rights reserved

References to Internet websites (URLs) were accurate at the time of writing. Neither the author nor New York University Press is responsible for URLs that may have expired or changed since the manuscript was prepared.

Library of Congress Cataloging-in-Publication Data
Names: Sturken, Marita, 1957– author.
Title: Terrorism in American memory : memorials, museums, and architecture in the post-9/11 era / Marita Sturken.
Description: New York : New York University Press, [2021] |
Includes bibliographical references and index.
Identifiers: LCCN 2021011564 | ISBN 9781479811670 (hardback ; alk. paper) | ISBN 9781479811687 (paperback ; alk. paper) | ISBN 9781479811717 (ebook) | ISBN 9781479811700 (ebook other)
Subjects: LCSH: September 11 Terrorist Attacks, 2001—Social aspects. | Terrorism—United States—History—21st century. | Collective memory—United States. | Memorials—United States. | Museums—United States. | United States—Social conditions—1980–
Classification: LCC HV6432.7 .S785 2021 | DDC 363.32509747/109051—dc23
LC record available at https://lccn.loc.gov/2021011564

New York University Press books are printed on acid-free paper, and their binding materials are chosen for strength and durability. We strive to use environmentally responsible suppliers and materials to the greatest extent possible in publishing our books.

Manufactured in the United States of America

10 9 8 7 6 5 4 3 2 1

Also available as an ebook

In memory of my mother
Marie Ryan Sturken
1921–2018

CONTENTS

Introduction: The Politics of Memory in the Post-9/11 Era   1

1. Monuments and Voids: The Proliferation of 9/11 Memory   25

2. The Objects That Lived, the Voices That Remain: The 9/11 Museum   77

3. Global Architecture, Patriotic Skyscrapers, and a Cathedral Shopping Mall: The Rebuilding of Lower Manhattan   129

4. Visibility and Erasure: Memory and the Global War on Terror   172

5. The Memory of Racial Terror: The Legacy Museum and the National Memorial for Peace and Justice   221

Conclusion   265

Acknowledgments   269

Notes   273

Bibliography   289

Index   303

About the Author   321

Introduction

The Politics of Memory in the Post-9/11 Era

In late May and June of 2020, in the midst of the COVID-19 pandemic, the cities and towns of the United States erupted into protests over the killing by Minneapolis police of George Floyd on May 25, a killing that was documented on video and shared widely on social media. Protests in opposition to police violence against Black citizens, many of them led by Black Lives Matter, had been taking place for years, but what happened in the summer of 2020 was different. Not only did very large numbers of people turn out, conveying the sense that anger over these ongoing deaths had accumulated, but these protests also began to turn to the Confederate monuments, the statues of Christopher Columbus, the numerous symbols of white power and history that had been set in stone over long periods of time. People had been agitating for the removal of many of these statues for decades, arguing that they were symbols of racism in the present. In the summer of 2020, these monuments suddenly began to fall, either through the collective action of the crowds or as institutions and political officials made rapid decisions for their removal. The removal and destruction of so many monuments revealed a shift in public discussion about race, nation, and memory and a surging of memories of racial violence that had long been suppressed. Was this a new era in the politics of memory in the United States?

In the months that followed, a time of enormous political drama and upheaval, the grim and frightening toll of the COVID-19 pandemic continued to rise, the tallies of the dead climbing daily. Media commentators attempted to make sense of the numbers by comparing them to previous crises in American history. Throughout December 2020 and into January 2021, they noted that more people were dying each day than had died on 9/11. When the death toll reached over four hundred thousand in January 2021, many observed that the number of dead now exceeded the number of US soldiers who had died in World War II. As the historical comparisons continued, they began to seem futile, if not absurd. As cartoonist Rob Rogers notes, the 3,124 deaths on December 9, 2020, compared to the 9/11 dead, was "just another Wednesday." Such a comparison revealed, of course, that the deaths from the pandemic had been dramatically undervalued and unmourned in the national context, compared to the 2,977 victims of 9/11 whose deaths have been the subject of an enormous number of memorials and tributes.

The entire first two decades of the twenty-first century were a time of remarkable upheaval—culturally, economically, and politically—resulting in dramatic changes to national self-identity and to the image of the United States in the world. During these two decades, the country endured terrorist attacks, engaged in ongoing wars of aggression, divided into increasingly polarized factions, and was extraordinarily preoccupied with memorialization. The country's obsession with memorialization and debates about memory reveal the ways that national identity is often negotiated, fought over, projected, and asserted through conflicts over who is remembered and how. This era began with the terrorist attacks of September 11, 2001, soon encapsulated in the term *9/11*, which immediately produced a demand for memorialization, and culminated in 2020 with the protests over police brutality that demanded the removal of historical monuments to racist historical figures. It also led to a reassertion of traditional American history myths as a form of backlash to these demands and a right-wing attack on the US Capitol, the symbol of the government, on January 6, 2021. In these events, cultural memory became a battleground for negotiations of national identity because it is a field through which the past is experienced in the present. This leads us to a set of questions: How do the processes of memorialization of traumatic events shape our current understandings of nation, race, and the United States as a nation and global force? How does the process of collective memorialization transform the victims of violence, war, and trauma into figures of a national narrative? What roles do design and architecture play in the shaping of these memories? And why does memory continue to matter so much in the post-9/11 era of the United States, an era of upheaval and social change?

In her sweeping history of the United States, *These Truths*, Jill Lepore defines the last two decades of US history as an era of disruption. The

Cartoon by Rob Rogers. Rogers © 2020. Reprinted by permission of Andrew McMeel Syndication. All rights reserved.

shocking event of 9/11 is merely one of many events that define disruption for Lepore in this era, which followed several decades of relatively stable political and economic shifts since the upheaval of the 1960s. This included not only the potential crisis of Y2K at the end of 1999; the 2008 election of Barack Obama, the first Black president; the emergence of social movements such as the Tea Party, Occupy, and Black Lives Matter; the Patriot Act and the wars in Afghanistan and Iraq; and the election of Donald Trump in 2016.[1] This era also included disruptions of entire industries, from journalism and publishing to advertising and retail to travel and transportation; saw the rise to dominance of the tech industry and social media; and felt the pain of widespread job loss in the manufacturing sector as a result of automation and global outsourcing. It has also seen the disruptions of the financial crises of 2008, the rise of financialization as a global force, the class divisions and increased inequality arising from economic hardship in whole areas of the country, and the global climate emergencies of wildfires, melting Artic ice, increasing numbers of hurricanes and typhoons, and crippling drought. In the last few years, these disruptions have only been magnified, with the impeachments of Donald Trump, the devastating impact of the pandemic and global economic crisis of 2020–21, the uprisings and protests over police brutality of Black citizens, the chaos of the 2020 election, and the attack on the US Capitol in January 2021. Disruption can act as a force that demands more of national narratives, which bend toward themes of heroism and sacrifice to restore pride and provide comfort. Disruption can also bring out divides and divisions, scapegoating and othering, because of the fear, insecurity, and desperation it can sow. And it can open new feelings, new ways of thinking, and demands for change.

The overabundance of 9/11 memory, which I discuss in chapter 1, demonstrates the powerful role of social unity and communalism that memory is intended to play, in particular in moments of disruption. The need to memorialize those who died on September 11, 2001, was immediate and politically charged from the beginning. Memorialization can operate as a form of social cohesion that is needed more during times when other modes of cohesion are failing; 9/11 memory, which has largely been a patriotic and nationally affirming enterprise, has provided comforting narratives of national unity whose coherence required that many aspects of the event be excluded. Memorialization can also be a site for contestation, disruption, and intervention. The Legacy Museum and National Memorial for Peace and Justice in Montgomery, Alabama, which opened in 2018 to commemorate those who were lynched in the South and beyond, which I discuss in chapter 5, is the polar opposite of 9/11 memorialization in terms of its relationship to concepts of national unity. It is a radical intervention into the narratives of the history of race relations in the United States, exposing the absence of memorialization for those Black people who were oppressed, terrorized, and lynched. In other words, it disrupts the uplifting story of race relations in the United States, demanding a rewriting of the script. These two examples, the memorialization of the victims of 9/11 and the memorialization of the victims of lynching, demonstrate the polarized strategies of memory in this era, with 9/11 memory as a form of nationalistic exceptionalism and the memorialization of racial terror as a form of memory activism that critiques the nation. These memorial projects anchor the beginning and the end of the book. My aim in coupling them is to examine both how they define the beginning and the end of the post-9/11 era and how seeing them on a continuum of national-memory projects challenges the divide between traditional US definitions of foreign terrorism and domestic terrorism.

That the public act of memorialization is manifested within particular forms—memorials, museums, and buildings—is key to the analysis in this book. Architecture and design have been particularly burdened with the role of shaping and guiding the emotional weight of traumatic events, designing both for loss and grief and for renewal and resilience. This book thus aims to understand the defining features of the post-9/11 era—and what characterizes its beginning and end—in relation to memory responses to terrorism within the framework of design and architecture. This spans not only the design of the 9/11 museum, the Legacy Museum, and other memorials but also the architectural rebuilding at Ground Zero and the complex negotiations of the demand for symbolism in those buildings.

Memory politics reveals the dynamics of collective grieving, an unearthing of the guiding ethos that determines who among us are considered worthy of being remembered, mourned, and grieved and who are seen as outside the category of the "grievable life," as defined by Judith Butler.[2] But those deaths that are defined as being outside the grievable life haunt the national story, for they are never fully erased, never unremembered. Their stories infiltrate; they are in the dirt, as the lynching memorial soil collection project contends. As Avery Gordon has written, haunting "alters the experience of being in time, the way we separate the past, the present, and the future. These specters or ghosts appear when the trouble they represent and symptomize is no longer being contained or repressed or blocked from view."[3]

Grief, loss, grievance, and anger are all emotions that emerge in these contexts of memorialization. Erika Doss argues that events like 9/11 demand a response of "public feelings." She writes:

> Contemporary American memorials embody the feelings of particular publics at particular historical moments, and frame cultural narratives about self identity and national purpose.... The affective conditions of contemporary commemoration—and public culture in general—do not foreclose the possibilities of social and political transformation. Rather feelings are cultivated and as such can be mobilized; affect has agency.[4]

The public feelings activated by processes of memory can thus be generative. The proliferation of 9/11 memorials gave rise to a complex array of public feelings about those killed that day that then produced additional feelings of patriotism and revenge. The battles over the Confederate monuments and memorials of racist pasts are as much about feelings—of grievance, of being left out, unseen, and threatened—as they are about affirming the ideologies of the Confederacy. The feelings of grief and injustice evoked by the lynching memorial in Alabama are activated toward social justice actions in the present.

The post-9/11 era gave rise to intensely patriotic and nationalistic sentiments in response to the 9/11 attacks and the threat of global terrorism at the same time that it released the ghosts of domestic racial terrorism embedded within US history. The first two decades of the twenty-first century were defined by the fear of foreign-based terrorism, a fear that shaped US policy and xenophobia. Yet at the end of this era, it was an uncontainable virus rather than terrorists that would bring the country to its knees and that constituted the broadest and deepest disruption. By the end of the century's second decade, the crisis of the pandemic exacerbated existing tensions, and the divisions of the country exploded into view. If the nation seemed to crack open in 2020, it was the dramatic shock of the pandemic—the deaths, the lockdowns, and the economic turmoil—that opened a space in which norms could be questioned, because norms had ceased to exist. And within that disruption, new stories emerged, new memories were unearthed, and the story of the nation was challenged.

The Post-9/11 Era

The post-9/11 era can be defined as the time period in which the 9/11 event, and all that followed in its wake, was the primary shaping aspect of US culture and society. From this one event, which shocked a nation oblivious to its capacity to engender such hatred for its foreign policy and its imperial strategies, emerged a culture of nationalism and excess patriotism, of revenge and Islamophobia, of fear of the racialized Other, of securitization and defense and a ramped up bellicosity that fueled two wars and the so-called global war on terror under the guise of national defense. The tide of nationalistic fervor provided significant public support for the wars in Afghanistan (begun in 2001) and Iraq (begun with the invasion of Baghdad in 2003), which were some of the first full-scale wars of volunteer armies in US history and whose forces also included National Guard troops who had not signed up for war duty. These wars propelled the country into deep imperial ventures for years before the US public began to sour on them, in particular on the war in Iraq. By the mid-2000s, as awareness of the conflict's futility and false national-security pretext grew, the powerful narrative of 9/11, now instantiated in memorialization, began to break free of the narrative that the wars in Afghanistan and Iraq would resolve the conflict that the US public believed had begun on that day and not before.

In this era, the integration of security procedures into daily life was a constant reminder for US citizens that they were under threat. The truth, however, was that the populations who were most under threat and would suffer most in the aftermath of 9/11 were far from US borders and outside America's dominant mainstream culture—the hundreds of thousands in the Middle East, in Iraq and Afghanistan, in Yemen and Syria, who were killed, maimed, and displaced and the tens of thousands of Muslims and immigrants within the United States who were othered and threatened.[5] By 2020, it was estimated that at least thirty-seven million people had been displaced by America's war on terror.[6] The election of Barack Obama in 2008 signaled a potential shift toward progressive politics after the hard-right politics of the Bush-Cheney administration. Yet Obama was both unwilling and unable to fully pull back from the post 9/11 wars or to close the appalling, illegal, and globally criticized prison in Guantánamo, and he amped up the troops and the drone war during his administration as a result. The financial crisis of 2008 pulled the national conversation back from the post-9/11 wars to the domestic front and exposed inequality and the precarity of vast numbers of the US population, which further fractured and polarized US politics. Outrage over the bank bailouts of 2008 and the lack of protection for ordinary mortgage holders gave rise to both the right-wing anti-government Tea Party, which began electing representatives to political office, and the radical intervention of the Occupy Wall Street movement, which would create a string of political initiatives focusing on debt and inequality. So into the second decade of this era, the nation turned away from the 9/11 event and the wars that followed. By the time Donald Trump was elected in 2016, the shift of national attention from 9/11 as a shaping event to the polarization of the national publics was fully underway. By 2020, it seemed clear that the factors defining national identity were undergoing a seismic shift from a nation defined by foreign enemies to a nation at war with itself over race, ideology, immigration, and concepts of liberty.

At the core of defining the 9/11 era is 9/11 exceptionalism, which itself forms part of the larger and more enduring myth of American exceptionalism. American exceptionalism is a national narrative that defines the United States as an exemplary nation that not only stands apart from other nations but also imagines itself as outside of international and global norms. American exceptionalism is an argument about the uniqueness and virtue of the United States, its capacity to be an ideal nation. I have argued elsewhere that this exceptionalism has enabled a narrative of American innocence that has the effect of absolving the US from responsibility for the outcomes of its actions.[7] The narrative of 9/11 exceptionalism defines 9/11 as a unique event, one of a kind, and thus without parallel in the history of violence in the United States if not the world. It also functions to mask the aggression of the wars that followed. It is through such exceptionalism, whose narrative affirms the nation's innocence and sees any attack on it as unprovoked, that the deaths of three thousand on September 11, 2001, were valued higher than the deaths of hundreds of thousands in the wars that followed.

9/11 exceptionalism is also a key factor in the political aftermath of the terrorist attacks. The post-9/11 wars that were fought in revenge came with staggering costs: more than seven thousand American lives—more than double that of 9/11—estimates of up to eight hundred thousand lives in the Middle East (Iraq, Afghanistan, Pakistan, Syria, and Yemen), and $6.4 trillion in costs to the US.[8] The narrative of 9/11 exceptionalism justifies these human, economic, and social costs and also justifies the changing of legal norms and moral stances that followed in 9/11's wake with the Patriot Act, the condoning of torture, and the secretive systems of illegal incarceration at sites like Guantánamo. In this story, 9/11 is narrated not simply as a different kind of violent event but as an unprecedented one. As I will argue in the chapters that follow, this has had deep consequences at Ground Zero in lower Manhattan, where the rebuilding has been shaped by the belief that the site could be rebuilt only in reference to the violence and loss of that day. This has resulted in a kind of

CDC poster in New York City, 2019. Photo by author.

travesty of urban renewal, with an oversized memorial, a heavily fortified and banal skyscraper, and an overpriced transportation center that is essentially a shopping mall, all paid for with taxpayer dollars.

While I want to critique 9/11 exceptionalism, I also want to make clear how the overdetermination of 9/11 and all that was invested in and projected on it does seem to fit the devastation that followed. When we consider all that emanated from it—the destabilization of the Middle East, the security culture, political dysfunction, the rise of xenophobia and anti-immigrant trends, and the financial burden of the wars that it spawned—that day in 2001 did change the nation, if not the world. That day does demarcate a before and an after, not because of innocence lost but because of the brutal response to the attacks that effectively shaped the post-9/11 era that followed.

It is now evident that the events of 2020–21 have marked the end of the post-9/11 era, have bookended it in a certain sense, signaling a new era with a different set of needs, demands, and motivating factors. This was enabled by the presidency of Donald Trump, in his isolationist, anti-internationalist, and anti-cosmopolitan provincialism and nativism, signaling a retreat from the global reach of the 9/11 wars. The public health and economic crises brought on by the COVID-19 pandemic in 2020, on top of the depletion of the US infrastructure and social welfare system, the Trump administration's wholesale dismantling of the norms of governance and diplomacy, the cruel detentions at the US border, and the political attacks on democracy, made the United States look like a failed state. In particular, the initial inability of the US, because of its political dysfunction, to adequately deal with the virus, and the country's COVID-19-related death rate, which in 2020 was one of the highest among developed nations, revealed a broader collapse of the functioning of the state. In this disruptive and dysfunctional context, the nation erupted over ongoing and visibly present police brutality that revealed long simmering anger and social divides, giving rise to protests and unrest throughout the country.

Writing in April 2020, former Obama administration official Ben Rhodes narrated the end of the post-9/11 era as the end of "September 12." Rhodes writes that early in his tenure, he saw a sign at the CIA that stated, "Every day is September 12." He narrates his personal trajectory from a New Yorker witnessing the attacks to working on the 9/11

Commission and losing his innocence about the false premises of the war. Assigned to research al-Qaeda's motivations and to read Osama bin Laden's fatwas, he was forced to see the myth of the Bush administration's narratives of the hijacker's hatred of American democracy. "The people who attacked us didn't seem focused on America's 'democratically elected government,'" he concluded. "What they hated was American foreign policy. What they sought was the overthrow of their own governments—chiefly that of Saudi Arabia, where bin Laden and 15 of the 19 hijackers came from, and that of Egypt, where the plot's ringleader, Mohamed Atta, came from."⁹ He defines the second term of the Obama administration as a "tug of war between Obama's desire to move into a new era and the pull of post-9/11 America." Rhodes sees Trump as "tapping into America's post-9/11 fears of a faceless 'other' and the frustrations of Americans who had been promised great victories in Iraq and Afghanistan but found only quagmires." Yet, he notes, the world order that emerges at the other end of this current crisis is likely to be permanently altered. In other words, the threats going forward are not about terrorism but about pandemics, climate change, authoritarianism and Chinese-style totalitarianism, and the inability of the US political classes to summon even remotely adequate responses to any of these challenges. As I aim to demonstrate in the chapters that follow, the crises of 2020-21 marked a turning point in the priorities of the nation that demonstrated, a full generation after 9/11, that its primary sites of conflict and contention are internal rather than external. This shift does not allow the narrative of American innocence to command the same power that it had in the post-9/11 years.

The Proliferation of Memory

An embrace of cultural memory as a social force expanded around the world starting in the 1980s. For the last few decades, there have been an extraordinary number of memory projects built and proposed, including memorials, memory museums, countermonuments, countermemorials, and artistic projects on memory, primarily, though not exclusively, in the United States, Europe, Latin America, and Africa. In many ways, this preoccupation with memory, which has been termed the "memory boom," has involved a reckoning of some kind with twentieth- and twenty-first century violent events, from World War II and the Holocaust to state terrorism throughout Latin America, genocide in Rwanda, 9/11, and global terrorism.

Why has memory emerged as such a powerful global cultural force in these last few decades when it had not been prior? Is this, as many have argued, an embrace of victim culture, a postmodern rejection of history, a response to the disappointments of modernity?[10] Perhaps it is simply that once loss is expressed in these cultural forms, it opens up long repressed needs to give form to pain and grief. The memory boom has been global in all senses of the word; aesthetic and strategic influences have traveled transnationally, with a Euro-American tendency toward minimalism and modernism being particularly influential. Yet memory projects in South Africa, Rwanda, Vietnam, Cambodia, and elsewhere demonstrate a range of aesthetic strategies for memorialization. The design of the National Memorial for Peace and Justice in Montgomery, Alabama, was influenced, in its modernist pillars, by the Holocaust memorial in Berlin, but it also incorporates figurative sculptures that speak to a broader range of global memory aesthetics, including those from Africa.

Situated within this global context, this book is specifically focused on cultural memory in the United States in the first two decades of the twenty-first century precisely because I am interested in unpacking the role of memory in US national identity and in relation to American exceptionalism. Through this focus, I aim to show not that the United States is the most important or exceptional site for memory but rather how memorialization in the US reflects broader changes in its national culture that have global implications.

Once it began, the global memory boom proliferated, because discourses of memory tend to produce competitions of commemoration. Memorialization inherently gives rise to intense debates about who is included and excluded. Michael Rothberg has written about the ways that collective memory is often viewed within a framework of scarcity, with the memory of one particular traumatic event literally crowding out other potentially equally important memories of trauma. He asks, Does memory have to work like "real estate development" in this way? He proposes, "Against the framework that considers collective memory as *competitive* memory—as a zero-sum struggle over scarce resources—I suggest that we consider memory as multidirectional: as subject to ongoing negotiation, cross-referencing, and borrowing; as productive and not privative."[11] Rothberg's entreaty is also about understanding how the overdetermination of memory can have detrimental political effects, whether intentional or not. If we are mired in memory, can we imagine futures?

In the United States, the memory boom has been a prime example of what Rothberg would see as competitive memory, with new memorials prompting more memorials. The decades after the opening of the Vietnam Veterans Memorial on the National Mall in 1982 saw the design and construction of an extraordinary number of national memorials, a significant number on the National Mall, many of which were promoted by those who felt left out by existing memorials. In terms of war memorials, this boom culminated in the construction of the World War II memorial in 2004, a huge, aesthetically conventional monument set in the middle of the mall, between the Washington Monument and the Lincoln Memorial, a memorial that for sixty years—until the memory boom—had not seemed a necessity.[12] By 2021, a World War I memorial had been opened near the mall (more than a hundred years after the war ended) and several others were in progress, including a National Desert Storm and Desert Shield memorial, a memorial to African American who fought in the American Revolution, a National Native American Veterans memorial, and, as I will discuss in chapter 4, a planned memorial to those who died in the ongoing global war on terror. Given its lack of closure, this last memorial was given an exemption by Congress from the mandate that memorials be built only after a ten-year period had passed since the war's end.[13]

Following two decades of memorial building since the construction of the Vietnam Veterans Memorial, the events of 9/11 were greeted almost immediately with a call for memorialization, even before the numbers of dead were established. As I discuss in chapters 1 and 2, the memorialization of 9/11, not only in New York, with its huge memorial and museum, but in Pennsylvania, at the Pentagon, and in a vast number of memorials nationally and internationally incorporating the steel of the destroyed twin towers, has been prolific. Not since the Civil War has an event been memorialized to this degree. Many of these memorials were subject to intense debate and competing claims of ownership, but rarely was this proliferation of memory questioned. Increasingly, toward the end of the post-9/11 era, the memory boom expanded to debates of inclusion of those traumatized beyond the framework of wars, to a broader recognition of the stories that memory politics had left out. This led in Washington, DC, to the long-anticipated 2016 opening of the National Museum of African American History and Culture and to the 2018 opening of the Legacy Museum and National Memorial for Peace and Justice in Montgomery, Alabama, which seek to extend the therapeutic aim of US memorialization to Blacks who were subject to racial terror. It is perhaps revealing that the political goals of the Equal Justice Initiative, which built the memorial and museum to raise awareness about mass incarceration and the racism of the criminal justice system, found that memorialization was a key avenue toward changing public views.

This "memorial mania," as Erika Doss calls it, is also intricately caught up in tourism (often referred to as "dark tourism"), and the popularity of memorials and memory museums as tourist sites has given rise to industries of memory souvenirs, gift shops, and organized tours. As I will discuss further, the 9/11 memorial and museum in New York have been a huge draw for tourists, who spend $26 to enter the museum and more at its gift shop. In New York, the integration of memory tourism into a rebuilt downtown has created a kind of mecca of global tourism and memory consumerism, where a visit to the memorial leads directly into the Santiago Calatrava–designed Oculus shopping mall, itself a tribute to 9/11 memory. The contradictions of the site are extreme: "A celebration of liberty tightly policed," Adam Gopnik writes, "a cemetery that cowers in the shadow of commerce; an insistence that we are here to remember and an ambition to let us tell you what to recall; the boast that we have completely started over and the promise that we will never forget—visitors experience these things with a free-floating sense of unease."[14] Similarly, the Flight 93 National Memorial draws visitors to Shanksville, Pennsylvania, and the Legacy Museum and National Memorial for Peace and Justice draws those traveling the civil rights tourist route through the South.

At this moment when the post-9/11 era appears to be shifting into a new era, in which issues of domestic conflict and racial divides are increasingly dominant, the memory boom has coincided with a debate within US culture about the presence of Confederate and other monuments to historical figures who owned slaves or were known for their racist ideologies, often the very figures in the name of whose "heritage" lynchings were carried out. These debates have been building in places such as Charlottesville, Virginia, where in August 2017, a violent protest defending the Confederate monument of Robert E. Lee from removal resulted in the death of Heather Heyer, who was among those protesters who came to demand that it be removed. Battles over these monuments, which included many commissions to study them and some states enacting laws to protect them, reached a peak in summer 2020 when protests over police brutality in the wake of the death of George Floyd took aim at monuments, subjecting them to graffiti, projecting images of victims on them, and beheading them. In the momentum that followed, many Confederate monuments and statues of former slave owners were destroyed or removed not only in the United States but in the United Kingdom, and many long-debated statues seemed suddenly to need to come down. In addition, discourses of memory have been integrated into the protests over those killed by police, with Black Lives Matters protests demanding that we "Say Their Names." As at the lynching memorial (the less formal name for the National Memorial for Peace and Justice), these actions transform memorialization of those forgotten or erased into political action, insisting that their lives be experienced as grievable. As the COVID-19 crisis continues, there are many discussions about how it might be memorialized, with activist memorials like the AIDS quilt seen as potential models.[15]

The articulation in the memory boom of what cultural memory means and why memorialization matters has been shaped through design and architecture. The memorialization of 9/11 has thus been shadowed by debates about design, architecture, and aesthetics. Similarly, the rebuilding of Ground Zero, which I discuss in chapter 3, has largely been a publicly funded private venture in which architectural design and contestations among architects have played a central role. Architecture thus emerges in these contexts as a crucial force in the experience of memorialization and renewal, a profession charged, in many ways, with the role of providing symbolism to these events and as an avenue for expressions of trauma, memory, and renewal. With the rise of abstraction and minimalism as key aesthetic strategies for memorialization and the broad turn within the US away from figurative monuments—precisely the kind of monuments that are being protested, taken down, and destroyed at the end of the post-9/11 era—memorials have been increasingly designed by architects rather than artists. Architecture has thus been deployed to shape *experiences* of memory, not simply objects designated to evoke memorialization. Artistic engagements with the cultural memory of the wars in Iraq and Afghanistan have also played an important role in responding to and processing the erasure of wars from public view and the deaths covered over and forgotten. In this, the now-named global war on terror has challenged conventional timelines of war and memory, given that it is a conflict across many nations that has no end in sight. Similarly, the demand for the National Mall to acknowledge the history of Native American genocide and slavery in the United States has made clear that memorialization via the memory boom has been a means for various constituencies of citizens to demand recognition within the script of the nation.

Redefining Terrorism

The memory of victims of terrorism unites many of the memorials, museums, and art projects that are pulled together in this book. As I discuss in chapter 5, within the myth of American exceptionalism, terrorism has been narrated as something that came from elsewhere, that threatened the nation, that attacked "our freedom." The terror attacks of 9/11 are thus an iconic example of the way in which the US public tends to understand terrorism—as an attack from the outside on an undeserving, innocent nation. Terrorism in this framework is seen as irrational and evil, without any discernable motive except to destroy "the American way of life." With the rise of right-wing militias in the 1990s and in the wake of the Oklahoma City bombing, the terms *domestic* or *home-grown* were used to describe our special brand of terrorism, conjuring aberrant acts of violence and images of rogues and misfits. It was not until the attack on the US Capitol on January 6, 2021, that US domestic terrorism would be more broadly acknowledged as a key threat to US society.

Terrorism, whether international or domestic, is officially defined by the United States government as the "the unlawful use of force and violence against persons or property to intimidate or coerce a government, the civilian population, or any segment thereof, in furtherance of political or social objectives."[16] Yet it has been the case that terrorist acts of white supremacy exist within the US without being defined as terrorism, and the terroristic practices of racial terrorism, such as lynching, have evaded being labeled and understood as terrorism in the broader public discourse, despite the efforts by civil rights advocates to define them as such. The point of terrorism is to alter life through fear, with specific acts of violence that aim to terrorize broad populations. Terrorism aims to undo life, to unmake the world, to shake the foundation of life as the everyday. For Blacks in the United States, two centuries of racist policies, laws, and practices created a terrorism of the everyday.

As a term, *terrorism* can be utilized for many long-term war projects. The post-9/11 wars were initially narrated as the "long war" by the wars' architects but were then rebranded by the Bush administration as the global war on terror, an expansive rubric that not only globalizes the role of the United States but also creates a more generalized, non-nation-specific category ("on terror") than did the wars in Afghanistan and Iraq. I prefer to use the term *post-9/11 wars* to refer to the wars in Iraq and Afghanistan and the regional conflicts that emanated from them in Pakistan, Yemen, and Syria because of the ways the term *global war on terror* constitutes a vague justification for a whole range of aggressive actions. Such a definition simultaneously erases the terroristic strategies deployed by the United States in fighting that global war on terror—war atrocities, sanctioned torture, extralegal detention, secret prisons, and the brutalization of prisoners at Abu Ghraib prison and at Guantánamo Bay. The artistic memory projects of the post-9/11 wars, which I discuss in chapter 4, often aim to draw these connections, to demonstrate that the actions of the US constituted terroristic practices intended to terrorize populations. These practices also include the drone wars that increased dramatically under the Obama administration and continued under the Trump administration—machines hovering constantly in the sky that target Islamic fundamentalists and kill civilians—that terrorize great swaths of Pakistan and Afghanistan.

Within the narratives of US history, there has been little recognition of state terrorism as a force. This is in contrast to Latin America, where the state terrorism of the dictatorships of the late 1970s and 1980s was a crucial factor in the memory projects that emerged in the memory boom. This has also meant that human rights discourse has been deeply integrated into memory projects in Argentina, Chile, Colombia, and Peru. Understanding terrorism not as a foreign project only but as a US-based and generated force would require grappling with the history of racial terrorism as state-sanctioned terrorism. In Montgomery, Bryan Stevenson and the Equal Justice Initiative explicitly situate lynching as a form of racial terror, one that aimed to terrorize whole communities in the South with the threat of lynching and which forced many blacks to flee the South in the Great Migration of the early twentieth century. To define slavery, lynching, and mass incarceration, as well as the genocide of Native Americans, as forms of terrorism, is then to understand terrorism as an integral active force in the origins of the United States and its very social fabric. The intervention of the Equal Justice Initiative to enact this narrative through memorialization is especially powerful because it aligns the trauma of the lynching victim with the trauma of the war dead and the trauma of the victims of 9/11. The demand that US actions be understood as forms of terrorism rather than as justified actions of a nation threatened is a radical one that is facilitated through memory.

The shifting terrain of the end of the post-9/11 era is a time of enormous upheaval, generational shifts of power, and norm-defying events that challenge not only the narratives of national identity but raise the question of the project of American empire itself. Of course, much of the infrastructure of US empire remains largely in place, with US military bases still broadly ensconced around the world and US political incursions into other nations still an active force. Yet a confluence of factors—economic, political, and social—has challenged the capacity of the US to remain an international imperial force and to sustain its national identity of American exceptionalism. The US public has grown fatigued with the ongoing post-9/11 wars, which have failed to produce narratives of triumph and patriotism. Even the 2011 assassination of Osama bin Laden, which, had it taken place in the early years after 2001, would have been an occasion to celebrate a successful retaliation, elicited only a muted response, as the ongoing conflict and the continued presence of US troops in Afghanistan blunted any expression of definitive triumph. As was exposed during the pandemic of 2020–21, the social infrastructure of the country in terms of health care and social welfare systems had been decimated after decades of war spending, government indifference, neoliberalist policies, and increased economic inequality. With its extreme political polarization and the threat to democratic institutions in the administration of Donald Trump, at the end of the post-9/11 era the nation had reached a new height of political dysfunction that undermined American empire.

The project of American empire has historically been one of disavowal in American culture. As Nikhil Pal Singh writes, there is a long history of defining the US empire as a different kind of empire.[17] American empire has thus been narrated by historians and policy makers as a project of global power unlike European and Asian empires. Daniel Immerwahr writes in *How to Hide an Empire* that the US form of empire is based primarily on a vast network of military bases rather than numerous official colonies. He writes that the United States "did not abandon empire after the Second World War. Rather, it reshuffled its imperial portfolio, divesting itself of large colonies and investing in military bases, tiny specks of semi-sovereignty strewn around the globe."[18] While non-US countries have thirty military bases overseas in total combined, the United States alone has eight hundred, with additional agreements granting it access to foreign sites. As Immerwahr notes, "The Greater United States, in other words, is in everyone's backyard."[19] This empire of military bases is, in fact, a direct cause of anti-American Islamic fundamentalist terrorism and the attacks of 9/11, as Osama bin Laden was specifically motivated by his outrage over the existence of US military bases in Saudi Arabia and near the holy sites of Mecca and Medina. Bin Laden stated, "Your forces occupy our countries. You spread your military bases throughout them."[20]

This configuration of American empire allows it to be hidden from broader concepts of national identity that circulate in the American public. In previous writings, I have used the phrase *tourism of history* to characterize the ways in which a disavowal of empire has functioned in American culture to create a tourist relationship—a distanced position of innocence without complicity—to global politics and the effects of US empire. American exceptionalism is a key narrative in this detached, anti-cosmopolitan position, in which the idea of the United States as an exemplar nation provides a script for absolving it of the impact of its imperial incursions throughout the world. I have argued that US comfort culture and the tourism of history are key factors in the disavowal in US society about both its project of American empire and our current fragile state of being. There are many complex and interrelated aspects to this disavowal that resist connecting the dots, so to speak, of the actions of the nation and the consequences of them.

To be palatable to an American public with strong isolationist tendencies, American empire must hide in the shadows of a culture of comfort and innocence. Singh argues that the disconnect between the foreign and the domestic is where we need to focus attention "if we are to understand the evolution of empire in the U.S. global age—not the refusal of the temptation of empire but the equally persistent claim never to have been one."[21] The eruption of domestic conflict and domestic terrorism in 2020–21 opens the possibility of understanding and reckoning this foreign/domestic disconnect in US culture.

Disavowal of US empire has also enabled the costs of the post-9/11 wars to be erased from public view. As the Taliban have regained control in Afghanistan and Iraq remains a dysfunctional state, the costs of these wars—human and economic—can barely be acknowledged. The crimes of former president George W. Bush, vice president Dick Cheney, and secretary of defense Donald Rumsfeld in perpetrating these wars based on lies and ignorance of the countries they invaded have never been fully exposed, and Bush himself has undergone a rehabilitation in his reputation. The US public thus continues to mourn those who died on 9/11 and to largely ignore the struggles of injured and traumatized veterans of the wars that followed or the ongoing health effects that the trauma of 9/11 continues to exact from the survivors of that event and its recovery operation. When the US closed its borders to refugees in the years of the Trump administration, the US public remained in extraordinary denial about how many of those would-be refugees were people displaced by the wars the US fought in the Middle East and beyond.

My argument that the post-9/11 era has come to an end is based in part on the belief that the fervency of that disavowal has eroded in the disruptions and upheavals of 2020 and beyond, which have exposed the fragility of US democracy, the failures of social and governance systems, and the loss of US power and prestige. The video images of police brutality brought into public view forms of racism at the core of American society, and the coalitions that emerged in response to this recognition were unprecedented. At the same time, there was a parallel recognition that histories needed to be retold, national stories needed to be rewritten, and monuments needed to fall. Sometimes, ideas wait for their moment and then take hold with deep and immediate effect. It may be that the disavowal of the consequences of American empire and of the systemic injustices embedded in an imaginary and idealized American way of life that empire purports to defend, once released from its hold, cannot be re-contained.

The decade of the 2020s will reveal where the nation takes this era of disruption next. The pushback from the Right to these demands for change has been predictably extreme. There can be no doubt, however, that public discourse has shifted in dramatic ways. As I have noted, disruption can open doors to new modes of being, but it also induces fear and scapegoating in the anxieties it gives rise to. If we have, finally, begun to move beyond the 9/11 era, with its two tragic and devasting wars of aggression and the broad public support and media acquiescence through which they were narrated, then we can only hope that aspects of the American tourism of history have been disrupted as well.

This book engages with these issues at the intersections of cultural memory, national identity, architecture and design, and terrorism. The first three chapters focus on 9/11 memory and its effects. Chapter 1 examines the proliferation of cultural memory and memorials to 9/11 around the world and analyzes its three official memorials at the Pentagon, at Ground Zero in New York, and in Shanksville, Pennsylvania. It aims to unpack the reasons for the excess of 9/11 memory and how that memorialization worked to affirm national unity and cohesion in the post-9/11 years. A key factor in the extended production of 9/11 memorials that I examine was the distribution of pieces of steel from the twin towers to far-flung towns and cities for memorial building in a program that ran until 2016, a full fifteen years after 9/11. In this chapter, I examine the aesthetics of the many 9/11 memorials and the contrasting effects of the three official memorials. Whereas the 9/11 memorial in New York is vast, with two enormous pools of water in the footprints of the former twin towers that function both as dark spaces and as sites of tourist picture taking, the Pentagon memorial is structured around aspects of the moment the flight hit the building, and the memorial for Flight 93 in rural Pennsylvania is a complex mix of landscape and modernism. Hovering over all of these memorials is the question, Why were so many 9/11 memorials built around the country, and what purpose do they serve?

The primary site of 9/11 memory is without doubt the memorial and museum that were built at the site of Ground Zero in lower Manhattan. Chapter 2 is an in-depth analysis of the 9/11 museum, an institution with contradictory goals. It aims as a memorial museum to honor the 9/11 dead, yet it also attempts to tell a historical narrative about the meanings of 9/11. In this chapter, I look in particular at the architectural design of the museum and how it shapes the experience of visitors, and I explore the objects and media through which the museum tells its story: the very large and very small survivor objects, the archaeological aspects of the site, the videos and photographs, and most movingly, the audio recordings of the spoken words of survivors and those who died. I also look at the complex digital projects at the museum that aim to engage visitors in a kind of collective digital memory of 9/11. The 9/11 museum tells a very nationalistic story of this event, in which the sacrifices of the unknowing victims of that day hold sway. This emphasis prevents it from engaging in effective historical analysis, yet its telling of the story of the day, and how people responded to crisis, is moving and human. Finally, I examine the museum's much-criticized gift shop, which reveals the deep contradictions of its commercial enterprise.

In chapter 3, I situate the memorial quadrant of the memorial and museum at Ground Zero within the broader context of the rebuilding of the area and the role of architecture, in particular high-end celebrity architecture, in how this destroyed area of the city was rebuilt. In what I ultimately conclude was a travesty of failed architectural vision and the unseemly transfer of $25 billion in public funds to the private sector, the rebuilding of downtown resulted in a heavily fortified skyscraper and a glorified transportation center that provides a spectacular cathedral structure for what is essentially a shopping mall. In this chapter, I aim to understand how the world of corporate name-brand architecture, which the private real estate interests and governmental agencies, such as the Port Authority of New York and New Jersey, wanted to deploy, ultimately produced a rebuilt downtown that had little interest in the needs of the public. This chapter situates these architectural projects, all enormously expensive, in relation to the shifting terrain of New York real estate and the reshaping of the city skyline through illicit global capital. The rebuilding of downtown is a cautionary tale in how the discourses of memory can get highjacked by the world of private interests, and in particular, the world of real estate development.

While 9/11 has been intensely memorialized, the wars that were fought in response to it have posed a set of problems for memorialization, not the least of which is the fact that they dragged on for two decades without clear endings. Chapter 4 turns to the memory projects that have emerged in response to the so-called global war on terror and to the attempts over the last two decades to memorialize those who died and were injured in those post-9/11 wars. I argue that the post-9/11 wars in Afghanistan and Iraq have largely been erased from US culture since the early years of the war, with the veterans—in particular, the high numbers of veterans who were wounded and who suffer from PTSD—rendered invisible within the fabric of the nation. Many art projects that have engaged with the wars in Iraq and Afghanistan have been preoccupied with counting the dead and laboring to make them visible through such media as drawing. Artists and photographers have created images that expose the painful afterlives of severely wounded veterans. Finally, this chapter examines efforts to create an official memorial on the National Mall to the global war on terror and the problems of memorializing two wars that have appeared unresolvable.

I turn in the last chapter of this book to the Legacy Museum and the National Memorial for Peace and Justice in Montgomery, Alabama, which opened in 2018, because I see them as an indication of a shift in national memorial culture. The museum and the memorial, created by racial-justice advocates and criminal justice reformers, form a bookend of the post-9/11 era in ways that signal a new era to follow. The lynching memorial commemorates the over 4,400 victims of lynching from 1875 to 1950, whose deaths formed a kind of racial terrorism targeting broader populations of Blacks in the South and beyond. The memorial and museum are both activist memory projects that intend, through the work of Bryan Stevenson and the Equal Justice Initiative, to demonstrate that slavery did not end but rather evolved into systems of lynching, segregation, and now, mass incarceration. While it may seem that this memorial and museum stand apart from the 9/11 projects analyzed in this book, I argue that in fact they are emblematic of a shift in how memory is deployed in US culture that signals an end to the 9/11 era.

The lynching memorial and Legacy Museum engage with issues of racial injustice that are completely aligned with the Black Lives Matter protests of the summer of 2020, and the demand that Black lives be remembered and mourned. The memorial and museum are both radical projects that stand in contrast to the nationalistic projects of the 9/11 memorial and museum. In contrast to the many 9/11 memorials that allow the narrative of American innocence to remain intact, the lynching memorial and museum demand a reckoning of the nation's guilt and complicity in order that we can move forward from these histories of violence by addressing the inequities and injustices that exist today.

In this book, I seek to demonstrate the connections between these memory projects and what they reveal about US national identity—the struggles over who is memorialized and how, who is forgotten, and what that politics of memory reveals about the United States as an imaginary and as a nation. My aim is thus to help illuminate how we got to the precipice of history at which we stand today, to explore the role of memory in shaping and contesting concepts of the nation that brought us here, and to imagine, as alternative futures, where we go next.

1

Monuments and Voids

The Proliferation of 9/11 Memory

In the vast black granite pools of the 9/11 memorial at Ground Zero in lower Manhattan, there is a gravitational pull. Waterfalls cascade down the pools' sides and descend into a central square hole where the water disappears from sight, pulling the gaze of the viewer downward into the voids. The void has been a trend of contemporary architecture that conveys a sense of loss through negative space. These pools are experienced by many visitors as vistas to be gazed upon (what one critic notes is akin to "mourning at Niagara Falls").[1] For others, they convey hopelessness. As Witold Rybczynski writes, "There is nothing comforting about gazing into the vast pit—or, rather, two pits—of the 9/11 memorial, the water endlessly falling and disappearing into a bottomless black hole."[2] The memorial's gravity is both metaphysical and emotional, with a somber tone and a physical pull downward.

Downward movement at Ground Zero has an inescapable set of associations attached to it, in the downward collapse of the buildings and, most harrowing and shocking, in the images of people jumping from the buildings to their death on the plaza below, captured in the seconds of their falling to the earth. In these images, we witnessed their desperate attempts to retain humanity in the face of death—a woman holding down her skirt, two people holding hands, people with their limbs extended outward to brace the fall. Diego Cagüeñas writes hauntingly of seeing the memorial voids in relation to those who jumped to their death that day: "It looked to me that, unintendedly, the memorial made their fall longer, if not endless. Indeed, no matter where one stands, it is not possible to see the bottom of the pools, as if signifying that once in the grip of their gravitational pull a body will fall forever without ever hitting the ground."[3] Gravity is a force that pulls downward without interruption, never ending—never, in a certain sense, at rest.

North pool of the 9/11 memorial (2011), New York, by Michael Arad. Photo: Francois Roux/Alamy Stock Photo.

The 9/11 memorial in New York is the primary memorial to those who died on September 11, 2001, and its massive size, with two enormous pools replicating the original twin tower footprints, is intended to convey the enormity of the event of that day. But this memorial is merely the most central of more than one thousand 9/11 memorials, memory projects, and museum exhibitions. 9/11 has created a surfeit of memory, an excess of memorialization that testifies in its proliferation and ubiquity to the ways that this event exceeds its own meanings. Such excessive memorialization points to the fact that the memory of 9/11 does much more than memorialize. Rather, it becomes a force through which contemporary concepts of the national unity are asserted and negotiated and through which a position of national innocence is affirmed. A 9/11 memorial in Laguna Beach, California, or Palm Beach Gardens, Florida, built far from the sites of 9/11 but with steel from the twin towers, is a means for these locales to connect to the powerful ways in which this event shaped the nation in its aftermath and affirmed a sense of patriotism. Throughout American history, few events have received this level of memorialization and memory production, with the exception of the Civil War. In that case, Civil War monuments and memorials were built in the decades after the war to assert racial power and affirm the "lost cause" in response to the challenges to white supremacy. The proliferation of 9/11 memorials, especially in the second decade after 9/11, can also be seen a kind of return, in this case a return to the moment of patriotic unity that the event produced in its immediate aftermath.

In this chapter, I examine this surfeit of 9/11 memory and the ways that memorialization became a vehicle for assertions of what America means in the post-9/11 era. The events of 9/11 accomplished an undoing of the fabric of the United States, a deep rupture made greater by the catastrophic response to it. There are many narratives attached to this disruption—the loss of innocence of the United States, the before and after as a demarcation of American history, the changing of norms to a constant state of emergency—yet none succeed in fully defining the meaning of the event. That is because 9/11 actually constitutes a whole series of events that preceded and followed from that one day in September 2001. One of the things that memorialization tends to do is to define time frames for events, and the memorialization of 9/11 has largely focused on that one spectacular, devastating, shocking day. As I will argue in the pages that follow, this emphasis on September 11 the day obscures many aspects of the post-9/11 era that follows.

Material Transformations and 9/11 Exceptionalism

As a global media event, 9/11 is often narrated as looming over the geopolitical landscape of the years that followed, as if it were located everywhere. Yet memorialization is most potent when enacted at the sites where memory is perceived to reside, at the actual site of loss and in the presence of material remains. Notions of the authenticity of site specificity have been crucial to the production of 9/11 memory. The events of September 11, 2001, took place at three specific sites: in lower

Manhattan in New York City, at the Pentagon in Arlington, Virginia, and near the small town of Shanksville, in southwestern Pennsylvania. Thus, while 9/11 has often been characterized as an event of spectacle, of shocking images and global media reach, its cultural memory has often taken on material forms and foregrounded material objects and site specificity. For instance, much of the proliferation of 9/11 memorialization was contingent in part on the dissemination of the bent steel from the twin towers as a material remain of the event. Debates about the memory of 9/11, in particular where and how it should be remembered, have often been focused on the designation of sacred ground and on material remains as the most meaningful elements for memory.

The terrorist attacks of September 11, 2001, in particular the destruction of the twin towers of the World Trade Center in New York City, were events in which material objects and structures were transformed in extreme ways. Materiality, in the form of buildings, furniture, emergency vehicles, and human bodies, was dramatically and irrevocably altered that day. While this material effect is certainly not unique to 9/11, the destruction of the outsized twin towers has meant that material transformation is a key framework through which the meaning of 9/11 has been constructed. One of the primary narratives of 9/11 that emerged from this material disruption is the sense that the alteration of the physicality of the site was unprecedented in its scale and speed.

In New York, the sense of matter transformed was powerful. Bodies were hurled through space, vaporized without a trace, or reduced to bits and pieces. Two 110-story buildings were pulverized in their descent to the ground, reduced to atom-sized bits of debris. Massive objects and emergency vehicles were crushed as if they were children's toys. Powerful steel beams were bent and twisted into strange shapes. Not only was there very little recognizable debris in relation to what had once stood there, but the swiftness of the destruction was unusual; the moment the towers fell has often been described as transforming the world in a matter of mere minutes from a "before" to an "after." Before, the buildings were standing; after, they were erased from the skyline. Before, the story goes, we were innocent; after, we were shocked, mourning, and angry.

9/11 exceptionalism puts forward the narrative that this event was transformative and beyond comparison, an exceptional historical moment in terms of loss, violence, trauma, and political impact. It is narrated not simply as a different kind of violent event but as an unprecedented one, one that marked the beginning of the post-9/11 era. 9/11 exceptionalism means that this event is seen as a moment when history changed, allowing for a new set of actions and rules to follow in its wake. This has deep political consequences, given that 9/11 effectively changed legal and moral norms in the United States. In New York this has meant that all the rebuilding at Ground Zero has been contingent on the narrative that it is a site with few parallels in history, thus producing the dominant belief that the site must be rebuilt in reference to the violence and loss of that day rather than as a multiuse urban area that incorporates memorialization. This narrative was so powerful, girded as it is by a moral discourse of mourning, that it overpowered alternative visions for the site and attempts to rebuild it with a more cosmopolitan urban vision.

9/11 cultural memory and the proliferation of 9/11 memorials since 2001 have been shaped by the destruction at Ground Zero and in particular by two material forms that emerged from it: the dust and the bent steel of the buildings. Each became a substance through which memory, grief, and loss were articulated and experienced. As I will discuss further, the huge number of 9/11 memorials that have been constructed around the United States and in the world use the steel from the destroyed towers as key features of their design. Thus, the dramatic material transformation at Ground Zero became a key element in how 9/11 memory was produced.

Dust and Steel

In New York, it was the dust that most powerfully evoked the material transformation of 9/11 and the pervasive feeling that things had changed irrevocably. The deathly cloud that enveloped the streets of lower Manhattan was the pulverized material result of the collapse of the two massive buildings. The dust was everywhere after the buildings came down, falling and gathering like snow. It quickly became the dominant aspect of the strange landscape that emerged in the area around the smoking pile of rubble at Ground Zero. In the testimonies of those who survived that day, many of whose stories are told in the 9/11 museum, a primary narrative is surviving the onslaught of the dust that coated their clothing, blinded them, and clogged their lungs. This was not ordinary dust; it was experienced as a new kind of substance.[4] We could say, then, the transformation of material objects on 9/11 resulted in new forms of materiality that demanded meaning making. Things remained, but they were not the same things. This transformation constituted the shock that has been associated with 9/11. How could those objects, those things, be not only gone but also transformed so quickly? The dust signified a world undone. It was also a toxic substance that would be the cause of illness and early death among those who breathed it that day and in the aftermath.

Within the cataclysm of the destruction, most of the bodies of those who died were either obliterated, leaving no discernable trace, or rendered into fragments. Both states of being or unbeing are horrific, and both pose problems for mourning. There were 2,753 victims killed at the World Trade Center that day (though it is believed by many that the actual number was higher, with undocumented workers unreported by their families). Of those, 1,113 have never been identified. Of the 1,640 who have been identified, only 293 were found intact.[5] The remaining 1,347 were identified in bits and pieces scattered in the broad pile of debris that was left at Ground Zero after the destruction, which was sifted through at the site and in later months at the Fresh Kills landfill on Staten Island where the debris was relocated. There have been ongoing battles over the status of the dust, with some family groups demanding that the dust be relocated back to Ground Zero from the landfill.[6] As I will discuss further in chapter 2, the status of these bodies remains largely unresolved, haunting Ground Zero in their liminal status as lost, destroyed, or never found—as *disappeared*.

While the dust was a key material substance in the meanings of Ground Zero in its immediate aftermath, the material extension of the site of Ground Zero outward into a vast network of memorialization has taken place through the buildings' steel. The exhibition of the 9/11 museum at Ground Zero contains a large steel column and several pieces of bent steel, and numerous memorials incorporate the steel. The journey of the steel into many different sites well beyond Ground Zero demonstrates its capacity to evoke the brutal material transformation of two airplanes crashing into the steel-girded buildings and the shock that the collapse of those buildings produced. Its metonymic quality, its capacity to stand in for 9/11, and its dual capacity to evoke brutal violence and resilience are constant narratives in the descriptions of the steel.

Technically owned by the Port Authority of New York and New Jersey, the steel from the twin towers was sorted in its aftermath to several destinations: landfill, in particular the Fresh Kills Landfill on Staten Island; recycling, in which steel was shipped to destinations around the globe to be melted down and reused; and preservation for memorial purposes.[7] A significant amount of the steel was preserved by the Port Authority and housed initially in Hangar 17 at John F. Kennedy Airport along with many other very large artifacts from the site.[8] A team of designers and architects (including architect Mark Wagner, who would later join the team of architects at Davis Brody Bond who designed the 9/11 museum), were brought in to Ground Zero in the immediate aftermath to tag objects and steel for preservation.[9] Some of those objects and pieces of steel were designated for the collections of the 9/11 museum and the New York State Museum in Albany, yet a large amount remained. Starting in 2010, the Port Authority began a program to distribute the steel and some artifacts—in their words, "to find them homes." Recipients had to apply to the program and commit to using the artifacts in a public display. By the time the program was closed down in 2016, they had distributed 2,660 objects, of which 1,890 were pieces of steel, to 1,585 fire and police departments, museums, municipalities, schools, community groups, and non-profit organizations in the US and several international locations.[10]

Throughout the process, the steel was narrated as a symbol of the heroic sacrifice of public servants. In the Port Authority press release, Port Authority superintendent of police Michael Fedorko stated, "This highly successful effort has allowed communities throughout the world to keep alive the memory of the heroic acts and ultimate sacrifices made by our police force, other law enforcement agencies and firefighters who lost their lives that day." Joseph W. Pfeifer, chief of counterterrorism and emergency preparedness for the Fire Department of New York (FDNY), stated:

> Each artifact from Hanger 17 is a piece of history that tells a special story about 9/11 such as firefighters and rescuers running into the burning Towers to save those who were in the greatest need. . . . The 9/11 steel,

whether small or large, represents the 343 firefighters who were lost, as well as all victims of terrorism throughout the world. Not only do these artifacts help us to never forget, but it also represents our hope for an end to terrorism.[11]

Additionally, the Port Authority requested that the following credit, or something similar, be included in any memorial made with the steel or other artifacts: "Artifacts recovered from the World Trade Center after September 11, 2001, courtesy of The Port Authority of NY & NJ and displayed in memory of the 2,752 victims, including: 343 NYC Firefighters, 37 Port Authority Police Officers, 23 New York City Police Officers." While this statement came from the quasi-governmental institution of the Port Authority, which lost many employees that day, including many who were not Port Authority police officers, the constant affirmation of the deaths of public servants here speaks to a larger narrative of heroism that functions in crucial ways to define 9/11. This was an event that dealt the country a double blow: the profound loss of life, and, by exposing the vulnerability of the United States to attack, the destruction of its symbolism of power. The stories of public servants who died saving others is enormously powerful in mediating this story of vulnerability.

The steel was designated for memorials in many disparate destinations, though a significant amount of it was distributed in the tristate area. Amy Passiak, the archivist and curator of the program, states, "The project has definitely created a network that will continue the memory of 9/11 through history." Passiak explains that when the steel was handed out in person at the hangar, multiple groups would come at the same time and make connections to each other. She says, "Through this project, I have met hundreds of people affected by the events of September 11, 2001, bringing both a rewarding but also humbling experience. . . . I feel that through memorials built with material from this project, I know that still more people will learn about these events, and the legacies of all those involved." Much of the salvaged steel was very large, but they instituted a "cutting program" to produce pieces less than 150 pounds that could be shipped to recipients who could not come retrieve the steel themselves.[12]

One can see in these statements the pervasive sense that the presence of the steel itself is understood to evoke the meaning of 9/11. In the aftermath of 9/11, there were many who argued that the ruins of bent steel visible at the site should inspire a memorial, that its brutal evocation of the violence of 9/11 spoke most profoundly to the meaning of the day. Philippe de Montebello, then director of the Metropolitan Museum of Art, wrote in the *New York Times* that "the huge, skeletal and jagged steel fragment of the World Trade Center and its façade" was a "relic of destruction" that could become "a testament to renewal. As a symbol of survival, it is already, in its own way, a masterpiece."[13] Memory scholar James Young has argued, to the contrary, that a memorial incorporating ruins would be a triumphant memorial to the terrorists and not to the victims.[14] The steel was paradoxical in its meaning; its shockingly bent frame was testimony to the extreme level of brute force that came from the airplanes hitting the buildings and the buildings' collapse, and yet its durability was understood as symbolic of survival and resilience. As Chris Ward, who would later run the Port Authority, states, "They are not sculptures. You don't want them to be beautiful. . . . [They are] brutally functional artifacts of heavy industry, battered and fire-scarred. . . . They are something more than beautiful: They are sacred."[15]

Steel is also a material of significant national meaning. The US economy throughout the twentieth century was symbolically fueled by steel, in particular with the development of stainless steel in the early twentieth century and during the war years. In its production, steel is a highly unsustainable process, dependent on coal and emitting high amounts of greenhouse gases, although it is also, as the WTC steel's journey makes clear, an industry that involves a significant amount of recycling and re-melting.[16] In the Trump era, a desire to return to the pre-1980 era of steel production, before Japan and China surpassed the US production of steel and many steel mills closed, became not only a symbolic component of the Trump slogan "Make America great again" but also the first act in the Trump tariff war. Steel thus came to represent American manufacturing dominance and stability to a working class that had been devastated by the outsourcing of manufacturing jobs worldwide, symbolic to a much broader population than former steel workers. It is ironic, then, that the first steel used to build One World Trade Center, known at the time of construction as the Freedom Tower, was announced by Silverstein Properties on April 26, 2006, as being manufactured in Luxembourg.[17] Since 9/11, the use of reinforced concrete, the primary structural material for the new One World Trade Center, has been on the rise, in part because of safety concerns raised by the collapse of the steel-dependent twin towers.[18]

Steel was an essential element of the rise of the modern skyscraper and a key component of the boom in skyscraper building in the 1920s and 1930s, with such iconic steel buildings in New York City as the Empire State Building and the Chrysler Building, whose hubcap-inspired top is made of stainless steel. The twin towers of the original World Trade Center were built in the early 1970s with a new kind of skyscraper design that allowed them to have significant height and an open floor design. Most skyscrapers are designed to be supported by an array of internal columns, which also break up the interior space. The twin towers were designed to be supported by exterior columns, which allowed for large window spaces and open floor spaces. The steel "skin" of the buildings, which is the source of the memorial steel, was both a design element, a kind of gothic play on the linear modern boxy shape of the buildings, and a structural element. The World Trade Center towers thus displayed their steel structure as part of their aesthetic, and many of the most famous pieces of their steel in the aftermath of their destruction, such as the trident steel at the entrance to the 9/11 museum, evoke the look of the towers. The gothic-inspired modernist design element of the steel façade of the original World Trade Center buildings was even a feature of some of the souvenir merchandise initially sold at the museum's gift shop.

Steel may exude a sense of permanence and durability, but it is also, as I have noted, a material often reused and repurposed. This took on a particular meaning in the aftermath of 9/11 with the Pentagon project to reuse steel from each of the three sites in US Navy warships. The USS *New York* had its bow forged from steel from the fallen twin towers, which was characterized as "strength forged through sacrifice."[19] Twenty-two tons of steel from a crane near the crash of Flight 93 in Pennsylvania were used for the bow of the USS *Somerset*, named for Somerset County, where the crash took place. Finally, steel from the Pentagon is on display in the USS *Arlington*, as the third of the Navy's ships in commemoration of the September 11 attacks.

The steel that was handed out by the Port Authority for many 9/11 memorials was thus freighted with these multiple meanings. But what does it mean when that steel becomes a key element of a memorial? It exudes strength, durability, survivor status. It is also a stand-in for the violence of the destruction that day. But how can a piece of bent steel represent a hope for an end of terrorism?

The Proliferation of Memory

The 9/11 museum maintains a crowdsourced worldwide registry of memorials, each of which can be located on a digital map.[20] There are more than 1,200 entries in the registry, with locatable memorials across the US—in New York, New Jersey, Texas, California, Florida, and Boston—and throughout the world, in such places as Israel, New Zealand, Canada, Italy, and London. These international 9/11 memorials are somewhat unusual for an event that took place elsewhere in a single nation. Some express allegiance with the US; others seem a bit arbitrary and idiosyncratic. Similarly, while some of the many memorials that were built in the US commemorate individuals who died, most are simply ways for localities to make a statement of solidarity and national unity through 9/11 memory.

There are so many memorials that have proliferated in the wake of 9/11 that it is hard to find a historical equivalent in the context of US history. While there are numerous memorials to World Wars I and II in towns and cities throughout the US, often as shared memorials, it is, as I noted, probably only the Civil War that reaches this level of proliferation (though as has been noted in the battles over Confederate monuments, many were built at times of racial conflict in the century that followed the Civil War rather than in its immediate aftermath). One of the key aspects of 9/11 memory is its focus on the specific day of September 11, 2001, in ways that tend to separate it from the context of the conflicts that built toward it—US forms of colonization in the Middle East, foreign policies based on petroleum economies, the rise of al-Qaeda—and all that continues to emanate in its wake, including the post-9/11 wars in Afghanistan and Iraq and the rise of ISIS. So the focus in 9/11 memorialization on that specific day, with its drama, its spectacle, its shock, and its grief, creates a distortion of the global political forces that defined it and contributes to what I have called a "tourism of history" in which the American public and its politicians can perpetuate a narrative of American innocence.[21]

The proliferation of 9/11 memorialization can be seen in the context of what Erika Doss has termed "memorial mania": "an obsession with issues of memory and history and an urgent desire to express and claim those issues in visibly public contexts." She writes, "Today's growing numbers of memorials represent heightened anxieties about who and what should be remembered in America. If wildly divergent in terms of subject and style, contemporary American memorials are typified by adamant assertions of citizen rights, and persistent demands for representation and respect."[22] Doss argues that events like 9/11 demand a response of public feelings and that such an event must be memorialized within the codes of sacrifice and heroism in order for it to exist within the broader narratives of American history. In the case of 9/11, that means a justifying narrative for the wars that were fought in response to the attacks, at the expense of more than seven thousand American lives and many hundreds of thousands of lives in Iraq, Afghanistan, and Pakistan.[23] While many of the 9/11 memorials focus their affective language on sympathy for the victims, others engage in the language of revenge and defiance. There is also a noticeable emphasis on designating those who died as heroes, which draws on a long tradition of memorialization. As Doss notes, "In both political and memorial cultures, those killed by terrorism are not remembered as murder victims but as freedom fighters and national martyrs, as the price all Americans must pay to defend the American way of life."[24]

Memorializing 9/11 is often about connecting a local context to the larger global event. For some memorials, that is about honoring a particular person who died, who had some connection to the place where the memorial was built. In others, the steel fragments function to create a connection of place between a memorial, which might be in Florida, Texas, or Illinois, and the site of 9/11, almost always represented by New York and the World Trade Center. The tristate region has the largest number of memorials, many of them honoring those from their localities who died. There are, for instance, over 150 memorials, including small plaques and larger memorials, in New Jersey. The shrines and memorial altars that proliferated throughout lower Manhattan and at fire stations were erected in the immediate aftermath of September 11, thus weaving the commemoration into the everyday from the very beginning. Some New York City fire trucks are still traveling memorials, with the names of lost firefighters and pictures of the twin towers painted on their sides, and many murals and smaller memorials remain, including the Tiles for America project in Greenwich Village and the fifty-six-foot bronze frieze of firefighters at work at Engine Ladder Company 10 near Ground Zero, designed by Viggo Rambusch.[25] The harbor of New York is dotted with memorials with a view of lower Manhattan (from Jersey City, Liberty Park, and Staten Island), with many of these memorials facing views of lower Manhattan. The memorial *Empty Sky*, designed by Jessica Jamroz and Frederic Schwartz, sits by the water in Liberty State Park in Jersey City, pointing directly toward the site of the former twin towers. The memorial consists of two long metallic walls that are engraved with the names of the 746 victims from New Jersey who died that day. The site specificity of the work, which is elegant in its minimal design (it also has a piece of steel on display at the entrance, though this seems unnecessary to its effect), effectively situates the names in relation to Ground Zero and the empty sky created by the towers' erasure from the skyline, now filled by the One World Trade Center building. The name *Empty Sky* is a reference to a Bruce Springsteen song about 9/11; Frederic Schwartz also designed a memorial in Valhalla, in Westchester County, that is named *The Rising* after another Springsteen song.

The many 9/11 memorials display an extraordinary range of aesthetics and styles, from minimalist plaques to larger monumental works. Many of the memorials are parks, street names, and small, unassuming grassroots projects. Several are named for one person, such as the Captain Kathy Mazza Park for a Port Authority police officer and nurse in Oyster Bay, Long Island, or the memorials created for the young children who were on the planes that day, such as Christine's Tree, for two-year-old Christine Hanson who died with her parents on Flight 175. Many are unofficial projects, such as the Memorial Garden in Georgia created by Bob Hart on his eighteen-acre property, which includes ninety-nine poles with the names randomly placed on them, or the twin towers created out of scrap steel in Oak Ridge, Tennessee. Boston College built a labyrinth for the twenty-two alumni who died that day. Several airports have memorials, including Boston's Logan Airport, which has a large glass cube sculpture that one can sit inside, designed by Moskow Linn Architects, with the names of the passengers and crew of American Airlines Flight 11 and United Flight 175, which departed from the airport. Los Angeles

Empty Sky memorial (2011), Liberty State Park, Jersey City, New Jersey, by Jessica Jamroz and Frederic Schwartz. Photo by author.

International Airport, for which three of the four flights were bound, has a work titled *Recovering Equilibrium*, designed by BJ Krivanek and Joel Breaux, which is a rotating mirrored compass form which has patriotic phrases along the edge.

One of the most monumental 9/11 tributes is *To the Struggle against World Terrorism* (also known as the Tear Drop memorial) in Bayonne, New Jersey, by Russian artist Zurab Tsereteli, which is ten stories high and made of 176 tons of bronze. The story of this memorial/monument shows the arbitrary and convoluted processes by which many of these memorials were built. In this case, Tsereteli, an outsized figure who has created many monumental works, some of them controversial, and who has his own gallery in Moscow, approached Jersey City about creating a memorial. After problems arose and local artists objected, the project was moved to Bayonne, where it now looks out into New York harbor, coming into view before the Statue of Liberty. To reach the memorial, one has to drive to the end of an industrial terminal pier with many empty marine buildings to where the memorial/monument sits at the end by the water. Otherwise, the primary viewership for the monument in person is from cruise ships coming to dock in the channel next to it or from container ships headed into the port of Newark. William Finnegan, who wrote a bemused essay about the monument for the *New Yorker* in 2007, noted that the $12 million memorial was financed by the "bogglingly prolific" Tsereteli himself, with funding from the Russian government.[26] In an ironic twist, it was dedicated in 2006 by Vladimir Putin (in person) in honor of our "unity of struggle against common threats."

The Tear Drop memorial-monument is perhaps the most bombastic on the aesthetic spectrum of 9/11 memorials, but it also points to the larger context of official, quasi-official, and unofficial memorials. There are no rules, of course, on who gets to create and dedicate a memorial to the 9/11 dead. It is an open terrain, onto which different forms of public feeling, as Doss notes, can be projected, which also taps into fears about terrorism and feelings of nationalism. The Tear Drop memorial is powerful in its kitchification of those feelings—the single tear that stands in for sorrow and grief in a monumental form. It conveys the sense that a memorial functions not simply to honor (and sometimes name) those who have died but also to elicit sorrow and grief from visitors, an emotional demand that pervades many of these works.

To the Struggle against World Terrorism (the Tear Drop memorial) (2006) in Bayonne, New Jersey, by Zurab Tsereteli. Photo by author

Tumbling Woman (2002), by Eric Fischl. © Eric Fischl/Artist Rights Society (ARS) New York. Photo courtesy Skarstedt Gallery.

For the most part, figurative statues commemorating the 9/11 dead have focused on firefighters and recovery workers and largely depict men. Brian Hanlon's 2004 memorial *We Shall Never Forget*, in Pennsauken, New Jersey, features a bronze businessman, a firefighter, a police officer, an emergency medical technician, and a rescue dog. Yet when artist Eric Fischl created a figurative work, *Tumbling Woman* (2001–02), as a tribute to a friend who had died on the 106th floor of the North Tower (and who might have jumped), he was roundly attacked for being exploitative and insensitive. *Tumbling Woman* depicts a figure in freefall in a graceful yet dynamic pose. It would later be included in an exhibition at the 9/11 museum, *Rendering the Unthinkable: Artists Respond to 9/11*, in 2016–17. Initially put on display at Rockefeller Center in September 2002, it was removed after only eight days because of negative responses. Fischl would later reflect on this when the finalists for the 9/11 memorial were revealed, in December 2003, in what he saw as a fetishizing of the towers over the dead themselves: "By trying to honor the buildings' footprints, and by placing the intimate and sacred memorial spaces underground, covered with a false sense of tranquility, they are regrettably doing what the attack did to the people inside: making them disappear."[27]

The distribution of the steel, in pieces large and small, has helped shift the aesthetics of many 9/11 memorials away from figurative representation. In some cases, this has resulted in modernist abstraction, in which the steel itself, often bent into shapes that evoke abstraction, seems to shift in its aesthetic identity, appearing to be scrap metal one moment and sculpture the next. For instance, the memorial *Tempered by Memory* in Saratoga Springs, New York, designed by local artists John Van Alstine and Noah Savett, is a twenty-five-foot high "progressive, forward-looking" sculpture of five pieces of World Trade Center steel fused together into an abstract form. It was commissioned by Saratoga Arts, a local arts organization, but then became the source of controversy when some residents objected to its placement in the center of town and its aesthetic, saying it belonged in a "scrap heap."[28] In the battle over the work, it was called a "twisted monstrosity" and an "embarrassment."[29] It was finally dedicated one year later, on September 9, 2012, after the town chose the less central site of High Rock Park.

The controversy over the aesthetics of *Tempered by Memory* demonstrates the kinds of design challenges the pieces of steel had for these hundreds of memorials. Just as much of the World Trade Center steel did end up as scrap steel, many of these pieces of steel do look like scrap metal, even while their bent shapes can powerfully evoke the violence of that day. While the salvaged pieces were not chosen for their aesthetic quality, when they became components of a public art sculpture, they were inevitably subject to questions of aesthetics. Their size and brute qualities often contrast with other elements of these memorials. The *Memoria e Luce* memorial, built in Padua, Italy, and designed by Daniel Libeskind Studio in 2005, is a tall, luminescent set of glass walls shaped like an open book, into which a piece of scrap steel is inserted, like an artifact. The memorial was sponsored by Permasteelisa, a steel contractor.[30] In Rosemead, California, in the San Gabriel valley east of Los Angeles, *Reflect* is a memorial in which two large sculptural hands,

Tempered by Memory (2012), by John Van Alstine and Noah Savett, Saratoga Springs, New York. Photo: James Nesterwitz/Alamy Stock Photo.

Reflect (2011), by Heath Satow, Rosemead, California. Photo by Heath Satow.

composed of stainless-steel bird shapes, one for each person who died, cradle a piece of steel. It was one of two designs that sculptor Heath Satow, who has created numerous works of public sculpture, presented to local residents for a vote. Here, the outsized form of the two hands gives the steel the appearance of a smaller, almost domestic scale, turning the steel girder into something that can be held. This is a gesture of humanizing the steel, transforming it into a hand-held object, while also symbolizing the spirits (as birds in flight) of the almost three thousand people who died that day.

These various memorials point to the problem of the steel. Because it was preserved and then handed out by the Port Authority, it became a command artifact for memorialization, but what it represents in each of these hundreds of memorials is often quite ambiguous. Is the steel a symbol of resilience, as it is often narrated to be, or is it a stand-in for the drama, the brutal violence, the epic quality of the event? Does it function as a kind of relic that creates a connection between these often distant locations and the site of Ground Zero, perhaps even imbued with religious overtones from that "sacred" site? It is worth noting that the dominance of the steel as a design element also affirms the ways that Ground Zero dominates the memory of 9/11 and overshadows the sites of the Pentagon and in Pennsylvania. Many of the memorials that have no direct relationship to the events of 9/11, whether through location or in honoring specific victims, exhibit a kind of incongruity. Large pieces of steel sitting among palm trees in Palm Beach Gardens, Florida (designed by Mark Fuller), or two pieces of steel leaning over a silver ball with a view of the ocean in Laguna Beach, California (Jorg Dubin, *Semper Memento*), while well intentioned, have an out-of-place quality to them.[31] Many of these memorials thus evoke a kind of general meaning of national unity and patriotism through which the steel conveys resilience and post-9/11 patriotism.

One cannot help but look with suspicion at this surfeit of memory, its excessiveness, its proliferation as a kind of overdetermination. In other words, while the hundreds of memorials testify to the powerful sense of loss and shock of this event, their proliferation in so many places with no particular connection to 9/11 is testimony to something much more diffuse and inchoate. While the urgency of the loss of 9/11 resulted in some memorials being built and dedicated within a few years of 2001, many of these memorials were completed for the 2011 ten-year anniversary of 9/11 and the years afterward, as more than 2,600 pieces of the steel were distributed until 2016. The building of these thousands of memorials was thus a prolonged process because of the distribution of the steel. What did building a 9/11 memorial mean in 2016, when the event itself had faded after fifteen years, when the wars fought in response to it were already many years too long?

Place, Authenticity, and Official Memorialization

The three official memorials to 9/11—the National 9/11 Pentagon Memorial, the National September 11 Memorial and Museum in New York, and the Flight 93 National Memorial in Pennsylvania—are understood to be the primary authentic sites of 9/11 memory. This is because those sites are places where the destruction took place and where people died. There are unrecovered bodies from each of these sites, and massive efforts at identifying remains have been undertaken at each (the Flight 93 memorial and the 9/11 museum in New York contain unidentified remains, and unidentified remains from the Pentagon are buried with a memorial in Arlington National Cemetery). Yet while these three are official memorials, only one has an official relationship to government entities. Both the Pentagon memorial and the 9/11 memorial are run by private foundations, and only the Flight 93 memorial is administered by the National Park Service. This means that the "official" memory created at these sites is not simply being created by government entities, and in the case of New York, that the memorial and museum are a commercial and expensive enterprise.

Dedicated in September 2008, the Pentagon memorial was the first national memorial built to 9/11, a process that was expedited by the fact that the Pentagon controlled the space and that the families had become organized relatively quickly, in part because of the previously existing Pentagon family outreach. The memorial was designed by two relatively unknown architects, Keith Kaseman and Julie Beckman, whose design was chosen by a committee from over 1,100 proposals in 2002. It consists of 184 cantilevered benches of steel, spread across two acres across the path of Flight 77 before it hit the west wall of the Pentagon. Each "memorial unit," according to the designers, contains a bench with the name of one victim inscribed on its edge, and with a pool of water under it. The benches for those who died in the building are placed so that one sees the building when reading the names, and the benches for those who died on the plane are arranged so that one sees the sky behind them when viewing their names. In this sense, one could say that the memorial participates in a reenactment of the crash of the airplane into the building, one that also separates the dead into two separate groups of victims. In addition, those who were in the military have their military titles included.

The placement of the names of the dead is a key factor in the narratives constructed by any memorial. For the Pentagon memorial, the designers made the decision to arrange the benches both in relation to the victims' locations—whether on the plane or in the building—and along

National 9/11 Pentagon Memorial (2008), by Keith Kaseman and Julie Beckman, Arlington, Virginia. Photo by author.

a timeline that marks the years of their births. Thus, the benches are positioned along lines demarcating the years 1930, that of the oldest person who died, John D. Yamnicky, a Navy veteran who was on the plane, to 1998, the birth year of three-year-old Dana Falkenberg; the sloped "age wall" on one side of the memorial edges up one inch per year following this pattern, from three inches to seventy-one inches. This designation by age gives emphasis to the five children who were on the plane—Dana Falkenberg and her eight-year-old sister Zoe, and three sixth graders, Asia S. Cottom, Bernard C. Brown II, and Rodney Dickens, who were on their way to California for a special National Geographic conference. The designers describe their work as aiming to convey the sense of individuals—hence the emphasis on the specificity of years of birth—whose lives on that day became a collective by chance. They write, "Both individual and collective in nature, the Memorial intends to record the sheer magnitude of that tragic day by embedding layers of specificity that begin to tell the story of those whose lives were taken."[32]

The design's arrangement by age places particular emphasis on the youngest victims because there is a large gap between them and the next oldest victim at age twenty-two (demarcated in the design as "the gap"). Julie Beckman states that they felt that listing the names alphabetically would not have added meaning to the memorial but "understanding people's ages and where they were in their lives when their lives ended is something that can live on for generations."[33] In this sense, the foregrounding of age asks visitors to think of those who died within the specificity of how long they had lived and, by extension, how long they were unable to live.

This design choice reveals how naming challenges all memorials. If the names are not random, which can seem arbitrary to the extent of appearing meaningless, and they are not alphabetical, which can make them appear like statistics, then how should they be listed? It is a well-known feature of the Maya Lin–designed Vietnam Veterans Memorial that the listing of names is chronological by date of death, which creates a narrative of the war, in particular as the casualties mount in certain years. At the Oklahoma City memorial, the names of the dead are displayed on chairs that approximately replicate where people died. For the Pentagon memorial, such arrangements would have made no sense. The Pentagon memorial's choice of emphasizing age also means that those family members who were traveling together, such as the Falkenberg family, are memorialized separately across the benches. The designers aimed to compensate for this by listing, below the benches in the memorial unit, the names of their additional family members who died.

There is an overemphasis of detail and explanation here, one particularly evident in the audio tour that explains all the design elements in meticulous steps, what Bradford McKee, writing in *Slate*, states is a design "laden with the disaster's statistical aspects, detailed like a program on CNN."[34] In other words, since the design elements are not particularly intuitive to visitors, they require explanation—in handouts, on plaques, and in audio commentary. There are also many of

Pentagon memorial bench for Dana Falkenberg. Photo by author.

the same design elements that typify contemporary memorial design. The Pentagon memorial evokes many of the design elements of the Oklahoma City memorial, with its chairs for each victim and its pool of water. People are invited by the design to sit on the benches, as they are with the use of chairs in memorial designs. Water as an element to evoke larger natural forces is present here, even within the understated modernist design of the benches; the water forms a constant aural backdrop at the memorial, as if a river were flowing underneath the benches. Water, as a common feature of memorials, can signify renewal and the continuity of life and nature.

The memorial emphasizes in its design the trajectory of the plane into the building, demarcating its flight toward the structure, which was so low to the ground at that point that it came close to cars on an adjacent road. As an extension of the memorial, and visible from it, a blackened stone of the structure from that day was reinserted into the rebuilt wall at the point of impact, with the date September 11, 2001, carved into it. The specificity of the site as the designated place for the memorial seems almost to call out for some reference to the dramatic narrative of the crash, yet it is unclear what this narrative accomplishes. These site-specific elements ask visitors to think of the horror of those final moments for the plane's passengers, when they must have known that they were about to die.

This site specificity raises important questions for the memorial. It is in a very inaccessible place, a long walk around the enormous Pentagon building from the nearest Metro station and near an overcrowded parking lot. It is crammed between the building, which by its very nature is a high-security zone, and a busy highway ramp with a constant stream of traffic and with the sounds of aircraft from Reagan National Airport constantly overhead. It is, in short, not a site particularly conducive to contemplation or easily accessible to the public. In his critique, McKee writes:

> After the trek to the isolated memorial, pilgrims will have to contend with the noise from an expressway feeder road running right against the west edge of the site.... With the speed of commuter life on one side and the prohibitions of the Pentagon on the other . . . where are visitors supposed to find the quietude of their own thoughts? ... The people who need a memorial most deserve a spot where they can shut out the noise from the world and wrestle with the unexplained.[35]

The presence of the Pentagon, effectively the seat of the US military, looms over this memorial physically and thematically. The Pentagon is a massive horizontal bunker of a building that does not reach into the sky so much as sprawl spatially and bureaucratically, facing inward. Symbolically, it is a place of secrecy, the center of the military machine, hardly a site conducive to mourning. It is the place from which the post-9/11 wars were launched, so the mourning of these dead, many of them civilians, seems out of place here. It may be that the emphasis on the children allows for narratives of innocence to emerge at the memorial, but these conflict with the complex meanings of the site itself.

Clearly, the imperative to put the memorial at the site where the crash actually took place guided this choice, though a memorial could have been built nearby in Arlington National Cemetery. (There were five people whose remains were never recovered, and on September 12, 2002, the unidentified remains from the Pentagon crash were buried at Arlington.) The social demand that a memorial be constructed at the crash site points to the powerful ways that the authenticity of place has shaped the memorialization of the three site-specific 9/11 memorials. Despite the fact that the Pentagon building is minimally accessible to the public, the idea that the memorial had to be here, on site, where it happened, was dominant.

Absence and the Void: The 9/11 Memorial at Ground Zero

Ground Zero looms over all other 9/11 memorialization. The largest number of people died there, it was the site of the most spectacular and devastating destruction, and it memorializes all the victims of 9/11. It is also the primary site through which the narrative of absence emerged as a framework for 9/11 memory. From the moment the two buildings fell, there was an obsessive preoccupation with their erasure from the New York City skyline. The construction of a memorial at Ground Zero, a long and tortured process, was shaped by this dominant sense of absence and, in the mode of 9/11 exceptionalism, by the belief that the site needed to be rebuilt only in relation to the events of that day. That is, instead of being redesigned as a rebuilt city of mixed use public space, housing, and commercial entities with a memorial within it, Ground Zero was imagined to be primarily a site of 9/11 memory. Although the memorial and museum are now adjacent to an array of office buildings, shopping malls, and projects of high architecture, as I will discuss in chapter 3, even some of these projects, such as the Santiago Calatrava Oculus transportation center, were designed in reference to 9/11, and the renaming of the buildings as One World Trade Center, Three World Trade Center, Four World Trade Center, and so on inscribes the newly built space in relation to the time frame of 9/11.

Ground Zero had an extraordinary number of visions and imaginaries projected on it before its redesign was in place. In the first two years, there were numerous design contests, both official and unofficial, that were testimony to a grief-stricken fervor to reimagine the site of destruction, to fill up the space, to reinsert the missing two towers, and to use design for repair and renewal.[36] As with the 9/11 memorials built elsewhere in the US and around the world, the range of aesthetic strategies, mediums, material forms, and engagements with the site was vast. The official memorial competition, run by the quasi-governmental Lower Manhattan Development Corporation (LMDC), which had a deadline of June 2003, resulted in 5,201 proposals. It is worth noting, however, that very few of these proposals considered the use of the Port Authority steel remains, though the guidelines stated that designs could include "surviving original elements." At this stage of the aftermath, very few of the design imaginaries conceptualized the steel as a part of their memorialization. Management consultant Lester J. Levine, who was one of the entrants into the memorial design competition, decided in 2012 to interview many of those who proposed designs, which he published as a book in 2016.[37] Levine's own populist interest in the range of design strategies and the different kinds of people, most nonprofessionals, who felt compelled to enter the contest, demonstrates a particularity of the design competition for the 9/11 memorial in New York, that it was the most high profile and also most public competition, subject to much discussion and debate. James Young, who was a member of the jury, which also included architect/artist Maya Lin as well as several artists, art professionals, and a family member, has written about the complexity of the design selection process, including the public discussion of the eight finalist designs that were put on display, and largely greeted by the press as banal and too "light."[38] The jury was under intense public scrutiny and felt beholden to many constituents, including the families.

The prospect of designing a memorial for the site of Ground Zero was shaped by elements of the existing site and by the fact that Daniel Libeskind had won the highly scrutinized competition for the master plan for the site in early 2003 that established a layout for buildings and a memorial. Libeskind's plan, entitled Memory Foundations, won over competing proposals in part because he was able to articulate at such an early stage of rebuilding a memory narrative for the site that resonated with a grieving public. The actual master plan became less and less of a factor in the rebuilding of the site, with most of its more specific design elements eliminated and, as I discuss in chapter 3, the large architectural commissions handed over to other architects with different design intentions. Yet the Libeskind master plan effectively established an aesthetic ethos for the memorial aspects of the site, in particular in his articulation of Ground Zero as a place of absence. The early declaration of the sacredness of the tower footprints (by New York governor George Pataki) thus intersected with Libeskind's vision to make it almost inevitable that the final memorial would echo the footprints of the original towers. Among the stipulations of the guiding principles for the design contest was to "create a unique and powerful setting that will . . . make visible the footprints of the original World Trade Center towers." At the same time, designs that departed from the master plan were encouraged by the jury.[39]

The dominance of the narrative of absence has led to an architectural preoccupation with the aesthetics of the void, one that is an integral part of both the memorial and the museum. The final design, by Michael Arad (with additional design on its plaza by landscape architect Peter Walker), was originally named *Reflecting Absence*, and it defines the space as one of absence (of the towers) articulated through voids.[40] As the announcement of the selection by the jury articulates, "In its powerful, yet simple articulation of the footprints of the Twin Towers, 'Reflecting Absence' has made the voids left by the destruction the primary symbol of our loss. . . . The memorial is thus anchored deeply in the actual events it commemorates—connecting us to the towers, to their destruction, and to all the lives lost that day."[41] The memorial's primary feature, as I have noted, is two extremely large voids in the former footprints of the towers with waterfalls cascading down toward a central square hole in each. The pools are lined at the top with bronze parapets onto which are inscribed the names of those who died on 9/11 and in the 1993 bombing of the towers. The two pools are voids in a large plaza lined with trees, in the center of which is the pavilion entrance to the 9/11 museum, which effectively bifurcates the memorial. Arad had spent the year after 9/11 obsessing about a memorial of voids in the Hudson River, to evoke the absence of the towers.[42] The design of the memorial creates a series of tensions, between absence and presence, the massive and the intimate, the solid and the fleeting.

The design of the pools as voids thus essentially reinscribes the presence of the original twin towers into the memorial plaza. One of the

Pool at the 9/11 memorial, by Michael Arad, New York. Photo by author.

features that endeared the twin towers to many while they stood was their two-ness, the sense that they were a pair of buildings, in dialogue with each other (only one would have been banal, as the solo One World Trade Center building now makes clear). Yet the two-ness of the memorial pools has an odd effect. Studies have shown that visitors tend to spend fifteen to twenty minutes at the first pool they come upon and then five minutes at the second, since while the names are different on each, the second pool is design-wise just like the first.[43] The fact of the matter, of course, is that if there had not been two towers, it would never have made sense to have a memorial with two pools. As architect Philip Nobel writes, the design thus immortalizes the twin towers as "architecture remembering architecture."[44] The voids of the two footprints effectively transform the memorial plaza into a space not so much to be in as to look down from. The plaza is thus primarily defined as a site of observation into the voids that one cannot enter and as a waiting area for visitors entering the museum.

Just as the Libeskind master plan was transformed and reshaped over the years by the complex negotiations that governed the rebuilding of the site as it progressed, with politicians, real estate developers, the LMDC, security professionals, and architects all weighing in, the design of the memorial has been dramatically transformed from its initial plan. While the primary feature of the pools with water survived the process, a key element of Arad's memorial design was underground chambers, imagined as intimate spaces, where visitors would see the water falling with the pools behind them and where the names of the dead would be inscribed. After extraordinary cost overruns, the intervention of security consultants who saw the underground area as a high-security space necessitating security checkpoints, and unhappy family members who felt the signification of going underground was too somber, the underground chambers were eliminated. As a consequence, the names now ring the pools above ground.[45]

The Arad memorial is a study in minimalism, with its spare lines and metallic polished bronze aesthetic.[46] In 2002, *New York Times* critic Michael Kimmelman wrote a much cited essay about how minimalism "of all improbable movements of the last 50 years" had become the aesthetic of contemporary commemoration. He notes that minimalist abstraction "in all its allegorical pliancy, turns out to function in a memorial context as the best available mirror for a modern world."[47] This "pliancy" has been the source of much of the debate about modernist and minimalist memorials, which are often accused of being essentially antiheroic. Erika Doss notes that "terrorism memorials" have embraced a minimalist aesthetic in part because of the nature of trauma itself, that it is "dissonant, confusing, and chaotic, a kind of dismantling." She writes, "Minimalism is often selected to commemorate trauma because it simultaneously evokes this disorientation and resolves it: it conjures trauma's profound dissonance and also speaks to the recovery and reaffirmation—the remaking—of individual and collective harmony."[48]

Perhaps one of the most interesting aspects of minimalism's pliancy is the way in which it has often been integrated with forms of monumentality—not a style one would think of as minimalist. Kimmelman, like many others, uses Maya Lin's Vietnam Veterans Memorial as a touchstone for a minimalist and abstract memorial that creates an intimate space for mourning.[49] Yet many of the other minimalist memorials, such as the Oklahoma City National Memorial and Museum, have elements that are also monumental (such as monumental gates), a feature that we will see as well in the Flight 93 memorial. This raises the question of how minimalism operates perhaps ambiguously in relation to scale and monumentality.

Scale is a key feature of the 9/11 memorial. The two black granite pools of the memorial are vast. Each is nearly an acre in size, two hundred feet squared, housing what the memorial website bills as "the largest man-made waterfalls in North America" and filled with 550,000 gallons of water. As a consequence, they overshadow, physically and sonically, all the other elements of the memorial, including its most important feature, the names etched on the pools' edge. In this sense, the memorial design equates the scale of the event in New York with the scale of the pools, the vastness and overwhelming quality of the void spaces. The pools, Adam Gopnik writes, are "wildly out of scale with the rest of the site in their immensity ... two huge sinks spilling chlorinated water from their edges ... their constant roar interrupts any elegiac feeling that the lists of engraved names of the dead which enclose them might engender."[50]

Of course, there is nothing arbitrary about the size of the memorial, which was guided not only by the discourse of sacred ground but also by 9/11 exceptionalism, which demanded a big memorial, a memorial that took up space, to reiterate the importance of the event and also the overwhelming grief that emerged from that day. So much of what has been built at Ground Zero is informed by the fact that basic plans were put into effect very early in the process and were guided by a deep, abiding, and unprocessed sense of loss. As the rawness of the grief subsided, the ways to reimagine the site expanded, but it was basically too late. It is now impossible to imagine that the site could have been rebuilt as a multiuse site incorporating public space and a smaller, more intimate memorial. Young notes that monumentality was an inevitable part of the process: "It's clear that together with the mandate to articulate the towers' footprints, a corollary mandate to memorialize the towers' sheer monumentality was established as well.... It may also be the unhumanly proportioned scale of the waterfalls that creates unexpectedly intimate spaces among small groups and families as they cluster together in the plaza and at the edges of the voids."[51] Here, the density of the sound of the water, which is omnipresent, can create sonic spaces of intimacy as it is hard to hear what nearby visitors are saying.

Naming is a crucial aspect of memorialization, as I have noted, and the final arrangement of the 2,983 names along the bronze parapets of the memorial, which includes six people killed in the 1993 bombing of the buildings, is the result of many changed design plans and complex negotiations over order, arrangement, and the special status of public servants. Inherent in these broader debates about naming are narratives about the meaning of lives and of deaths—what matters, where people were when they died, how old they were, if they worked together, if they were public servants, how they were grouped and connected in life. The primary groupings that organize the names at the memorial relate to where people died and what plane they were on, as well as what tower they were in, though it is a grim fact that the remains were scattered over the entire area and that more than half of the dead have never been recovered in any form. Names from a particular corporation might be grouped together, but the corporate names are not on the memorial. The public servants, such as the 343 firefighters and the police from various forces, are identified by these affiliations and their units within them, such as engine companies. The stories of the firefighters and other public servants who died on 9/11 have been enormously powerful in defining narratives of heroism for that day, and their organizations succeeded in having their names highlighted in this way that separates them from others who died.

After much negotiation, the names are also arranged in complex "meaningful adjacencies" that include familial relations, work connections, and other connections requested by families. Examples that are often shared by Arad include a woman's father, who was on Flight 11, and her best friend, who was in the North Tower; and two men, former strangers, who were attempting to descend the stairs together, one helping the other, who both died.[52] Much has been made of the complex algorithm that was used by Jake Barton and Local Projects, who designed the digital media in the museum, to create these meaningful adjacencies, for which there were 1,200 requests, some of which are only known to friends and families. The algorithm is here given a mystical quality, with the idea that only a mathematical formula could sort through and affirm this many very complex human connections.

Names on the south pool of the 9/11 memorial, New York. Photo by author.

The names are etched into the bronze, and visitors can touch them, make rubbings of them, and photograph them up close. Yet there is a tension between the vast pools and the intimacy of the names. Critic Martin Filler writes, "The propulsive aural and visual excitement of the three-story-deep waterfall and its mysterious disappearance captures and holds your attention in a way most unusual for the static medium of conventional architecture. That distraction makes one's next perception all the more shocking, as you focus on the names of the victims, incised into the continuous tilted rim of bronze tablets that surround each pool."[53] The memorial swallows up the names in its voids; it is difficult to register the presence of a name with the roar of the waterfalls and the vast pit of the pools looming behind them and drawing our gaze away from them.

The 9/11 memorial has become a primary tourist destination in New York, visited by millions of people every year; it has a broad media presence and is the source of a constant flow of social media reviews and images. Within the "sacred" quadrant of Ground Zero, the memorial plaza, with the museum pavilion in the middle, is on the same grade as the streets but ultimately because of security design is designated as a separate city space. The plaza is ringed by security bollards that would prevent any vehicle from driving onto it, and it is governed by an extensive list of forbidden activities. As Kimmelman writes, "The memorial permits no recreation, no loud noise, no 'behaving in a way that is inappropriate,' according to the memorial's online rules list. You can't sing. At a site celebrating freedom and liberty, protests and demonstrations are prohibited."[54] There are also no street vendors or food vendors, a common feature of New York City parks and plazas, allowed on it. It goes without

Flags and flowers on names on the 9/11 memorial on September 11, 2019. Photo by author.

Plaza at the 9/11 memorial. Photo by author.

saying that the memorial would never be a site of protest, and so when protests have marched through downtown, they have occupied adjacent spaces; the original site of Occupy Wall Street is just two blocks away at Zuccotti Park, and many of the 2020 protests against police brutality were at Union Square and further north. It is patrolled by an array of security personnel, including the New York Police Department (NYPD), the Port Authority Police, and private security personnel, the cost of which has been a constant source of tension with the family members who monitor the foundation's finances. The plaza is thus a highly securitized area, with commercial business kept at its perimeter (the Oculus shopping mall/transportation hub can be entered just across the street, past the security bollards). Architecturally, the remade site of Ground Zero thus bears the modernist legacy of the World Trade Center buildings whose destruction created it. The World Trade Center complex was a notoriously inhospitable site at ground level, with a windswept plaza cut off from the street grid of downtown by the design of a superblock, popular in the mid-twentieth century. The memorial plaza is better integrated into the city, although it is not exactly a public space.

The landscape architecture of the memorial plaza is geometric, with patches of green that are laid out in strips that cannot be accessed by pedestrians and rigid rows of grass and trees, what Kimmelman calls "military ranks of trees" that make it feel very little like a park. The stone benches are severe and few. He adds, "This place doesn't feel like New York, it feels like a swath of the National Mall plunked in downtown Manhattan: formal, gigantic, impersonal, flat, built to awe, something for tourists."[55] Visitors tend to cluster around the few areas where one can sit or where there is minimal shade. This effect is particularly ironic when one considers Michael Arad's narration of what inspired him to design a memorial—his profound experience of community and mourning in public spaces like Union Square and Washington Square Park in the immediate aftermath of 9/11—and that he imagined the plaza area as a "place for residents on their way to work or play."[56] While the trees will continue to grow and perhaps a sense of the memorial plaza as more park-like might emerge, the convergence of tourism and security means that casual activity at the site is constantly under surveillance and that it is an unlikely place for workers to congregate for lunch or breaks (there are also no trash cans). As I note in chapter 3, the design of the transportation hub funnels commuters into underground passageways so that they are not encouraged to walk across the memorial plaza on their way to work.

The memorial plaza is likely to become a site for further memorialization. On May 30, 2019, the Memorial Glade, composed of six stone slabs placed in the southwestern corner of the plaza, was dedicated to honor those 9/11 recovery workers and first responders who have struggled with the effects of their exposure to toxic substances at the site and those who have died from that exposure. The result of a campaign spearheaded by political comedian Jon Stewart, the final design was created by Arad and Walker and includes steel from the towers as well as large stones that, in Arad's words, "are rough and worn, and their angle suggests a forceful resistance, an answer to the violence that brought

9/11 Memorial Glade (2019) for first responders, by Michael Arad and Peter Walker. Photo by author.

them forth." He adds that they represent "firmness, stability and faithfulness through adversity, pointing skyward, referencing how the recovery cleared the way for rebuilding and renewal."[57] The tilted slabs of rock that line the glade create an odd almost primordial effect, compared to the sleek modernism of the memorial and plaza.

It is perhaps fitting that the memorial that was built on the site of an event defined by images has itself become the site of an immense amount of picture taking. Like Niagara Falls or the Grand Canyon, the memorial's vast scale invites photography, and in the complex world of social media photographic practices, it is a favored place for tourist pictures, posed before the vast abyss. It is inevitable that the taking of selfies at the memorial have often circulated and that they have become the subject of a moral debate about what constitutes acceptable behavior at a memorial (similar debates have emerged at the Holocaust memorial in Berlin). The selfie is often understood to be a kind of cheerful and self-involved photographic genre. A memorial selfie is thus understood as a conflict in tone. *New York Post* reporter Steve Cuozzo writes that "selfie snapping hordes" make the memorial seem more "celebratory than solemn."[58] We can also see how the design of the memorial seems ideal for picture taking—not all memorials are—in its viewpoints of gazing into the pools. Its destination as a site of tourism effectively enables a sense that one should engage in the social media practice of sharing an image on Instagram or Facebook or Snapchat that says, "I was here." As Young and others have pointed out, most of the visitors to the memorial are tourists; rarely do they include those who were there on September 11, 2001, except at anniversary ceremonies. The memorial, Young notes, is primarily not for "those who can never forget." It is for those "whose experience of the day will always and blessedly be a vicarious one."[59]

The Flight 93 Memorial

The site in western Pennsylvania where United Flight 93 crashed is a study in contrasts to Ground Zero in New York City. Here the landscape is shaped by family farms and coal mining, both in pits underground and in strip mining operations that have reshaped the hills, and by wind turbines on adjacent hills that signal the end of the coal era. There are many stories told about the extraordinary actions of the passengers on Flight 93, including the story, confirmed by at least one phone call, that they waited in their attempt to take over the plane until it was over a rural area and away from large towns and cities. The plane was turned near Cleveland, Ohio, and passed south of the city of Pittsburgh and the relatively large town of Johnston, Pennsylvania, before it crashed at the end of a field that had been created by a reclaimed strip mine, with debris filling the trees beyond the field. No one was on the ground where the plane hit, though several people saw it flying low in the air before it crashed, and a farmer on the opposite hill was almost knocked off his feet. It crashed not far from the Shanksville elementary school, which was filled with children, and in the religious narratives about the crash that dominate in the area, that is one factor among many that testifies to locals about God's hand that morning. These religious narratives extend to many of the family members of the dead; for instance Lisa Beamer, widow of passenger Todd Beamer, wrote a best-selling memoir and became a public figure for a number of years, and her story is told as a profoundly religious one.[60]

This rural area of western Pennsylvania, a landscape of fields, woods, lakes, and farmland, is only eighteen minutes flight time via commercial airplane from Washington, DC, and the apparently intended target of Flight 93, which is believed to have been the US Capitol building. One can see in that simple fact how modern air travel has reconfigured landscapes in the same way that modern railroad travel reconfigured towns as either railroad destinations with train stations or towns that were traveled past. This part of western Pennsylvania is under the flight paths of airplanes as they travel from the East to the West and back. In one story told, the children at the local school were allowed by the principal to watch the events in New York on television before the plane crashed. When one asked the teacher if they should get under their desks and hide, she replied, "Nothing can happen here; we are in the middle of nowhere."[61] In the narratives that created what Alexander T. Riley calls the "myth" of Flight 93, with its construction of heroism, the loss of innocence of the small towns of Somerset County is one.[62] The extraordinary events of September 11, 2001, broke that fly-over status, with the violent crash of this high-tech travel machine into the field, disrupting life defined here as sheltered from the world and transforming it into a site of tragedy and war—and then of tourism.

The story of Flight 93 is impossibly dramatic. As the plane was taken over by the hijackers, who killed the pilots and a flight attendant, the thirty-three passengers and remaining crew members, alerted by phone conversations on their mobile phones, realized that their plane was part of a larger plan that included the planes that had already crashed into the World Trade Center towers and the Pentagon. Faced with almost certain death either way, they decided to attack the hijackers with knives, hot water, and a rolling cart. Most of what is known about the flight comes from the phone calls that were made by passengers and flight attendants in the thirty-five minutes from the hijacking until the crash. As I note in chapter 2, there is a chilling audio collage of those minutes, taken from phone conversations, cockpit recordings, and voicemail messages, in the 9/11 museum in New York, and the visitors center at the Flight 93 memorial has a number of recordings that visitors can listen to individually. While it was not recorded, one of the most famous of these calls is one that Todd Beamer made to a Verizon operator, who recited the Lord's Prayer with him at the end. Several of the women left messages for their husbands and families, telling them they love them and that they love their children. These messages are powerfully moving glimpses into humanity and to the powerful need to express love for others when faced with death. Yet these audio recordings provide only small snippets of what took place, which has meant that the story of the flight, in the absence of survivor testimony, has been one of constant projection. These narratives construct several of the men in particular as robust heroes—narratives that have been affirmed by numerous memoirs written by their widows—because a number of them were sports enthusiasts; Jeremy Glick had a black belt in judo, and Mark Bingham had been a rugby star (Bingham, who was gay, became an icon for the gay press because of his image as a strong gay hero).[63]

There are no images of the flight or its crash, except a photograph of the plume of smoke that was taken by local real estate agent Val McClatchey, who then immediately copyrighted it and titled it *The End of Serenity*, that shows a picturesque rural landscape with a red barn that has a dark cloud of smoke rising behind it. (As is sadly predictable in such contexts, she became the focus of attacks and conspiracy theories and then had to fight the Associated Press over copyright claims.)[64] Flight 93 has been the subject of several films, the most effective being Paul Greengrass's *United 93* (2006), which is shot like a cinema vérité documentary. The film premiered at the Tribeca Film Festival in lower Manhattan in 2006 and was screened near Shanksville, both times with family members present. It is based on a significant amount of actual testimony, and Greengrass is credited with a deep level of research, so the film makes claims to authenticity and as a vehicle for commemoration. In realist mode, it features many air traffic controllers and members of the military playing themselves, but it also speculates on what actually took place once the passengers decided to attack the hijackers, a scene for which there is no audio record. It is precisely the absence of actual images, as John W. Jordan writes, and the fact that it was the "least visible" of the four flights, that spurred the film about it.[65] The imaginaries produced by the flight are thus powerful.

Poster at Flight 93 memorial with *End of Serenity* photograph. Photo by author.

From the very first weeks after the crash, a temporary memorial emerged organically on the hillside above the restricted crash site area, where people left objects and flags and then memorial benches with the names of the victims on them. At the same time, a charismatic, somewhat rogue priest, Father Alphonse Mascherino, took over a former chapel building eight miles from the site and created an ad hoc memorial chapel, one that blends religious discourse with patriotism and artifacts from families and souvenirs and that continues to this day, after Father Al's death.[66] In addition, the small town of Shanksville has constant reminders of the crash on display. Negotiations to build an official memorial took many years and were subject to the now expected list of obstacles—slow moving government agencies, Washington politicians with complex agendas delaying funds, and, in the region, a long and protracted battle over the land of the 2,200 acre site, most of which was owned by local mining companies. Key in this contest was the question of how the value had now changed in the wake of the crash, in other words, what it was worth because of the memory industry and the commercial potential of the tourist industry that would accompany a memorial. At one point, the Svonavec family company, which owned a large contested parcel of the land, estimated its value in the tens of millions of dollars because of its commercial potential as a tourist destination, while its value as a former strip mine was substantially less; they began to consider building their own memorial and talked with real estate developers who specialize in turning sites of tragedy into valuable assets.[67] The National Park Service (NPS), which had partnered with the families to run the site, is restricted by law in the amount it can pay to purchase land, and ultimately the federal government moved to take over the land through threat of seizure in order to finalize the deal. Through this complex history, the importance of the memorial's eventual stewardship by the NPS seems particularly important, especially in comparison to the 9/11 memorial and museum in New York, which is a commercial enterprise run by a private foundation with no relationship to the NPS.

A design contest was held in two stages, starting in 2003, with 1,011 entries in the first round and five finalists in the second. The decision to have the memorial include the full 2,200 acres, a very large area, rather than just the specific site of the crash, made the design challenges unique in many ways, since the memorial is also about landscape. The Flight 93 National Memorial, which was dedicated in 2013, with the visitor center dedicated in 2015, is a deliberately spare design that is in many ways absorbed into the larger fields and park land that form the entire memorial area. Architects Paul and Milena Murdoch of Los Angeles created an understated, modernist design that stands in contrast to the rolling hills and fields it sits among and to the distinctly rural context in which it stands. Yet its minimalist aesthetic is paired with monumentality, as several of its structures rise in almost brutalist fashion from the landscape. The Flight 93 memorialization process, which was a partnership of the families with the NPS and a federal advisory commission, was largely without controversy, except for the debate that erupted when the

The Flight 93 Memorial Chapel includes this memorial to the pilots and flight attendants, with an airplane on top. Photo by author.

original design, which was called Crescent of Embrace, had a grove of trees form the shape of a crescent. Right-wing bloggers began to peddle conspiracy theories about how the design was embracing Islam, calling it the Crescent of Betrayal.[68] After modifications by the designers to create a circle instead, the controversy quietly faded.

The memorial design asserts itself from the beginning in controlling the views onto the site from all angles. All visitors must enter the site from the approach road, where they are greeted by the Tower of Voices, a ninety-three-foot-tall tower of forty windchimes, one for each victim. The area is known for its winds, which is why it is now surrounded by wind turbines. The approach road arrives at the visitor center, which sits on top of the hill, from which visitors can either walk or drive down to the memorial itself at the bottom of the field. The design of the site deliberately restricts the view of visitors onto the memorial before they are within it. As Inga Saffron writes, "Every element in the Murdochs' design is aimed at controlling what you see and when you see it."[69] The large concrete wall of the visitor center building deliberately blocks any view of the crash site and memorial until visitors are at a designated viewpoint. From a narrow entrance in the concrete wall of the center, they can walk forward to the viewpoint that looks out over the field and the crash site. As Saffron notes, "The arrangement sets up a classic architectural progression, a sense of compression followed by an explosion of space. Beyond the wall, an enormous vista is laid before you."[70] Alternatively, visitors can enter the visitor center, where there is a window that stretches out toward the field. These design elements signify that the view of the crash site should not be accidental or incidental.

From the visitor center, visitors can walk down a winding path on one side or walk (or drive) along the allée of trees that defines a circle on the other side, to the memorial plaza. Entering the memorial space, visitors walk down a long, black-granite walkway to the Wall of Names, a white granite stone wall of angled panels, each of which contains the name of someone who died. The angled white marble wall follows the flight path of the plane right before it crashed, and points visitors toward the impact site. The walkway allows visitors to look out into, but not enter, the debris field and impact site of the crash (where only family members are allowed), designating that particular area of the crash site as sacred ground. The architects, after realizing that people felt the need for the

Flight path walkway and walls of visitor center before lookout, Flight 93 National Memorial (2013), Pennsylvania. Photo: National Park Service/Brenda Schwartz.

Visitor center lookout from below. Photo by author.

memorial to have a center, placed a large boulder at the impact site, which is presumed to be where the plane most directly hit the ground. In 2011, two coffins of unidentified remains were buried there.[71] (The possibility that those remains included the remains of the hijackers as well as the crew and passengers prompted significant concern among the families in its material reminder of the comingled fate of the hijackers and their victims, but ultimately other solutions, including their cremation, were deemed inadequate.)

View down Wall of Names at Flight 93 memorial. Photo: National Park Service/Brendan Wilson.

The broader space of the memorial is like a park, and the Murdochs collaborated with Nelson Byrd Woltz Landscape Architects to create groves of trees along the edge of the field, featuring a memorial grove of maples in a circular form around its edges. The field remains central to the memorial's aesthetic with its slogan, "A common field one day. A field of honor forever." The entire design has an expansive feel, as if it

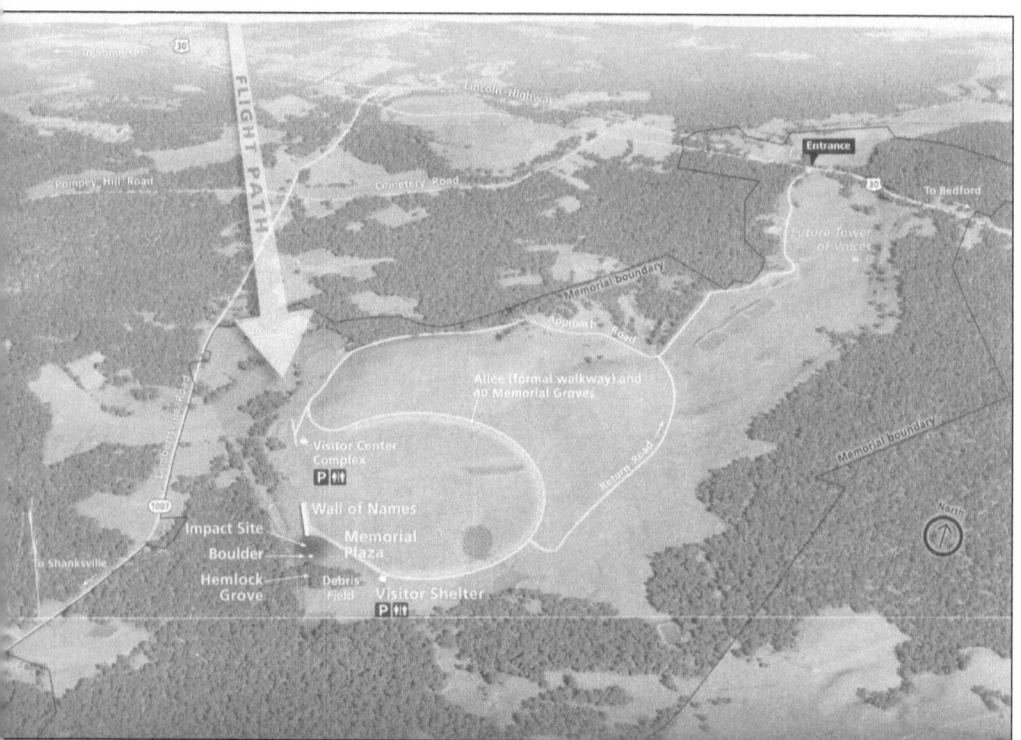

National Park Service map of Flight 93 memorial site. National Park Service.

is a space one is asked to wander through and walk about rather than stand in one place for reflection. Paul Murdoch has characterized the memorial experience as one that is open for visitors, not restricted to a particular view. He states, "Like freedom, this memorial design is open-ended, requiring each visitor to help sustain its legacy through commemoration, commitment, and engagement."[72]

The memorial thus finds a balance between minimalism and monumentality, between control and openness, and between modernism and the pastoral. Its expansiveness means that it does not actually photograph very well, with most images of it featuring the bright colors of the field and trees rather than particular elements of the design. It has often been described as a design of understatement if not severity, which is minimal on patriotic elements. Joshua Noel wrote in the *Chicago Tribune* that "where there could be excess, the memorial exercises restraint. Where it can aim for the heart, it heads for the mind. Instead of the sentimental, the memorial favors the spare."[73] He notes, "There is none of the Let's Roll chest-thumping often associated with the tragedy" but rather "simplicity is the root of the memorial's power." This is also why, predictably, it has been the subject of conservative critique as not patriotic enough.[74] Murdoch defines these aspects of the design as a response to the complexity of the Flight 93 story: "In its raw severity, we acknowledge their sacrifice. In its solemn darkness, we acknowledge their loss. In its calm serenity, we offer solace at their final resting place. In its monumental scale, we praise their heroic deeds."[75]

While the rural aspect of the site is dominant, one of the key aspects of the design is its incorporation of the history of the site as a former strip mine. Thus, any simple equation of this as a rural site that was suddenly transformed by a plane crash is disrupted by the region's history of coal mining in strip mines.[76] The pastoral aspects of the site are mediated by the sense that the land in this area had already been shaped by commerce and industry—mined, worked, managed, and extracted—before being shaped in the name of memory. Even the presence of a gravel yard next to the winding path is a reminder of the economy of the region and how it shapes its land and local politics. The field that sits at the center of the memorial land was disfigured by a strip mine—leveled and stripped—and then allowed to be reclaimed by nature, filling in as a field. This extracted landscape was reshaped yet again by the plane crash itself, which ironically put into motion a process by which an experience of nature, including ecological aspects of the design for wetlands planned for the future, would be created in the name of memory.

The contrast of the Flight 93 memorial with the other two official 9/11 memorials in New York and Virginia is emblematic of the divided nation. This is coal country. It is also deeply religious and remote from urban areas, twenty miles off the Pennsylvania Turnpike. The rolling farmland is beautiful, but the sense of financial hard times pervades. Local pride permeates the memorial, though no one who died was local. In addition to the NPS rangers, the memorial is staffed by a large number of ambassadors, now officially under the auspices of the NPS training as volunteers, who are mostly from the local area. Many of the ambassadors talk of how visitors to the memorial come with increasingly less knowledge about the story of Flight 93, often asking if anyone survived and when it happened.[77]

Merchandise at the Flight 93 memorial gift shop. Photo by author.

Also in contrast to the other two memorials is the presence of the NPS itself, which provides the understated tone of the site. The exhibition at the visitor center tells the story of the flight in a straightforward fashion, with a timeline that provides historical context and a focus on the passengers and crew. Families have contributed artifacts of those who died. There is a carefulness in the exhibition, one that avoids spectacle, voyeurism, and overt forms of jingoism despite its patriotic tone. The exhibition allows the speeches of various politicians from the anniversary ceremonies (Clinton, Bush, Obama, Biden) to do the patriotic work, and it stays close to the story of Flight 93. One feels, despite the extraordinary story undergirding this event, a refusal of 9/11 exceptionalism. As one might expect, however, there is a gift shop that sells Flight 93 merchandise alongside education materials and books, including many memoirs and religious narratives.

The story of what the passengers and crew on Flight 93 did in the face of almost certain death is a one of great courage, one that demands that each of us ask ourselves, What would I do in that moment? That the passengers on Flight 93 apparently took a vote, according to several phone calls, allows the story to remind us also of civic engagement. And in this act, they fulfilled the narrative of heroes so desperately needed in the face of the brutal and devastating attacks of 9/11. They are credited with sacrifice, with saving the lives of many people in Washington, DC, and at the Capitol, by refusing to be passive participants in the attacks against them. Because it is a story of a nation vulnerable and unprepared, unable to defend itself—Greengrass's *United 93* film shows in dramatic fashion how the lack of communication protocols between the FAA and the military meant that fighter jets made it into the air only after all four hijacked planes were down—the story of 9/11 needs heroes. The firefighters and police who died at the World Trade Center fulfill the role of heroes because they entered the buildings to save others; with Flight 93, the fact that it was ordinary people who chose to act rather than public servants who were acting in accord with their chosen profession, gives the story an even greater register of heroic narrative. As I have noted,

Flight 93 memorial coffee mug.

many stories of Flight 93 also couch these actions within religious narratives, a religious justification for what happened, that some of these passengers were destined for this role (there are many stories of premonitions of the flight) and to sacrifice for others, to be hero-martyrs.[78] As Erika Doss notes, terrorism memorials do the work of transforming individual heroic acts of courage into broader narratives that reaffirm national innocence and can render those individuals as justification for revenge. The story that the resistance of the Flight 93 passengers and crew was the first "victory in the war on terror," a phrase initially used by president George W. Bush and other politicians and now used by volunteers at the memorial, enables the ordinary people who died on the flight to be deployed as justification for the wars that followed.[79]

The surfeit of 9/11 memory, in not only the three official memorials but also in the proliferation of small memorials throughout the nation and beyond, can be seen as emblematic of a broader search for heroes in a time of trauma, loss, confusion, and shifting economic times. Yet this excessive memorialization often operates as a simplification, a smoothing over of the meaning of 9/11. Inevitably, mourning the innocent people whose lives were arbitrarily caught up in history on that day and whose lives deserve to be mourned enables narratives of innocence and heroism that are then activated in the actions taken by the nation in response to their deaths. The pervasiveness of religious narratives—the notion of sacred space, the evocation of these innocent people as guided by God—also functions to absolve what the state did in response to their deaths. Ultimately, in the post-9/11 era, an era of constant disruption to norms and structures, 9/11 memory has played a powerful social role of unity and communalism, with the reassurance provided by enacting rituals of commemoration.

2

The Objects That Lived, the Voices That Remain

The 9/11 Museum

In the vast Foundation Hall of the National September 11 Memorial Museum (commonly referred to as the 9/11 museum), which opened in May 2014, reside two objects that embody in many ways its complex, contradictory, moving yet problematic project. The first is the very large steel column that stands in the middle of the room, commanding the space. Known as the Last Column, this thirty-six-foot-high steel colossus is covered with messages, missing-person posters, pictures, and memorial inscriptions put there by firefighters, police, rescue workers, and other laborers who worked at the recovery mission at Ground Zero for nine months. The Last Column has been much written about, and as an object, it has been the source of a significant amount of emotion and ceremony. When the column was finally removed from the site of Ground Zero on May 30, 2002, it was draped with a flag and awarded an honor guard escort. The museum defines the Last Column as a symbol of resilience[1]

One could say that this steel column became an extraordinary object in the aftermath of September 11, one deeply invested with the grief, anger, and mourning of the site. As a symbol of resilience, *because it survived*, it is an object of affirmation that mediates the loss and vulnerability experienced in the events of 9/11. It speaks to the deep ethos of the public servants, engineers, and union workers who devoted themselves to the recovery and clearing of the site of Ground Zero, many of whom have suffered in the aftermath. Scrawled with names and messages, plastered with photographs, the column has been transformed into a totem of the loss that resides at Ground Zero; on display in the museum, it has been set up with a digital database so that visitors can go to screens and tap into the stories behind the messages.

The meaning of the Last Column is also about scale. It is huge, towering over the space of the hall, which itself stands seven stories

Last Column in Foundation Hall of 9/11 museum, New York. Photo by author.

underground. Its size is a reminder of just how tall the twin towers were as oversized skyscrapers that for decades dominated the New York skyline. It is also a reminder of the scale of the event, during which huge pieces of steel were twisted, bent, melted, and broken. This steel column embodies this massive scale and the shocking transformation of materiality that took place on 9/11, even as, at the same time, its inscriptions speak of intimacy, of compassion, and of sorrow.

The second object, which is on display not far from the Last Column, is a seemingly ordinary brick in a display case. This brick was taken from the compound in Abbottabad, Pakistan, where Osama bin Laden was assassinated by US Navy Seals in 2011, and it is now on display with the jacket of one of the Navy Seals, donated by the man who wore it, and a small CIA "challenge coin," apparently awarded in the agency for a mission accomplished, that was donated by the CIA operative "Maya" who led the intelligence mission to find bin Laden. There are many troubling aspects to the inclusion of this brick in the museum (it was added after the museum opened, in September 2014), not the least of which is that the historical exhibition of the museum has only the smallest mention of the killing of bin Laden, under the title of "Accountable." Unlike the Last Column, which is striking in its uniqueness, a steel column that could not be mistaken for another column, the bin Laden brick does not exude its historical importance in its objectness. It looks like an ordinary brick of a particular kind of sandy construction. The brick was donated by Fox News reporter Dominic Di-Natale, who chiseled several bricks out of the foundation of the compound before it was torn down while reporting in Pakistan. According to Fox News, he stated at the time, "America is the greatest country in the world. It's the least I could do."[2] Tragically, Di-Natale, who was originally British, took his own life in December 2014 after being diagnosed with brain damage related to injuries he received while covering the war in Iraq.[3] The layers of tragedy in this story speak to the bitter emptiness of revenge and the impossibility of closure of the events of 9/11. It is a reminder of another sad consequence of the wars that emanated from 9/11—the thousands of American veterans and journalists who have been disabled and killed since 2003.

The brick sits in the museum as a form of evidence, with a quasi-legal status, as an indicator that bin Laden's killing did indeed take place. Its presence in the museum is meant to signal a narrative end to the story

Brick from compound in Abbottabad, Pakistan, where Osama bin Laden was killed, on display in the 9/11 museum, New York. Photo by author.

of 9/11, if not closure then the restoration of national power. It has been referred to as an "artifact of justice."[4] We have no actual material confirmation of bin Laden's death, since the Pentagon apparently chose to bury him at sea, so it is only the popular culture imagining of the 2013 film *Zero Dark Thirty* through which most museum visitors would likely have learned the story of the woman CIA officer "Maya" who pursued bin Laden over the years.[5] The journey of the brick, via Di-Natale, from Pakistan back to New York, is imbued with retrospective meaning—that the brick's ultimate and most appropriate "resting place" is here, in this museum, among the objects of 9/11. Even so, the brick also exudes a foreignness, an out-of-place quality in this museum filled with artifacts of 9/11.[6] At the same time, the apparently necessary destruction of the bin Laden compound, perhaps intended to prevent precisely the kind of souvenir hunting that Di-Natale participated in, is a strange parallel to the material destruction of the towers. The brick sits in the museum as a form of justification, an object that affirms the capacity of the nation

Display of Navy Seal jacket and bin Laden brick. Photo by author.

for revenge. How could such a story ever have been imagined for this very ordinary brick when it was manufactured somewhere in Pakistan and placed by a worker within the building's foundation? The bin Laden brick exudes a kind of agency, so powerful is its embodiment of this particular political and historical tale.

The presence of these two objects near each other in the Foundation Hall demonstrates so many of the varied and contradictory aims of the 9/11 memorial museum. The museum states its mission as "bearing solemn witness" to the terrorist attacks on September 11, 2001. It has, in fact, two key goals: to commemorate those who died that day, not only in New York but also at the Pentagon and in Shanksville, Pennsylvania, as well as the six victims of the 1993 World Trade Center bombing; and to tell the story of the events of September 11, 2001, and its aftermath. The dual roles of the museum as a historical museum and a memorial museum are, however, in deep conflict. This is primarily because the memorial function of the museum to honor those who died inevitably restrains and restricts its capacity for historical interpretation. The museum succeeds in powerful ways in memorializing those who died on 9/11 and in telling the stories of heroism, sacrifice, and humanity of that day. As I will discuss further, beyond the story of that day, it is unable to provide a coherent narrative about why 9/11 took place and about all that followed in its wake, which included two long wars of enormous human and economic costs, terroristic actions on the part of the US government and military, and a destabilization of the Middle East. In other words, the stories of heroism and sacrifice of that day demand a kind of unambiguous moral clarity that the actions of the post-9/11 years are in conflict with.

The existence of a memorial museum at Ground Zero in New York now seems like an inevitable outcome of the events of September 11, 2001. Many aspects of the museum—its site specificity, its narrative, its material objects—cohere to make it seem as if it were always supposed to be at this site, now defined as sacred. Such a sense has been retrospectively constructed, however, since a memorial museum was not part of the first visions for the site. The museum is the result of many years of debate and controversy; its fate was often precarious and unpredictable. A memorial museum was only initially conceived in 2004, with its current form put into development in 2006. This was after many other cultural imaginings for the site had been proposed, including the International Freedom Center, a museum with a much broader aim to address issues of freedom throughout the world that was protested as being potentially anti-American. In these previous debates, it became clear that because of the fraught politics of the site, a museum at Ground Zero would have to be focused solely on 9/11.

Upon its opening, the museum immediately became a draw for visitors. In September 2014, it reported that it had reached the milestone of one million visitors a mere few months after its opening; by 2021, the number of visitors had reached 17.7 million. It has been the focus of an enormous number of reviews, much civic attention, and not a small amount of criticism. It has become the primary destination for visitors to Ground Zero in ways that have reshaped the experience of the memorial, which for many is now an auxiliary part of a museum visit. Because the pavilion of the museum sits almost between the two footprints of the memorial, it bifurcates the memorial, giving the impression that the memorial is built around it. The two entities are in fact intertwined, as the museum structure lies underneath the memorial plaza, and the voids of the footprints of the memorial descend into the museum space, with the two central galleries—the memorial gallery and the historical exhibition placed beneath each memorial pool.[7]

Like all the post-9/11 responses to that day, the museum was a messy and expensive project, with a price tag of $1 billion for the memorial and museum combined, an amount inflated by the cost of rebuilding damaged infrastructure at the site.[8] There were several design firms involved in its exhibition design. The original exhibition design was done by Thinc Design and Local Projects; Layman Design, which was hired in 2010, did the historical exhibition; the various digital media designs were by Local Projects; and the architects played a role that spilled over into exhibition design.[9] This means that there is some redundancy in the exhibitions—two parts of the exhibit, for instance, tell the story of the twin towers in popular culture—and that the trajectory through the museum is often filled with emotional and temporal swerves.

The shaping of the museum's various exhibitions was guided, as its director Alice M. Greenwald writes, by four key principles: "authenticity, engagement, connection, and storytelling."[10] One can also read in the museum's narrative that in its design, it was beholden to a large number of political interests and interest groups, including family members of those who died, representatives of the firefighter and police organizations, and donors, and that it is the result of design by committee in ways that were inevitable. As *New Yorker* writer Adam Gopnik writes, "Throughout the museum, the designers seem engaged in curatorial white-water rafting, struggling to keep the displays afloat while in constant peril from the enormous American readiness to be mortally offended by some small misstep of word or tone. They can be felt navigating the requirements of interested parties at every turn."[11] In a "conversation series" that ran from 2006 to 2013, each exhibition and stage of its design was shaped by intense consultation with a range of stakeholders.[12] The museum and the memorial are both enormously expensive to run, maintain, and police. They are operated by a private foundation, which is chaired by former New York City mayor Michael Bloomberg, with no relationship to the National Park Service or the federal government. While entrance to the memorial is free, the museum has an entrance fee of $26, which is waived for family members and 9/11 rescue and recovery workers. It has been heavily criticized for this price tag and its gift shop, but both reveal the ways that it is a commercial venture.

Designing the Experience of Memory

The design of the museum presented a significant challenge to the architects. Not only was it to fill in a preexisting and vast underground space constituting 110,000 square feet and seven stories below street level, but there were two acre-size footprints projecting down into the space from the memorial. The actual museum space is thus quite oddly shaped, dictated not by design choices but by the size of the hole left in the ground from the destruction of the underground complex of the original World Trade Center. There are several subway systems that border the space, with the PATH trains from New Jersey cutting directly into its lower level. As part of its status on the National Register of Historic Places, the museum design has to provide meaningful access to certain aspects of the site, including the slurry wall that famously held back the Hudson River that day and afterward and the bases of the columns of the original twin towers, as well as a number of smaller features.[13] In addition, because of its high-security status and underground space, the museum had special demands in terms of egress and access, and the entrance to the museum had to accommodate a security checkpoint. Entering the museum is akin to the experience of passing through security in an airport, with body and bag scanners. Some critics have analyzed this entrance as a kind of experiential museum exhibition to remind us of how airport security has been normalized since 2001 (it is not, of course).[14]

The vast museum space was designed by Davis Brody Bond (DBB), which was contracted in 2004 to work on designing a structure at Ground Zero before the museum director and staff were even hired. Snøhetta, an international design firm originally based in Norway, designed the museum's pavilion, which sits on the plaza between the two voids of the 9/11 memorial pools and houses the security-heavy entrance, an auditorium, and a café. The pavilion was originally supposed to house a restaurant serving gourmet comfort food by the well-known restaurateur Danny Meyer, but after criticism, this was downscaled to a café with pastries and coffee.[15] The Snøhetta structure appears to evoke an angled building on its side and is designed to provide horizontality to the site; it is bright and airy, bringing in light through its glass and steel structure.[16] Both architectural firms were actually working on previous projects at the site when the Lower Manhattan Development Corporation changed tack and put them together on the newly conceived museum project in 2005. The pavilion is a modified and reduced version of Snøhetta's original design for a cultural building housing the proposed International Freedom Center and the Drawing Center, which was rejected in 2005.[17] The combination of these two designs with their very different aesthetic experiences was thus based on the fraught management of the project rather than on aesthetic choices. Snøhetta's architect, Craig Dykers, characterizes the distinction between the pavilion and the museum as evoking the past and present: "As a reflection of the present, the Museum pavilion serves as a bridge between the memory of past events embraced by the Memorial design and the trust in the future, signified by the neighboring office towers."[18]

The pavilion houses two of the largest 9/11 artifacts, the "tridents," massive seventy-foot-tall remnants of the original façade of the towers (called tridents because they branch into three prongs as part of the gothic-inspired design). These tridents establish the massive scale of the

Museum pavilion, designed by Snøhetta. Photo by author.

space and its artifacts; they are so large that they had to be installed before the pavilion was completed. They loom over the escalators, and precisely because they are out of context, they look like two oversized forks standing in the entrance. Once visitors descend into the main space down the first escalators, the DBB design changes tone dramatically to a more somber one. Visitors descend into the concourse level, which effectively constitutes a second lobby, where the entrance to the exhibit leads from one side and the exit and gift shop lead on the other (the museum is designed to prevent those exiting the museum and those entering it from running directly into one another). The exhibit begins with a walkway through a collage of voices and images that evoke the global response as the events unfolded on the morning of September 11. Here, the shock of what happened is narrated by an array of voices, with images and place names from around the world flashing on screens. In this, the museum's most cosmopolitan moment, we see the event as a global rather than a local experience and as one that unified, however briefly, a worldview, as told through the voices of people who witnessed it via the media. This entrance effectively places visitors into the timeframe of the morning of September 11, 2001. This section ends with numerous images of faces looking up, presumably at the towers on fire, affirming one of the primary tropes of 9/11, which is that it was an event of awesome spectacle. This initial exhibition is dark and designed to act as a transitional space into the museum, thus setting a somber tone for the museum experience.

DBB's four guiding principles in the architectural design were memory, authenticity, scale, and emotion. The primary feature of the DBB museum design is a broad "ribbon" walkway that brings visitors down a journey toward the huge central space, stopping first at a vista point that looks into the Foundation Hall with the slurry wall on the left. The space is immense and awe inspiring in its massive scale.[19] The Foundation Hall is, according to architecture critic Karrie Jacobs, "DBB's best architectural moment," with the sixty-eight-foot-tall slurry wall dominating one side and the vast space both compelling to look at and to be within.[20] The architectural design of the museum, through the ribbon walkway, vista points, and large spaces, articulates the site itself as impressive, something to be gazed at. As one continues on the walkway, there is a piece of "impact steel" hung off the walkway on one side, and farther along, posters of the missing dead are projected on a wall. Farther down, the walkway reaches another vista point into the lower space and then brings viewers down to the floor below, next to the Survivors' Stairs, a preserved staircase that provided a way out to Vesey Street for thousands of survivors. This first part of the exhibition trajectory thus takes the visitor through the experience of the day from impact until the search for the missing. The ribbon walkway is a functional way to enter the museum, but it is also designed to allow visitors to approach the space slowly and gradually, with a "progressive disclosure" into the space.[21] The original "experience map" created by Thinc Design and Local Projects narrated the various experiences of the museum in first person as follows: "I arrive, I collect myself, I remember, I encounter, I explore, I honor, I engage."[22]

Tridents of World Trade Center steel in museum pavilion. Photo by author.

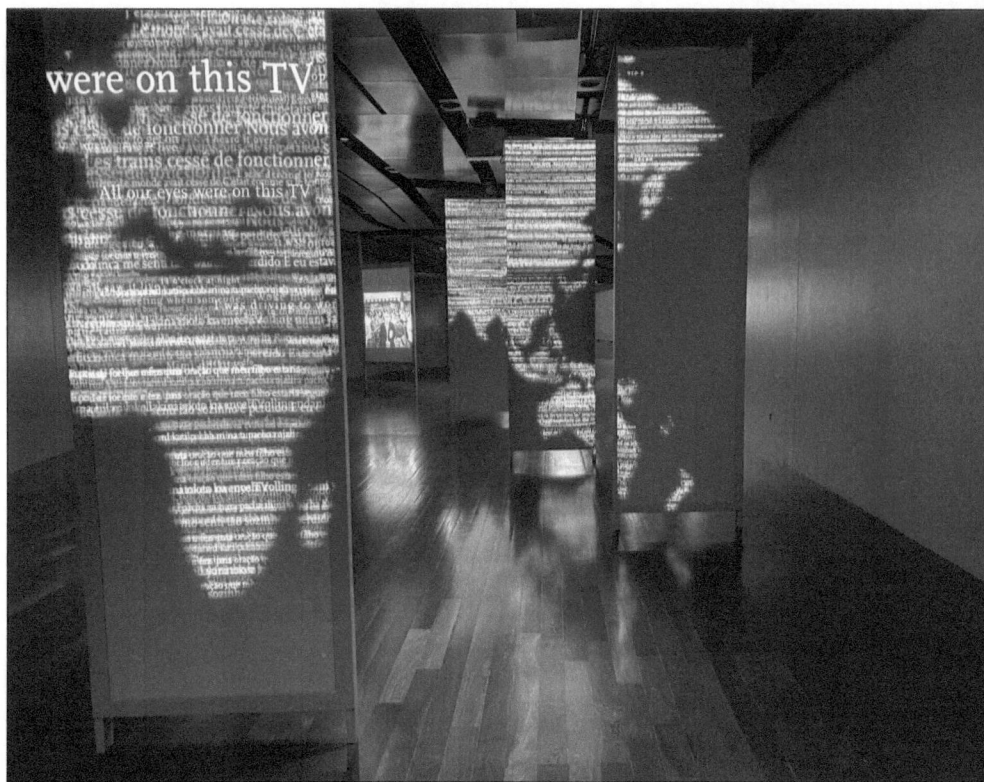

Initial corridor into museum with image and sound collage. Photo by author.

The underground museum incorporates the two enormous square structures that contain the "voids" of the memorial pools, with the memorial gallery and the historical exhibition housed below them. The architects designed these square structures to hover over the entrance level of the galleries and clad them in an aluminum mesh that provides a dynamic and textured surface.[23] (The space housing the memorial gallery is, in fact, only 57 percent of the actual footprint, because the lines of the PATH train cut into the space.) Beneath the hovering void structures, the architects made the decision to excavate the bases of the columns of the original towers so that one sees not only the footprints of the original columns but also the metal bases, worn concrete, and even the original wooden frames from when those columns were first erected in the late 1960s. These features of the museum design are surprisingly effective;

Vista point looking at slurry wall and Foundation Hall from ribbon walkway in 9/11 museum. Photo by author.

Foundation Hall with Last Column, slurry wall, and ribbon walkway. Photo by author.

Column footprints of original twin towers. Photo by author.

while one might want to question how the footprints of the original towers have taken on such symbolic power, the material artifacts carry a particular evocative power.[24] Stripped to the essentials of earth, rock, and dirt, the site has an archaeological feel.

The huge space of the underground museum, and the immense size of many of the objects on display all converge to convey the sense of 9/11 as an event of massive importance. The underground space constitutes not only the original underground of the World Trade Center complex, which has a large underground shopping mall, but also the site of its aftermath—the immense hole in the ground that remained after the debris had been hauled away. While the influence of the architect Daniel Libeskind as the master planner of the site has been eroded over the years, the public embrace of his plan in 2003 was in

Trying to Remember the Color of the Sky on That September Morning (2014), by Spencer Finch. Photo by author.

part because of his insights about how the site of Ground Zero itself was meaningful. Libeskind was one of the first to say that the design for the site should highlight rather than cover over the slurry wall and the bedrock.

When visitors descend from the walkway onto the main floor of the museum, they have a choice to turn to the right, where there is the memorial gallery in tribute to the dead and a "tribute walk" of memorial quilts, a memorial motorcycle, and other items, many of them folk art projects given to the museum. Visitors can follow these artifacts to the end of the corridor, where the second piece of impact steel stands. Then, the excavated footprints of the towers lead visitors along the perimeter, which includes explanations of the original building of the twin towers, and at the far corner, to a video about the World Trade Center and spaces for temporary exhibitions.

If visitors turn to the left at the bottom of the stairs, they come through a wide corridor that contains *Trying to Remember the Color of the Sky on That September Morning*, a large artwork by Spencer Finch of individual hand-painted blue sheets, each a different hue of blue to evoke the individuality of each person who died that day, in which a quotation from Virgil is embedded: "No Day Shall Erase You from the Memory of Time."[25] One follows this corridor with a number of large artifacts—a crushed fire engine, a portion of the towers' antenna—before arriving at the entrance to the historical exhibit and the Foundation Hall. As I will discuss further, the museum demands different modes of engagement from visitors at different times, everything from empathy and mourning, to awe at scale and spectacle, to historical reflection, to political anger. Cognizant that the museum experience can be overwhelming, the architects designed four places where visitors can opt out and leave.[26] The museum experience is thus understood, both in its size and its content, to be a potentially traumatizing one.

Survivor Objects

Within the museum exhibition, the sense of the dramatic material transformation of 9/11 is most directly manifested in the material objects that are on display. This raises the question, What happens when the material remains of violent events are placed in a museum context, in highly designed and orchestrated spaces, in the service of historical, memorial, and political narratives? The museum had many objects donated, such as clothing, that were covered in dust, now known to be toxic.[27] Its exhibition includes an enclosed shop window of Chelsea Jeans, a former downtown store, with the clothing on racks caked with dust. Narratives about these material objects and the archaeological features of the site are often couched in terms of survival. For instance, the slurry wall is often talked about in terms of heroic survival; it was damaged during the fall of the towers, but it held the Hudson River back as it was built to do, preventing even more catastrophic damage. The 9/11 museum tells many stories of individual survival that are deeply moving and powerful testimonies to the human condition. It also narrates the story of 9/11 through objects that survived that day ("survivor objects") that gained value in part through the fact—indeed, in some cases, the miracle—that they survived.[28] For instance, as I noted, the Last Column's special status is derived in part from the fact that it survived as a large, intact, and unbent piece of steel. One could take this further, as the museum does, to see it as a symbol of resilience, one that speaks to the values of public servants.[29] This object, massive and "unharmed," can provide its own counternarrative to the events of 9/11 by standing in for the city and the nation, an object that survived when people and buildings did not, a survivor with a story. As Nicholas Paliewicz writes, resilience is a mode that can help "shape collective identity without necessarily resolving trauma."[30]

Among the large survivor objects is the crushed fire engine of Ladder Company 3 that stands in one of the main corridors. Ladder 3, based in the East Village, was one of the first companies to respond to the first tower and suffered some of the highest numbers of deaths (the call came in during a shift change resulting in two shifts of firefighters going to the towers, a total of eleven firefighters who were all killed). The truck, parked on West Street next to Tower One, was damaged in the fall of the tower. Fire engines inspire awe in part through scale; they are big, lumbering machines that clear streets and fascinate children. Here the engine is stripped down, mangled, and battered. It is dramatic both in its partially destroyed state and in its state of survival. To look at the Ladder 3 fire engine is to think of the men, now gone, who once rode in it. The empty open doors, the crushed frame, the torn metal evoke the absence of those who once inhabited it. It is a sorrowful object, but it is also an object of affirmation—precisely because it survived.

The objects in the museum also raise questions about display and aesthetics. The 9/11 museum has on display two large, mangled pieces of impact steel, each about thirty feet long, that were taken from its first point of impact, when American Airlines Flight 11 hit the North Tower. The museum chose to display these two pieces of steel separately rather than place them next to each other (which could have been to great effect). One of them is situated strategically at the end of the Tribute Walkway, a long space where it can be seen from a distance. The impact steel signifies evidence of the massive destructive forces of that day, of the brute force of an airplane crashing at high speed into a steel building, yet the

Ladder 3 fire engine. Photo by author.

museum also narrates the impact steel as testimony to resilience.[31] How could this steel, formerly and even now so resolutely unbendable, have been twisted so irrevocably? Standing without context at the end of this long space, this impact steel is rendered into an aesthetic object.

One could argue that this is exactly what the process of museumization does: it turns objects—of art, of history, and of everyday life—into things that signify something more, with mystical and magical qualities. The transformation of survivor objects into fetish objects is an inevitable outcome of the processes of museumization that include modes of display—pedestals, lighting, barriers, and signage—and the valuing of objects as part of a museum collection. When such an object becomes museumified, it is transformed in profound ways. As Andreas Huyssen has written, the museum object projects an aura of authenticity in particular when it is isolated from its "genealogical context" and subject to the "museal glance of reenchantment."[32] Thus, the museum context inevitably transforms these objects through its gaze upon them, as in the case of the steel, which might otherwise have been melted down and recycled.

This piece of impact steel also raises the question of aestheticization. Standing on display in the museum, the steel looks like a work of

Piece of impact steel on display. Photo by author.

modern art, one that seems to signify the violence of modernity. It is Giacometti-like, evoking figuration with a sense of alienation that one might associate with artistic engagements with the modern condition. In other words, the impact steel looks as if its sculpturing was the result of aesthetic choices rather than an intentional act of violence. This might prompt us to ask, Does the experience of aesthetics disturb the memorial intent of the museum? It is worth noting that the other piece of steel that forms its counterpart is hung in such a way as to be impossible to see from a distance and is much more difficult to see in aesthetic terms.

Material objects that have survived a cataclysmic event manifest the very transformation that turned them from ordinary objects of everyday life into survivor objects; they quite literally become storytelling devices and stand-ins for the dead. So an object that is mangled, partially destroyed, and crushed stands in for the absent bodies that were subject to the same destructive forces. Survivor objects can have a powerful sensory effect through their material presence; we can see their textures, their battered and crumpled forms, and smell their material elements. This material presence thus imbues these objects with a kind of corporeality.

The smaller personal objects of survivors and those who died that are on display also create a corporeal presence; ID cards, watches, keys, shoes, wallets, and briefcases—these objects are evidence of the everyday that was irrevocably disrupted that day. The effect of these once ordinary objects is quite distinct from that of the large artifacts that inspire awe in part through size. Mundane objects, so familiar and yet so transformed, convey a poignancy in their altered states. Like the posters that sought the unaccounted-for dead when hope was still possible, these simple and unassuming objects evoke a prior innocence of a time when the events of 9/11 were unimaginable. With these small objects, we are reminded of the ordinariness of the lives lost that day, of the mundaneness of activities in the buildings before they were hit, of people going to work, riding in elevators, sitting at their desks, thinking of the small tasks of the day. On display in the museum, many of these ordinary objects evoke specialness not simply because they were once banal but also because they survived the violent fall of the buildings. In this, we can see that they fulfill the role of survivor objects, as objects that persisted to have afterlives. This quality awards an agency if not an aliveness to them.

They survived when people did not; in a sense, they are objects that "lived." In this sense, they evoke what Jane Bennett refers to as "vibrant matter"—material objects that challenge the notion that matter is inert. Bennett uses the concept of "thing-power" to define the "strange ability of ordinary, man-made items to exceed their status as objects and to manifest traces of independence or aliveness."[33] Objects that are transformed through violence offer a particular kind of aliveness through their evocation of survival.

This quality is perhaps strongest with those objects that were once worn by people. There is Giovanna Gambale's wallet, torn, crumpled, and burned, which was found on the roof of the Marriott hotel across from the World Trade Center. Gambale worked for Cantor Fitzgerald, a company on the 103rd floor of the North Tower that lost over 658 employees, and she died that day at the age of twenty-seven. The wallet itself reads like an extension of her personality, with credit cards and a Brooklyn library card—the detritus of an everyday life and its modes of identification. And there are Linda Lopez's yellow pump shoes, which sit in a display case, intact though bloody. There is a long tradition of using shoes to stand in for and evoke those lost, the most famous being those at Auschwitz, and more recently those memorializing the Boston Marathon bombing. From the museum display, we learn that Lopez escaped from the South Tower in part by carrying her shoes and going barefoot. Many of these objects explicitly embody the material transformations of that day; they are battered, torn, burned, crumpled. They are described as having journeys; often, they have been returned through extraordinary happenstance from the rubble to the families and then donated to the museum's collection of now more than ten thousand objects. Some commentators have also seen them as akin to religious relics.[34] These objects have moved from the realm of the personal and the ordinary into a realm of cultural memory and then to historical status in the museum.[35]

One of the most resonant of these objects is a watch that once belonged to Todd Beamer, a passenger on United Flight 93. Beamer has become famous as one of a small group of passengers who fought back against the hijackers; he is the one who apparently uttered the phrase "Let's roll" in range of a recorded cell phone call when the passengers moved forward. His watch is one of several on display in the museum, its

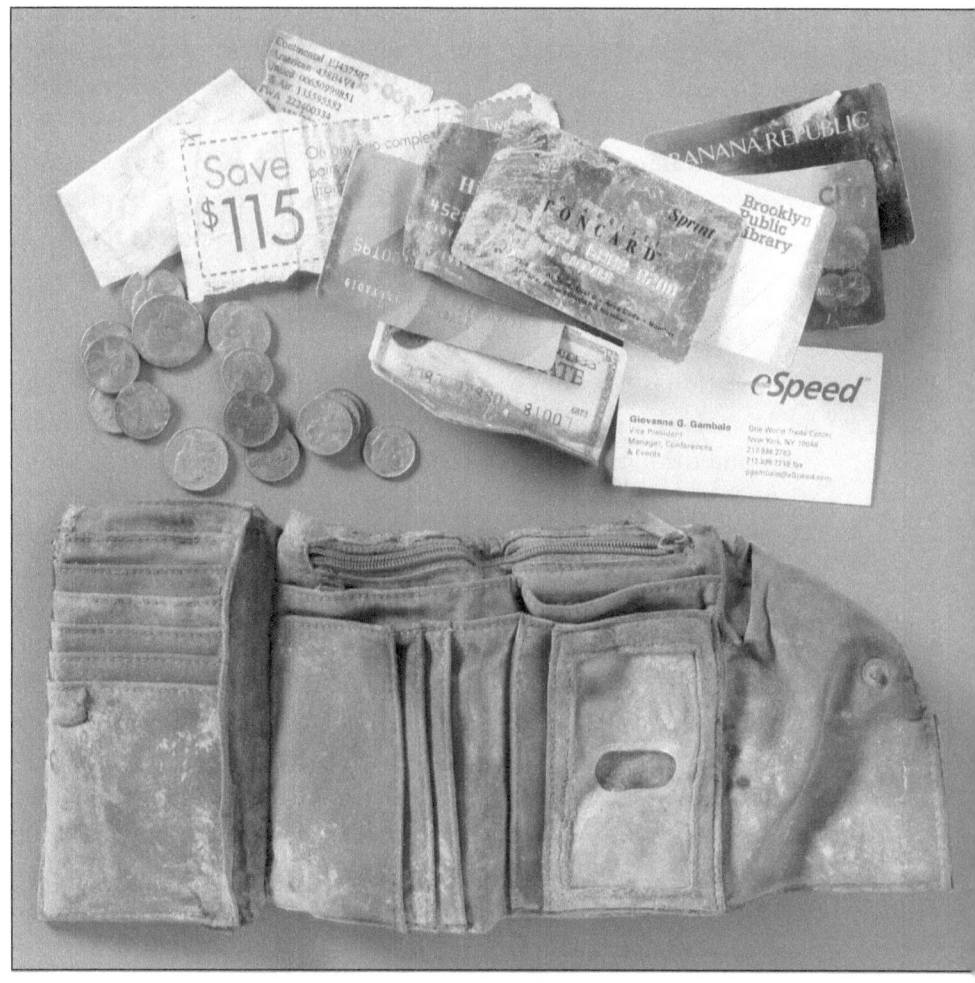

Giovanna Gambale's wallet. 9/11 memorial museum collection. Gift of Anthony and Maryann Gambale, in memory of Giovanna Gambale. Photo by Michael Hnatov.

battered frame (it was a $7,000 Rolex when first purchased) indicating the violence it was subject to and the frozen date of 11 and the stopped moment in time, 10:10, when the plane crashed.[36] In that it survived at least somewhat intact, that it belonged to this person who became famous in death as an American icon, that it held that fateful moment in time within its mechanism, the watch is itself a kind of miracle.[37] As Jan Seidler Ramirez, the museum's chief curator, notes, watches carry a particular power because they are intimate objects that have touched the body.[38] A watch is worn and thus stands in for the body that did not survive. On exhibit in the museum, the watch is also a deeply American object. In this context, we can see Beamer's watch as taking on a register of national meaning, evoking the tale of heroism and sacrifice that Beamer achieved in death and symbolizing a narrative of American identity that dominates in the museum—a can-do, never-give-up spirit of resiliency.

Material Remains and Making Presence

It is a defining aspect of 9/11 that a significant number of those who died that day have never been found. Because of this, the site of Ground Zero, and the museum, can be said to be haunted by the absent bodies of the dead, a collective absence that asserts itself as a present tension. There were 2,753 victims killed at the World Trade Center that day, and of those, 1,113 have not had remains identified.[39] A massive effort of DNA identification, led by the New York City Office of the Chief Medical Examiner (OCME), was undertaken to identify bodily remains, finally costing $80 million of federal funds. The official statistics of the OCME states that 21,906 remains were recovered, of which 14,254 were identified.[40] In the aftermath of 2001, a conflict over remains, identification, and debris from the site centered on the claims by certain family groups that the dust and debris that was taken to the Fresh Kills landfill on Staten Island had not been properly sifted and demanding that it be returned to Ground Zero.[41]

The intense demands for the 9/11 remains to be identified were fueled by a broader moral discourse enabled by science. As Jay Aronson, whose book *Who Owns the Dead?: The Science and Politics of Death at Ground Zero* is the definitive work on the story of the remains of 9/11, writes, "The World Trade Center was attacked just as large-scale DNA identification efforts were becoming possible." He notes:

> The primary goal, of course, is to link even the tiniest fragment of human remains to a person in an effort to provide proof of death for those families that hunger for such knowledge. But the massive forensic effort was also undertaken to demonstrate that Americans, as individuals and as a society, were dramatically different from the terrorists who so callously

disregarded the value of life. It was as much a political and moral statement as it was a scientific and legal one.[42]

In this context, the science intersects with affect and loss in ways that fuel the need to search further; a triumphant narrative of science feeds the belief that ultimately all remains could and would be identified. In those parts of the world where DNA identification is available in catastrophes, it has effectively altered how remains are thought of, and how societies lay to rest, or do not lay to rest, the dead. Science creates the promise of certainty in a situation of unknowingness, ambiguity, and absence.

Many families stated that the identification of even a small remain provided some comfort to what one calls the "vanish" factor. Some families buried symbolic objects or even a vial of blood as a way of substituting for the absent body.[43] Inevitably, this identification process raised the question of whether it was worth its extraordinary price tag and emotional effort. Aronson writes, "It is an open question whether the extreme measures taken to analyze miniscule and highly damaged remains were worth it. Have families benefited from continual identifications? Is it really therapeutic to receive a bone fragment the size of a thumb or even a thumbnail? Might it not have been better to bury the remains that could not be easily identified together in a respectful common grave?"[44] While it provided some families with a certainty of death, one could also argue that science could do little to allay the haunting presence of the dead.

On May 10, 2014, before the museum was opened, almost eight thousand unclaimed and unidentified remains were placed in a repository behind a wall on the lower floor of the museum. The procession of vehicles carrying three coffins of remains from the Manhattan OCME forensics lab on 26th Street to the museum was saluted by members of the FDNY, the NYPD, and the Port Authority Police, as well as many family members, as it passed by.[45] A number of family members also came to protest the placement of the remains within the walls of the museum, where many mistakenly thought they would be on view for tourists. As one protester's sign read, "Human Remains Don't Belong in a Museum." In this, the protester points to the tension of science, mourning, and the museum as an institution where objects are on display to be looked at.

While it is likely that most museum visitors do not see the discrete sign for the repository or even know it's there, the presence of the remains within the walls is haunting nevertheless.[46] Placing the remains within the site pulls in both the scientific (as they are still under the protection of the OCME) as well as the funerary. It also amps up the register of disapproval at museum activities that seem to push at the boundaries of memorialization, such as the black-tie VIP cocktail party that took place at its opening, which the *New York Daily News* called an "alcohol-fueled party" on "unidentified remains."[47] By comparison, at the Flight 93 memorial in Pennsylvania, the unidentified remains were placed in an area beyond the memorial that visitors are restricted from entering.[48]

While the disappearance of many who died haunts the site, both the museum and the memorial deploy strategies to render the dead and the bodies of the dead present. The memorial does this primarily through the presence of the names, etched into the bronze panels that form the periphery of the two voids of the memorial design. In the museum, the memorial gallery aims to render those who died present as individuals through photographs and storytelling. The walls of the gallery display photographs of the dead, including all those killed on September 11 in New York, at the Pentagon, and in Shanksville, Pennsylvania, and those killed in the World Trade Center 1993 bombing. These are individual portraits, each distinct, that the museum has gathered from organizations and families. Some are official portraits—of firefighters and police officers and those who worked for companies such as Cantor Fitzgerald, for instance—and others are casual images, but all are head shots, which gives them a certain uniformity. The names are listed alphabetically, unlike their complex arrangement on the memorial. As Steve Kandell narrates in his biting commentary on his visit to the museum in honor of his sister who died, "The crowded memorial hall is lined with photos of everyone who died and touchscreen consoles that call up their obituaries; my sister is found, as she has been for 12 1/2 years and will be forever, between Gavkharoy Kamardinova and Howard Lee Kane."[49] Kandell points, angrily and ironically, to the strange after-death relationships such lists produce.

The museum has made a huge effort to make the photo grid complete, but there a number of portraits that are empty, represented instead by

Memorial gallery. Courtesy 9/11 memorial and museum. Photo by Jin S. Lee.

the symbol of a leaf. Three families asked that their family member not be represented, and the museum was unable to find at least seven others. Ramirez states, "We're not about abstract statistics. We're about honoring each and every person who was killed that day, creating an opportunity for friends and family to see the faces they loved."[50] The absent faces on the grid potentially point to the class differences of those who died in New York that day and those who worked at the lower levels of food service industries who, as the *New York Times* reported after attempting to find some missing families, came from "lower-income families whose public footprint may not be too large."[51]

It is one of the goals of the museum to engage visitors empathetically, because it is decidedly a "memory museum" that functions to commemorate those who died that day. In the context of the post-9/11 wars, this privileging of the 9/11 dead set against the notable absence of commemoration of the multitudes who died in 9/11's wake raises issues of "grievable lives," as Judith Butler has put it. This discrepancy is sad and painful, of course, because the people who died on 9/11, ordinary people caught up in history, deserve the honoring they have received. As Butler writes:

> The differential distribution of public grieving is a political issue of enormous significance... Why is it that governments so often seek to regulate and control who will be publicly grievable and who will not? ... Why is it that we are not given the names of all the war dead, including those the US has killed, of whom we will never have the image, the name, the story, never a testimonial shard of their life, something to see, to touch, to know?[52]

Such an acknowledgment would demand that visitors to the museum, for instance, would be able to see those hundreds of thousands of civilians who died in the wars in the wake of 9/11, who were also ordinary people caught up in history, as also deserving of being mourned.

In the memorial gallery, although several display cases feature on a rotating basis particular objects that were important to certain individuals, it is primarily through digital media that the dead are made present. The main feature of the memorial gallery is a digital archive where visitors can touch a particular person's image, call up their digital profile, and ask for it to be played in the gallery. Here, families and friends can record their memories of someone, though the material tends to be variable, with some profiles narrated by someone, like a coworker, who doesn't appear to know the person very well. Presumably, this should change over time as more people participate. We see here the primary strategies through which people aim to conjure up the qualities of someone whose life was arbitrarily cut short, telling stories about them that give a sense of who they were, discussing their likes and dislikes, and mentioning those people they loved.

The digital aspect of the memorial gallery provides an interactive and deeper level of portraiture than the more traditional media, such as photography, represented in the memorial gallery. Perhaps because the photographs are in general posed and formal images, laid out in a grid, they are somewhat lacking in affect. The wall of photos has a homogenizing effect that negates the individuality and specificity of the individuals—something that the digital archive aims to mediate. Given how dominant visual images have been in the meanings of 9/11, it is striking how the photographs in the museum in general tend to be less evocative than the objects.

The material object that most embodies the fraught relationship to the bodies of the dead—absent, fragmentary, and present—is the "composite," which the museum decided to put on display after much debate and controversy.[53] This is a large chunk of debris that has been determined to contain several floors of one of the towers pancaked and compressed into a boulder-sized piece several feet high. The composite is, through its very naming, a liminal object. While it appears to still contain within it fossilized bits of paper, it was apparently formed by intense heat and pressure; the medical examiner determined that because the temperatures presumed to have created it would have destroyed organic matter, it does not contain any remains. This position is contested by many family groups, who see it not as an object but as entombed remains. Like many of the objects on display in the museum, the composite generates meaning through its textures and its material presence. It has an archaeological feel to it, as if it were dug up at the site of some lost civilization, replete with the clues to a way of life. Yet it also evokes Bennett's "vibrant matter." With its fused elements and the jagged steel cables weaving around it, it conveys an unknowability—it will never be possible to know what is contained within it. Its name defines it as a fusion of materials, an undefinable status that is about a mixing of material states to create something else. The wall text accompanying the composite, "Understand the Composite," reads: "As material evidence of the devastation and condition of the towers' collapse, the composite represents a unique historical record of these events. As objects connected to the unfathomable circumstances in which thousands died on 9/11, they also represent the unknowable."

The composite is treated by the museum as a controversial object, set aside in an alcove with careful explanations and accompanied by a box of tissues. One is inclined in looking at it to feel awe at the phenomenal material transformation that it evokes, all that is compressed within it recalling a scientific status of molecules and atoms rearranged. In this sense, its presence engages visitors sensorially and viscerally. The museum's wall text encourages visitors to see the composite in these terms, as an object of unique status. The box of tissues signals that it is also an object of mourning and of loss.

Narrating the Day

It should not be surprising that it is in telling the story of the actual day of September 11, 2001, that the museum is at its most compelling. This is, after all, an extraordinary story, dramatic, epic in its scale, and deeply moving in its stories of compassion, resilience, and sacrifice. In the stories told here, visitors see and hear details that are chilling, and they are reminded of the initial confusion as the events unfolded. Above all, the museum powerfully narrates this as a story of survival.

The primary gallery in which the museum tells this story is the historical exhibition, which is in the North Tower footprint and which was primarily designed by Layman Design. Visitors are greeted here and elsewhere in the museum with warning signs that the exhibit contains difficult material.[54] In fact, the entire experience of the museum visit was largely understood by its administrators and designers as a potentially traumatic one, with the fear that it could be one "massive trigger for victims and a trauma in its own right for everyone else."[55] The historical exhibition is demarcated not only by signs and guardrails, but also by the architectural design, in which the architects created a threshold effect. In order to enter into both the historical exhibition and the memorial gallery, visitors must traverse the excavated footprints of the original columns on a kind of bridge that design-wise indicates a transition to a different mode.

The historical exhibition begins with the morning of September 11 and narrates the story from the first moments when people begin to understand something is happening. The galleries are chock full of objects and media, from television clips to audio recordings to photographs and video footage, a kind of overload of information. The gallery is, by its placement within the footprint, narrow and almost claustrophobic, in contrast to the larger open spaces of the corridors and Foundation Hall. The exhibition moves from the morning of 9/11, with the towers hit, the Pentagon hit, Flight 93 brought down, the towers falling, and the shock of the day. It then moves, rather disconcertingly, into a section called "Before 9/11," which includes a day in the life of the twin towers, "The Rise of Al-Qaeda," then "After 9/11," on the recovery effort and clearing of the site and the aftermath. Viewers then exit into the large Foundation Hall where they can see the Last Column and the bin

View of historical exhibition with images projected onto steel. Courtesy 9/11 memorial and museum. Photo by Jin S. Lee.

Laden brick along with an interactive timeline about the journalism of the events. This means that the experience of the museum's trajectory is somewhat chronologically confusing, as the narrative of the story of 9/11 leaps forward and backward, from the event to before to after. The modes and responses that these varying elements demand—somber reflection, grief, intellectual engagement—can flip back and forth in disconcerting ways.[56]

Throughout the exhibit, there are numerous photographs of people gazing on horrific scenes that the visitors themselves cannot see. This image trope has proliferated in relation to 9/11, and as Laura Frost notes, "After 9/11, the substitution of eyewitnesses for the actual image they are gazing at was widespread in American media."[57] There are also images that are haunting and disturbing, especially those of the people trapped in the North Tower who fell or jumped to their deaths before the camera's gaze. These photographs were initially disseminated in the media and then effectively censored in the US media. One could see these images as crucial to the broad sense of global shock engendered by 9/11; when the rest of the world declared, "We are all Americans," the shocking images of people falling to their deaths from this supertall skyscraper were key to that response. The museum officials saw these images as highly sensitive material and considered many ways to warn visitors of the content and several strategies to avoid aestheticization.[58] They are presented on a side alcove with a warning sign that reads, "This area includes content that may be particularly disturbing." This phrasing acknowledges that the entire exhibit itself has the potential to be "disturbing," with these images being "particularly" so, according to Frost. The museum made a decision to only include images of those who were unidentified. The images of people falling are accompanied by testimony of witnesses, many of whom affirm the position of looking: "You feel compelled to watch out of respect for them, they were ending their life without a choice and to turn away from them would have been wrong." Witnesses tell of seeing a woman hold her skirt down before jumping, or two people holding hands. Here, as Frost notes, we are turned from the images to the voices of those who witnessed, and this testimony provides a humanizing and empathetic dimension to what could be a purely voyeuristic experience.

In the various media forms at the museum, it is the medium of audio that emerges as the most affective, with the most potential to evoke emotional responses. Within the historical exhibit, there are several alcoves where visitors can sit and listen to audio testimonies of survivors and voice recordings of those trapped in the towers. These audio retellings, which were curated by the media design firm Local Projects from several sources, are digitally sampled into groups of about six to twelve integrated retellings, as visitors look at a map of the twin towers that locates each speaker. The setting of low light allows visitors to focus on the voices, of the stories of those who arrived to the plaza level, with the dangerous crash of bodies at every turn, being told by firefighters to run and not look up or back, of the memories of the expressions of the firefighters who were climbing the stairs to their deaths. A second alcove integrates stories of people surviving the buildings' collapse. Here there are moving stories people being overwhelmed by the cloud of dust, of a group of strangers holding onto each other to form a human chain, of people picked up off their feet by the force of the collapse. Artist Vanessa Lawrence tells of thinking she is dying and then being protected by a firefighter who puts his coat over both of them as the cloud envelopes them. These stories narrate the experience of the world undone when the towers collapsed.

In these alcoves, visitors hear many voices of the dead, leaving messages on voicemail for those who are not home, speaking to 911 operators, trying to sound calm yet also saying goodbye. At the end of each segment, the screen notes in memoriam names for those whose voices were heard who died. There are calls from those trapped in the North Tower, begging for help, giving information, describing the smoke, and hoping for rescue, and there are emergency communications between firefighters who were doomed. James Gartenburg calls in to a local television station from the 106th floor, describing the scene of fire and smoke. One flight attendant tells her husband she hopes to see his face again. Laura Grandcolas on Flight 93 leaves a message for her husband: "We are having a little problem on the plane. . . . I am comfortable and I am okay, for now, it's a little problem. I love you, tell my family I love them." Her intonation and phrasing seem to reveal an entire dimension of her personality, attempting to sound upbeat and make it all sound better than it is to shield him from the reality. Some voices are extraordinarily calm as they narrate what they know are their last minutes. Orio Palmer, a Fire Department battalion chief who climbed to the 78th floor of the South Tower, shouts breathlessly into the radio to report "numerous 10-45s Code Ones"—Fire Department lingo for the dead. As Justin Davidson writes, "The realization that he will be next comes in a burst of weird, appalling immediacy."[59] These voices of the dead, preserved in this recording media, seem to come alive, to be alive, and to allow listeners to hear their fear and resolve, their desperation. It also allows visitors to glimpse their humanity and to hear their caring and expressions of love for those they know they are leaving behind. The simplicity of hearing these voices is deeply moving and emotionally devastating. One feels their presence through the timber, intonation, and vibrations of their voices. And what one hears most often is that people who fear they are going to die want those who are still living, whom they love, to know that they loved them.

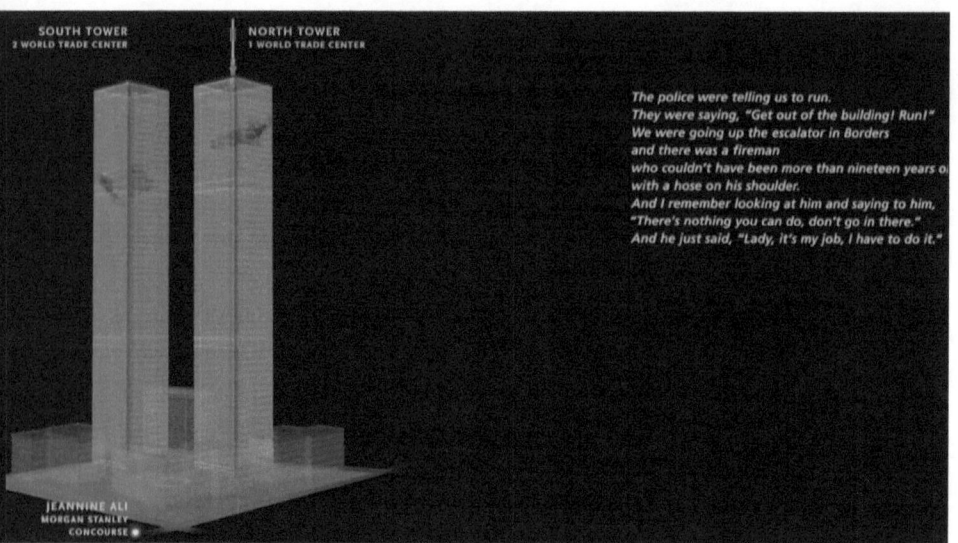

Screen in alcove for audio. Courtesy Local Projects.

Jake Barton, Local Projects director, sees these sampled combinations of shared audio stories as achieving an "epic simultaneity" that allows listeners to have a sense of the larger event. He argues that audio produces a particular kind of engagement because it "requires some form of active participation on the audience in terms of literally picturing what it is that is being described to you, which is quite different than video. It's not just listening, it's constructing meaning out of the words that are being spoken to you."[60] Barton notes that the designers were cognizant that one of the constituents of the museum would be visitors who were not alive in 2001, and that it is the "public memory" of these testimonies that "bring people back into the moment" of 9/11.

These audio collages also take the form of reenactment. The audio reenactment of Flight 93, in a separate alcove, is particularly chilling and dramatic, telling the story of this flight with a map of the airplane and audio clips from phone calls (thirteen people made thirty-seven calls from the plane), air traffic controllers, cockpit recordings, and voicemail messages. Some content is represented only in text on the screen rather than in audio. This is one of the few glimpses into the air traffic control story of that day; in one of the last moments, a controller is told that Flight 93 is down, and her voice rises in hope, asking, "He landed?

Because we have confirmation that . . ." The reply: "He did not land." She asks, "Oh, he's down, down?" "Somewhere northeast of Camp David." Here is also one of the moments when the museum fails to contextualize its narrative—the last statement, represented only as captioned text, is one of the hijackers yelling "Allāhu akbar" (God is greatest). Yet there is no place in the museum where it explains that this phrase, uttered by millions of Muslims each day as a religious statement of faith, has been distorted in its meaning by Islamic terrorists.⁶¹ As it stands now, the phrase hangs on the screen, justifying everything from the war in Iraq to the Trump Muslim ban.

These audio recordings offer visitors to the museum access to these intense and very personal moments of trauma and impending death. This inevitably raises the question of whether or not listening to them constitutes a kind of sonic voyeurism. In making decisions about what to include and what was inappropriate to make public, the museum staff and consultants negotiated a complex set of understandings of what was private and what public. The audio recordings of phone calls were donated to the museum by family members who wanted them to be shared (many of them are also used individually in the exhibition of the National Park Service center at the Flight 93 memorial). For instance, the family of flight attendant Betty Ong, who called in from Flight 11 to report that the plane had been taken over, demonstrating an extraordinary level of calm—and patience, as the ground control operators she speaks to frustratingly spend a precious minute trying to verify what seat she is sitting in—felt that it showed her impressive professionalism and revealed aspects of her personality that they wanted to share. The museum decided, however, not to play a call in which a 911 operator tried to comfort a young woman in her final moments; Greenwald told the *New York Times*, "This was not meant to be a public moment. We have to be careful not to be exploitative, to be sensitive to what's appropriate in the setting of a public museum."⁶²

The museum can be deeply moving in telling the stories of survival, resilience, sacrifice, and compassion that took place in response to the attacks of 9/11. It is significantly less effective in addressing the *meaning* of 9/11. That the museum was constrained in how it could address the political meaning of 9/11 was a given from the start, and the broad range of its consultancies during the design phase aimed to provide it more leeway in its narrative.[63] The aim of the museum to interpret the meanings of 9/11 has been particularly criticized, most pointedly by Muslim leaders and constituencies, for its representation of the Islamic faith. Complaints have focused most on the film, shown in the "Before 9/11" section of the historical exhibition, titled *The Rise of al-Qaeda*, which has been accused of equating all Muslims with jihadists and terrorists. Before the museum opened, its administrators refused to respond to the call by an interfaith group of religious leaders to change the film and to make these distinctions clearer.[64] The film is deeply inadequate in clarifying the aspects of American empire, in particular the presence of US military bases in the Middle East, including Saudi Arabia, that fueled anti-American sentiment within Islamic fundamentalism. Its short narrative is thus unable to grapple with the attack's being a response to US actions in the Middle East rather than an arbitrary attack on America.

In the gallery after the film, there are photographs of the 9/11 hijackers, an aspect of the exhibition that was much debated within the museum. As in other memorial museums, the question of representing perpetrators is a fraught one, and this has usually meant that such museums, such as the museum at the Oklahoma City memorial, are unable to explain the actions of those perpetrators in anything but Manichean terms of evilness versus goodness. Museum officials decided that to explain the motivations of the attackers might serve to humanize them, and so their presentation would be limited to evidence of guilt.[65] Nevertheless, they felt that photographic representation of the hijackers was needed. The photographs, with FBI evidence stickers attached, are small and placed low on a wall, at thigh level, so that one has to bend down to look at them. It was important to the museum that they not be placed for a "head-on confrontation." The decision, after much consultation, seemed to be that such placement would mediate the fraught feelings produced by the images. These decisions, which took into primary account the feelings of family members, indicate the dilemma of attempting to make sense of a historical event in a museum that is also designated as a memorial, exposing the ways that the discourses of grief and loss restrain the possibility of historical analysis.

The historical exhibition is an exhausting experience to go through, if not a traumatizing one. In this sense, the museum can be seen as transferring the memories of trauma to visitors in what Amy Sodaro calls a "prosthetic trauma."⁶⁶ If the museum experience is overwhelming and potentially traumatizing, it raises the question, To what end? Harvey Molotch writes, "Is it pathos for the sake of pathos or not even that, just another case of disaster porn?" Molotch notes that other museums, such as Holocaust museums, use these histories to craft lessons about dangers to be vigilant about. He continues:

> At the 9/11 Museum, we lack a similar moral arc or even a line of reasoning. We have the terrorists who did this somehow "Islamic" thing and the bric-a-brac of the deed: plane parts, building shards, wrecked vehicles. There is artifactual force. But now what? What's the history before the famous date? What could we have done, proximately or long-term, to have prevented it? What did we do afterward? How'd that go? Most important, what does any of this teach us about the nature of humanity or about politics, nations, cultures, countries, or even flight attendants?⁶⁷

What then, he asks, is the moral take-away of the museum, that we should be afraid of Islamic terrorists, that we should come together in times of attack and trauma, that it is tragic when innocent people are caught up in these attacks through no action of their own?

Part of the dilemma of historical narrative here relates to the broader question of chronology: When does 9/11 the event begin and end? Historians might argue that 9/11 begins with the rise of al-Qaeda in the 1990s, or with the Soviet Union's invasion of Afghanistan in 1979, or with the United States' political engagement with Saudi Arabia, and so on. Each step backward into the deep narrative of political decisions and events that produced the attack of September 11, 2001, itself the most spectacular in a series of terrorist attacks by al-Qaeda, can be perceived as spreading the responsibility for what happened that day. And then, when does the event of 9/11 end? Since the effects of 9/11 have dragged on for almost two decades, how is the story of what happened in the wake of that day to be told? Here is perhaps the museum's greatest shortcoming: a small room contains one image of Guantánamo, one poster about a protest against the war in Iraq, one small picture of Afghanistan, and one mention of the Patriot Act; visitors then exit the gallery to see the bin Laden brick. There is no discussion of the ways that the Bush administration leveraged the attacks to invade Iraq, a war built on lies to the US public, of systematic violations of human rights through illegal incarceration and torture, of abuse at Abu Ghraib, of thousands of US soldiers dying or committing suicide, of the drone wars, of the rise of ISIS, of the spiraling downward of the region into the destruction of Syria. That the events of 9/11 tragically drove this nation, with enormous public support, to enter two disastrous, costly, and lengthy wars that resulted in hundreds of thousands dead is not a story that can be addressed within the museum. We could say that this may be asking too much of the museum, to fully engage with the fact that the story of 9/11 is as much about its aftermath as what happened that day. But it is also the necessary work of historical interpretation.

Here it is worth remembering that the International Freedom Center (IFC) proposed for the site was imagined as a museum that would address 9/11 in relation to broader historical contexts. Informed by cultural historians such as Eric Foner, who was later demonized in the debate, the center was originally proposed by Tom A. Bernstein, president of Chelsea Piers, a sports complex two miles north of Ground Zero, and was conceived on the model of the United States Holocaust Memorial Museum in Washington, DC, aiming to be a place of "education and engagement" addressing issues of freedom throughout the world.[68] As Frost notes, "The IFC's mission was comparative and culturally diverse. It would have had the flexibility to address the interlacing of local and global factors around September 11."[69] Yet as Greenwald notes, the 9/11 museum was conceived in opposition to this broader aim: "The museum would not be a platform for a comparative analysis of terrorist acts."[70] It was precisely the ways that this reflective historical interpretation was seen as tainting the memorial function of the museum that ultimately fueled family groups, police officer and firefighter unions, and various politicians, including then senator Hillary Clinton and governor George Pataki, to call for the IFC to be cancelled. In pronouncing the IFC unacceptable, Pataki and others referred constantly to the memorial "quadrant" of the space as one that was sacred, a place where such reflection could conceivably not take place.[71] It's worth noting that the museum's expansive program of lectures and presentations could begin to look like what the IFC had imagined, but has been largely been 9/11 focused rather than more expansive comparatively.

Later, in 2010, a similar battle would take place over the Park 51 project, when real estate developer Sharif El-Gamal proposed to build an Islamic culture center two blocks from Ground Zero. Intended to be a place for interfaith dialogue, the site was branded the "Ground Zero Mosque" and the proposal erupted into a firestorm of protest.⁷² It was later quietly refashioned into a plan for a smaller cultural institution and then even more quietly turned into a condominium tower. As I will discuss in chapter 3, these kinds of policing over sacred ground seemed to fade away when the fully commercial elements of the site were opened, even though initially, that idea of sacred ground was seen to be threatened by shopping malls.

Digital Media and Collective Memory

One of the goals of the museum is to provide the possibility for many different stories of 9/11 to be told. There were many designers involved in the construction of the museum, as I have noted, and the digital material was produced by Jake Barton and Local Projects. Barton's design philosophy is based on what he calls emotional storytelling, literally crowdsourcing the story by collecting as many stories as possible. This follows the model of the StoryCorps project, created by audio producer Dave Isay, which Local Projects helped design, in which ordinary people are invited to record a dialogue together. Barton defines this collecting of stories as oral history that comes to us, and he sees it as a form of collective memory. As the Local Projects website states, "We are an experience design studio, we revolutionized the museum, we made everyone a designer, with the mission to push the boundaries of emotional storytelling."⁷³ Here the participatory rhetoric of digital discourse is clearly at work, in which digital media reassigns everyone new roles—listeners/viewers are not just consumers but producer-consumers, they are not experiencing design, they are making it.

The experience of the museum is thus in many ways a highly mediated one. As Mike Hill writes, "The museum is above all a hypermediated experience. It is as such a kind of walk-through apparatus of mourning; a manipulation of space, sight, and sound, that is by turns invasively intimate and inconceivably massive in scale."⁷⁴ One of the primary modes of distinction of digital media from previous media is the mode of interaction. Imagined within the framework of the museum, this interaction primarily takes the form of witnessing. As I have noted, the museum exhibition begins with an audio collage of voices from around the world, with images of global maps and people looking up at the towers from the street, establishing the status of 9/11 as a global event experienced simultaneously around the world. Sarah Senk notes that the museum design proposes an opening up of the category of the witness in which everyone is a witness, regardless of their proximity to the event (here this refers almost always to the events in NYC) or if they were even alive when it happened. Because the event itself was experienced live on global television, the category of the witness has become somewhat blurred, with those who watched the event on television or saw images of it online, as opposed to experiencing it in proximity, acquiring claims toward the status of witness. As Senk writes, "By framing every visitor's experience in this way [as an act of collective memory] the museum casts the physical space as an atemporal site of thereness."[75] In other words, "In the museum's formulation, anyone can be a witness merely by having opinions or feelings."[76] This is in many ways the function of a memorial or history museum: to provide experiences of prosthetic witnessing.

The designers were explicit in creating this experience of shared witnessing. Tom Hennes of Thinc writes, "We have sought to create conditions where people feel comfortable moving out of their own experience to witness these events and others' myriad responses to them with greater empathy."[77] Barton defines this in terms of the sharing of experience: "Our approach is to use the stories of those who lived through that experience to educate the people that didn't."[78] They also used digital media to extend the survivor objects as sites of storytelling. For instance, the Last Column is surrounded by digital touch-operated screens that provide the background, details, and stories behind many of the inscriptions and images on the column. Here, the digital media extends the artifact into this domain of "emotional storytelling."

Barton imagines the museum's digital media not simply as extensions of the artifacts on display or the stories told in the museum but as the essential transformation of the museum into a platform. A museum as platform can "continually evolve and dramatically change as

Museum visitors writing messages. Photo by author.

the story itself changes."[79] The digital is thus understood as flexible and open to change—hence the update as a crucial feature of social media. This incorporation of collective memories into the museum experience thus aims to democratize the memory of 9/11 and to make it sharable as memory. Amy Sodaro writes, "The 9/11 Museum takes memorial museum tropes to a new, twenty-first century level. The 'democratization of memory' ... is, in the 9/11 Museum, taking on a whole new meaning as individual memories become the foundation of the creation of historical narrative."[80]

There are numerous sites within the museum where visitors are asked to share their impressions and stories. There are booths near the historical exhibition where visitors can record their personal stories for the museum archive. The presentation *Reflecting on 9/11* intermixes these reflections of ordinary visitors, survivors, and families with well-known political figures (such as Hillary Clinton, George Pataki, former city council speaker Cristine Quinn, former US attorney general Eric Holder, and others) responding to questions: What's our responsibility

Messages written by museum visitors projected onto slurry wall. Photo by author.

to those with post-9/11 illnesses? How has the world changed since 9/11? Why do you think it's important to remember 9/11? Before visitors leave the museum exhibition via a long escalator, they are asked to write personal messages on screens that then project those messages onto the slurry wall before them. This collective storytelling and messaging aim to mediate the potential fixity of the museum and the memorial as institutions that tell an unchanging and distant story as history hurtles forward.

Primary in digital media is the dominance of data and the algorithm, and this is made clear in the digital projects at the museum and memorial though two projects, the "meaningful adjacencies" created for the names at the memorial (discussed in chapter 1) and for the Timescape project on display in the Foundation Hall of the museum, which is a map of all the journalistic references to 9/11 since 2001. Here, Barton can be seen as narrating a kind of algorithmic thinking. There is a sense, not exactly stated but implied, that the algorithm could be a crucial ingredient of truly collective memory in the ways that it can gather and connect at a scale well beyond human capacity. Just as the algorithm of the meaningful adjacencies is narrated as getting at some core truth of human connection, the Timescape project is seen as providing a potential overview of the meanings of 9/11.

The Timescape project is presented by the museum as an expression of objectivity, in which the algorithms sort through nearly four million newspaper articles from 2001 until today using key terms that are displayed in ten-minute cycles. Barton has stated that the algorithm "lets the curators say they haven't set an agenda." While some of the results are predictable, others have surprised the designers. Barton notes, "You have these unexpected timelines like the airline industry, or a terrorist event in Bali, or looking at the arc of Dick Cheney as it begins with the moment and then goes toward the end of his career. And that's what been interesting about it, is that the Timescape has both cut down on some of the work and labor that the museum might have to do to tell the post-9/11 world story."[81]

Since, as I have noted, the museum's inability to tell the story of the post-9/11 aftermath is one of its primary failures, this particular embrace of algorithmic history is revealing. As Lauren Klein points out in her analysis of Timescape, the dataset is Anglocentric, with a focus on mainstream news sources.[82] For Barton, however, the algorithm promises to extend the museum platform's mission into the future, to keep it from becoming a static institution: "We discovered that a museum doesn't need to be finished, that it can be a platform, an evolving dynamic changing set of experiences that hold truths and histories that evolve."[83]

While it is an appealing concept, Barton's idea of the museum as a repository of collective memory and as a flexible platform is only a partial story. Sodaro notes, "The story the museum tells is one of a wounded America, all visitors, because of the ethical implications of their role as witness to the events, are invited to identify with the individuals and values that were attacked." This position, she argues, is a Manichean one of "good 'us' (Americans, and by extension, visitors to the museum) attacked by the evil 'them.'"[84] Despite the production and sharing of collective memories in the museum, its exhibition tells, in fact, a very particular, heroic, and tragic story of 9/11 that is unable to fully grapple with the full history of US involvement in the Middle East that made it the target of Islamic fundamentalism, or to discuss the aftermath of September 11. As such, it constructs a very limited subject position for visitors, who are interpellated into a particular patriotic mode that divides into us and them. I never saw this more acutely than when I brought a class to the museum that included an Iranian-American student who wore a hijab and who was so profoundly alienated by the experience that a group of students felt the need to stay with her, revealing of the ways that the museum does not feel welcome to Muslim visitors. *Washington Post* critic Philip Kennicott attributes the museum's narrowed effect specifically to museum design: "It is the reigning ideology of museum design—in which the ideal is a museum 'experience' akin to the emotive, manipulative, collectively aggrandizing power of a Steven Spielberg film—that propelled this thing into a monster of cultural self-indulgence. Striving for catharsis and epiphany, they have created an oversized pit of self-pity, patriotic self-glorification and voyeurism."[85] This experiential aspect of the museum thus augments the tensions that already exist within its dual functions as a memory museum and an historical museum that aims to make sense of this event. As a consequence, visitors can leave the museum with little understanding of the broader political context of 9/11 and without any critical understanding of the devastating events of the post-9/11 era.

The Gift Shop

The 9/11 memorial museum is so many conflicting things: a memorial to those who died, a historical museum, a shrine, a sacred site, a tourist destination. It is also a commercial venture. A vast number of tourists visit the museum every day; in 2019, there were more than six million. The majority of these visitors are not from New York, and the fact that New Yorkers have tended to avoid the museum has on occasion been a concern for its administrators.[86] In 2016, the museum hired Gravity, a design agency, to oversee a branding campaign—"Our City. Our Story"—to encourage New Yorkers to visit the museum.[87] As the *Wall Street Journal* reported, the museum was thinking of ways to get New

Yorkers, many of whom say they won't go because they do not want to relive that day, to not only visit but to visit more than once.[88] As a private foundation, with no public funding and an annual budget of $111 million, the memorial and museum are constantly seeking funds through fundraising, ticket sales, and the sale of merchandise.[89] The museum has been particularly challenged in raising funds for its general operating costs, including security. The foundation is under constant criticism from watchdog family groups for its administrators' high salaries and for its spending on private security, especially considering that it is also patrolled at taxpayer expense by the NYPD and the Port Authority police.[90]

The commercial aspects of the museum are indicated not simply in its $26 admission fee but in its selling of merchandise related to 9/11. Just as the 9/11 museum now seems inevitable—though for many years, it was not—the presence of a gift shop within the museum now feels fated from the start; many, though certainly not all, contemporary memorial museums throughout the world have gift shops. The gift shop has drawn the most negative attention in all of the assessments of the museum, despite its discreet location, on the trajectory of viewers out of the museum but unobtrusive nevertheless. When it opened, the *New York Post* called it the "Little Shop of Horror," quipping, "Visit mass grave, buy a T-shirt."[91] The highest level of derision was aimed at the September 11 cheese plate, a plate shaped like a cheese-yellow map of the United States with hearts marking Shanksville, New York, and the Pentagon; it was withdrawn by the museum when the criticism reached a crescendo. Crass is a common adjective used to describe the merchandise for sale at the shop. For many family members, the offensiveness of the gift shop was equated with the problem of the remains also occupying the same space. "They're down there selling bracelets; they're making money off my dead son," Jim Riches, whose firefighter son, Jimmy, died at the World Trade Center on 9/11, told reporters. He added, "I won't go down there as long as those body parts are in the museum."[92]

The selling of 9/11 merchandise, much of it kitsch, has taken place since the first weeks after September 11, often as unofficial street merchandise of informal economies, some of it in more official stores (there have been a number of temporary official stores selling official merchandise since 2001, including coffee mugs, stuffed animals, T-shirts, and the

Merchandise in 9/11 museum gift shop. Photo by author.

like).[93] There are several categories of merchandise for sale in the gift shop. Much of the merchandise is pedagogical—books, films, photographic books. Another key category is that of comfort objects, intended for children and adults—stuffed FDNY teddy bears, rescue dogs, and animal-related merchandise. There are items that could be called souvenirs, many of which celebrate the FDNY and NYPD, merchandise of New York boosterism that existed long before the loss of many public servants that day. Much of the merchandise, however, is what we might call domestic merchandise. This is typical for museum gift shops in general, like the shops of the Metropolitan Museum of Art, which generate income by selling household objects, clothing, and jewelry. However in memorial museums this is a much trickier enterprise. While souvenirs in general are designed to be put on display, domestic merchandise is intended for use in everyday life. A hoodie or a T-shirt with the museum logo is intended to be worn. A coffee cup, through its very materiality, implies an integration into daily life, so that not only is its presence at the breakfast table appropriate but it is expected. What does it mean to drink one's morning coffee with a 9/11 memorial museum coffee mug or to sip from a 9/11 museum water bottle? Is it a way to integrate the memory of 9/11 into one's life, or does it function to domesticate and reduce the story of 9/11 to one of simple sentimentality? The museum logo, attached to items of daily life, signifies a trace of the site itself, awarding the everyday object a particular moral posture that an ordinary hoodie

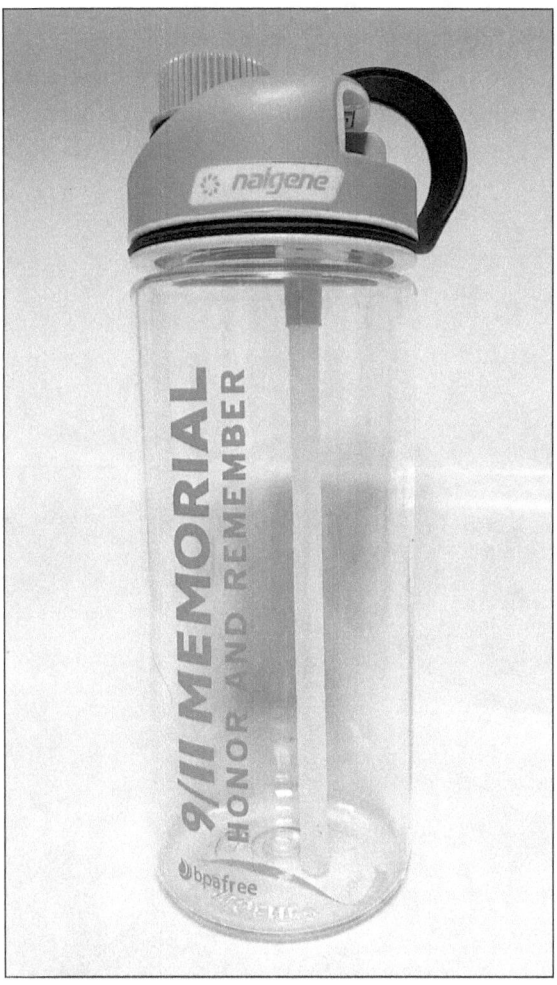

9/11 Memorial water bottle.

would not carry. It is certainly the case that souvenirs that align the story of 9/11 with patriotism, jingoism, and narratives of resilience are screening over the complexity of the story of 9/11, reducing it to one of unproblematic notions of strength and resilience.

Architectural style is also a factor in commodifying the story of 9/11 in the gift shop. The museum shop commissioned a range of merchandise by designer Josh Bach that uses the architectural form of the original twin towers as a design motif. Displayed in merchandise that sells "absence" and "honor," the familiar gothic shape of the steel outer skin of the towers is transposed into a design element for cups, trays, scarves, and men's ties. If we can think of the steel remains of the original building's outer frame as being survivor objects, this merchandise takes its materiality one step further. It recreates this design motif in miniature, packaged for consumption. If the twin towers live on at the museum

9/11 museum gift shop merchandise with architectural theme. Photo by author.

with their footprints, their materiality is remade into another kind of afterlife in the gift shop. Here, we have a domestication of the modern architectural form of the twin towers into merchandise at a gift shop at a museum that memorializes their destruction for political reasons. Who could have predicted such an outcome? It is an odd decision, but one that seems to deploy the nostalgia about the towers as a way to mediate the very selling of merchandise itself.

There are many ways that we can make sense of the merchandise for sale at the museum, including critiquing its depoliticizing effect and its crassness. As I have written elsewhere, such souvenirs sell a form of American innocence that obscures the complex machinations of global politics that produced the attacks of 9/11 not as something "out of the blue" but as a response to US foreign policy. In his biting essay "The Worst Day of My Life is Now New York's Hottest Tourist Attraction," Steve Kandell, whose sister Shari was killed at the World Trade Center, writes:

> Everyone should have a museum dedicated to the worst day of their life and be forced to attend it with a bunch of tourists from Denmark. Annotated divorce papers blown up and mounted, interactive exhibits detailing how your mom's last round of chemo didn't take, souvenir T-shirts emblazoned with your best friend's last words before the car crash. And you should have to see for yourself how little your pain matters to a family of five who need to get some food before the kids melt down. Or maybe worse, watch it be co-opted by people who want, for whatever reason, to feel that connection so acutely.[94]

Kandell writes that he was originally motivated to go to the opening family day by his outrage over the gift shop:

> By the time I finally reach the gift shop, the indignation I've been counting on just isn't there. I stare at the $39 hoodies and the rescue vests for dogs and the earrings and the scarves and the United We Stand wool blankets waiting for that rush and can't muster so much as a sigh. The events of the day have already been exploited and sold in ways previously incomprehensible, why get mad at a commemorative T-shirt now? This tchotchke store—this building, this experience—is nothing more than the logical endpoint for our most reliably commodifiable national tragedy.[95]

In contemporary American culture, we are accustomed to the ways that commercialism and branding permeate all aspects of life, from the most intimate to the most public. Indeed, some commentators greeted the gift shop with predictable cynicism about the central role of consumerism to the US as a nation. Writes Luke O'Neill, "What better way to memorialise that than by a store that sells useless, overpriced bobbles to people with too much disposable income, who have no need for, or really any idea why they'd want to buy, any of it in the first place? Forget a tower, that right there is the American dream writ large."[96] For some, the gift shop was a strange yet fitting outcome to the narrative of 9/11, which was that the threat to any American way of life—read, rampant consumerism—had now been triumphed over through consumerism. As the *New York Post* noted, the museum gift shop was funded in part by a $5 million donation from Paul Napoli and Marc Bern, partners in the law firm that gained $200 million in fees, paid for by taxpayer dollars, after suing the city on behalf of almost ten thousand recovery workers.[97] Such a factoid points to the economic complexity of the entire project, in which systems of compensation range from lawsuits to gift shop merchandise.

Why does the museum gift shop so offend? Why is it such a problem for this institution of memory to sell these items? Here, I think that we can return to the question of museumification and aestheticization, for the gift shop participates in a particular kind of fetishization. The objects in the gift shop are sold as commodities. This association of cultural memory with commodification creates anxiety; it is seen as inappropriate at a site dedicated to the memory of the dead. This reveals, among other things, that we have a romantic cultural association with memory as somehow unadulterated and unmediated, even though fetishization is inherent to memory objects. The moral discourse that shapes the museum's role as a memory museum defines the lives lost as priceless. Other discourses, such as compensation, have explicitly attached a value to the lives of those who were killed that day, but the museum's role is to define that loss as beyond valuation. The commodity, on the other hand, embodies a social life and will "live" as part of a system of exchange and valuation.[98] The museum fetish appears to transcend exchange value, according to Andreas Huyssen, so its relationship to the commodity souvenir troubles this valuation.[99]

It is easy to critique the museum merchandise for the ways in which it packages and makes money off loss and grief; that the income from sales go toward funding the museum does not change this fact. Yet if we are attentive to their effect and their appeal, we can see how these commodities convey a sense of authenticity; they signal the charged aspects of the site of Ground Zero, and this gives them a certain power. They stand in for the survivor objects, for the material remains of the site itself, and for the sense of afterlives they convey. As conservationists often note, people have a need to take objects away from sites of meaning, as talismans; better they should buy a souvenir rather than to chisel out part of a material object on display. Objects allow people to express their emotional responses to trauma, whether they are unique or manufactured.

In this sense, we can see that the experience of materiality in the service of memory can also be about comfort, about reassurance that material life goes on. These objects, whether survivor objects in the museum or souvenirs in the gift shop, tell us that the material cannot be destroyed but that it is remade, transformed, reinvented into new forms, even into replicas and souvenirs. In its enactment of modes of presence and absence, the 9/11 museum reminds us that cultural memory is mediated through many different material forms, through artifacts, survivor objects, audio fragments, photographs, architectural environments, and souvenirs. These material objects produce intangible, sensory experiences. They operate as agents, making demands on us, shaping affect, exuding vitality and vibrancy, asking of us that we think beyond the binary of matter and life.

It is worth remembering that most sites of violence around the world do not result in memorial museums. It is precisely the exceptionalism of 9/11, however, that demands its story be told as one of consequences—to frame it and make sense of it within the larger history of the United States and the world. In a post-9/11 era in which the tragic consequences of that day continue to emanate, the stories about this event continue to matter. At its best, the 9/11 museum is a work in progress, designed to accrue more stories, to hold conferences and events, and to function as an educational institution. But it fails in so many ways to provide historical analysis of what happened in the aftermath of that singular day that it ultimately reaffirms simplistic narratives of American innocence and the nation. In being framed with the discourse of memory, the museum is pulled constantly into the realm of grief for those who died that day, yet it is unclear where that mourning is intended to take visitors when they go through the museum's historical exhibit. In chapter 5, I will discuss the Legacy Museum, which takes a sharply different tack in demanding memory be deployed as activism. By contrast, the 9/11 museum affirms the nation as it was and will be.

3

Global Architecture, Patriotic Skyscrapers, and a Cathedral Shopping Mall

The Rebuilding of Lower Manhattan

The Sky Pod elevator that leads visitors to One World Observatory, the observation deck of One World Trade Center, rises 102 floors in forty-two seconds, an ear-popping ride upward in a whoosh of air pressure. As the doors close on the ground floor, the walls illuminate as high-definition screens that appear to insert passengers into a history of the landscape of lower Manhattan, facing eastward, from 1500 until the present. The rapid time lapse first begins in the bedrock underground and as it rises, it shows the pre-urban island of lower Manhattan, with early buildings such as St. Paul's Chapel appearing. As the years elapse, bridges emerge along the East River, and skyscrapers begin to rise in lower Manhattan. In the 1970s, the North Tower of the original World Trade Center appears, almost magically, to the right, and then just as quickly, evaporates as the clock passes 2001. Finally, as the elevator slides into place, the structure of the building it has risen within is built around it.[1]

As a journey into the sky of lower Manhattan with its destination at the top of One World Trade Center, billed on its completion as the tallest building in the Western Hemisphere, this video experience evokes the exuberance of the aerial view as the triumph of the modern city. In the rise of the urban center in the nineteenth century, the aerial view became a quintessentially modern way of seeing, aspirational and emblematic of the embrace of technology as a mode of human progress. In mid-nineteenth-century Paris, the photographer Nadar famously took a camera up in a hot air balloon to photograph the city from an aerial perspective, and the Eiffel Tower, constructed for the 1889 Paris World's Exposition, was built as much for the gaze upon it, with its resolutely modern construction of steel, as for the views that were possible from its upper decks, opening up to Parisians a previously unavailable view

One World Observatory elevator video.

of their city from above. The South Tower of the original World Trade Center had a well-known observation deck that was a prime tourist destination. Michel de Certeau ruminated in his much-read 1984 essay "Walking in the City" about the view from the South Tower, an essay returned to often after the towers came down in 2001. He wrote, "To be lifted to the summit of the World Trade Center is to be lifted out of the city's grasp."[2] De Certeau noted that this "looking down like a god" is in contrast to the urban practices, the "speech acts" (the meaningful actions) of pedestrians in the street.

The 360-degree view from One World Observatory replicates this earlier twin tower view, providing an expansive vista of the cityscape. It is marketed by the tagline "See Forever," a slogan that implies that the building will not be short-lived like its predecessors. Looking north presents an aerial view of the city grid, allowing the viewer to gaze up long vertical avenues heading uptown. It is a kind of pure spectacle, compelling precisely because of its status as an actual view of an actual cityscape. In a world in which access to aerial views, satellite views, and drone generated videos of cityscapes are common, the view from One World Observatory is likely to be one that visitors have seen before. As Caren Kaplan notes, today towns and cities are depicted in coffee-table books taken from the air, and aerial images are a part of our everyday life as consumers via Google Earth. She writes, "We absorb these views to such a degree that they seem to become part of our bodies, to constitute a natural way of seeing."[3]

Unlike the original observation deck view of the South Tower, the tourist experience of the One World Observatory view is one constantly mediated by digital technologies. Once visitors exit the elevator, with its multiple screens, they are immediately shuffled into a viewing room, where they are shown a digital film collage of images of the city, projected onto a screen shaped like buildings. At the end of the film, the screen rises up to reveal the view itself, as if the actual view needed to be introduced in a theatrical way as real.[4] Visitors are encouraged to rent a tablet screen to be held up before the view, which identifies different buildings and sites within each view, with links to additional information about landmarks and buildings. While much of this information is historical and contextually interesting, the device encourages viewers to look at the screen rather than at the view itself. Given that visitors are

View from One World Observatory looking north. Photo by author.

already taking vast numbers of photographs and selfies of themselves with their camera phones, the tablets add to a context in which the view is one of constant mediation through myriad screens. By contrast, the former observation deck of the South Tower had decidedly analog translucent maps on the windows identifying particular aspects of the cityscape so visitors could look through the maps onto the view. This contrast is a reminder of just how profoundly digital media has infiltrated the cityscape, in terms of how we navigate it, see it, and situate ourselves within it and how our worlds have been reshaped by digital media not only in the years since the twin towers were built but most significantly in the years since 9/11.

Even though this building is named after the original World Trade Center, there is little sense within the observatory space of the original twin towers except for their brief, magical appearance in the elevator video. The building's physical presence is one of weightiness, and visitors are protected from a vertigo-inducing sense by the thick glass windows. Because the observatory space is enclosed, as in many skyscrapers, with no access to the outdoors or fresh air, the observatory commissioned a scent, named "One World," a subtle mix of wood, trees, and citrus, to be diffused through the ventilation. As the *New York Times* notes, "The scent was made to resemble something that does not exist at the top of one of the tallest buildings in the world: trees, all native to New York State, including beeches, mountain ashes and red maples."[5] Ironically, the original design for One World Trade Center by architect Daniel Libeskind, now long rejected, had included interior trees and gardens at the upper levels.

The view from the 102nd floor is spectacular, even thrilling. One can see the George Washington Bridge, the Verrazano Bridge, boats going out the harbor, the Statue of Liberty, the Empire State Building, and numerous newly constructed glass towers in downtown and uptown. The city that one sees from One World Observatory is a city in constant flux, always under construction, with new skyscrapers reshaping the skyline every year, a city of volatile global economic shifts. The skyline of Manhattan has historically been a key factor in the city's identity, one anchored by particular skyscrapers, beginning with the Woolworth Building, built in 1913 in lower Manhattan. In the 1930s, the skyline was epically shaped by two skyscrapers in Midtown, the Chrysler Building in 1930 and then the Empire State Building in 1931, that rose above the clusters of tall buildings surrounding them. The New York City skyline was largely unchanged from 1931 until 1973 when the World Trade Center towers opened, anchoring the downtown skyline, and then, as other buildings, such as the slanted profile of the Citicorp building in 1977, were added to the Midtown skyline, it remained largely unchanged again until 2001. The twentieth-century history of the skyline was largely shaped by buildings that housed businesses and offices in the business districts of the city, Midtown and downtown. As I will discuss further, the skyline is now being reconfigured by tall, thin residential towers of high-priced condominiums, a reshaping into a cityscape affordable only to the wealthy, in a neoliberal economic context in which the profession of architecture has been complicit.

The sectors of memory at Ground Zero such as the memorial and museum are thus integrated into a rebuilding of downtown through which the power structures of New York have asserted their power to dictate the intersecting realms of real estate, high-end architecture, and consumerism. The financial structure through which private interests hold the primary power in decisions on how to rebuild the city is not new; as many commentators have noted, New York City has long been shaped by the outsized political influence of real estate developers. Indeed, architect Michael Sorkin dubbed the post-9/11 rebuilding process "the tragedy of business as usual."[6] The rebuilding of Ground Zero is fully integrated into 9/11 memory. While the museum and the memorial speak about memory in terms of heroism, sacrifice, and resilience, the architectural rebuilding of downtown defines renewal as consumerism. In this chapter, I focus on the role of architecture as a key factor in 9/11 memory and how what was built at Ground Zero constituted not only a profound failure of imagination of urban renewal but also an appalling hand-off of massive public funds to private interests. What this produced, in a city filled with smart design professionals and many innovative architectural projects, and after years of debate, is a banal corporate office park and shopping center with almost no public space.

In the context of the global history of urban destruction and renewal of such cities as Tokyo, Berlin, Sarajevo, and Baghdad, the rebuilding of Ground Zero seems relatively minor by comparison. The site of destruction in New York in 2001 is, famously, only sixteen acres in a very large city. Yet the events of 9/11 loom so large in history now that the site is one of extreme overdetermination. As I have noted, all the rebuilding at Ground Zero, from its memorial and museum to its office buildings has been contingent on the narrative of 9/11 exceptionalism, that it is the site of an event with few parallels in history. Thus, Ground Zero is dominated by the belief that this event was so important and so exceptional that it could only be rebuilt with all its elements in reference to the events of that day rather than as an urban area that incorporates memorialization. This means that the sense of the epic scale of the event has been translated *materially* even into architectural spaces that are designed to evoke awe, spectacle, and massive importance.

Like the wars that followed in 9/11's wake, the rebuilding of Ground Zero has also come with an extraordinary price tag, a significant proportion of which was paid from public funds. Estimates of the total cost of rebuilding the site weigh in close to $25 billion (most massive infrastructure projects are in the $5–10 billion range).[7] One World Trade Center, formerly the Freedom Tower, is at $3.9 billion the most expensive building ever built. The Santiago Calatrava–designed transit hub with the Oculus space, dubbed a "symbol of the boondoggle," cost an astounding $4 billion in public funds.[8] Additional costs bringing it up to the total figure include the underground infrastructure ($1.9 billion), the Vehicle Security Center ($1.3 billion), additional buildings 2, 3, and 4 ($6.7 billion), and retail development ($2 billion).[9] Key factors in these outrageous costs have been the rebuilding of destroyed infrastructure, mismanagement, demands for defensive design, expensive symbolic architectural forms, demands to meet anniversary deadlines, and the culture of starchitecture. Yet there was also the sense that the scale of the event demanded a massive, and massively expensive, response. As Sorkin writes:

> From the start, the governing powers had concluded that the only possible response to an enormous crime was an enormous—and enormously expensive—project, one that would replace all the architecture lost. Setting aside the thin film that this idea places over the desire of most of those empowered to reap huge amounts of money, there was a kind of potlatch in the riposte, a compensatory extravagance: throw money at the problem.[10]

The rebuilding of Ground Zero has been a time warp of architecture trends and real estate patterns, and its ultimate realization speaks to the conflicting power struggles over the ownership and meaning of the site. Because of the demand by its lease-holder real estate developer Larry Silverstein that the site be rebuilt with the equivalent amount of office space as the twin towers, a position fought by the city and various entities for almost two decades, the rebuilding of the site effectively re-inserts an earlier time frame when the demands of New York office real estate were quite different (though notably, the offices of the original twin towers were rarely fully occupied, which is why they housed the offices of the Port Authority of New York and New Jersey that built them). It is thus entirely possible that the architecturally branded expensive buildings that have risen at the site will struggle for decades to fill their office and retail shop spaces, especially given that the COVID-19 pandemic has prompted a rethinking of the very idea of working at an office instead of remotely, with many companies reducing their office footprints.

Ground Zero intermixes memorialization with commerce and consumerism, real estate development with tourism, in which architecture has been a key factor in the symbolism of renewal. The rebuilding of Ground Zero is thus emblematic of the contradictions and conflicts of post-9/11 America, a lens onto the state of the nation. In looking at the politics of architecture at this site, we can see the powerful ways in which the cultural capital of high-end architecture has been a key factor in the neoliberal reshaping of the urban landscape, one that has depleted a sense of the public and its right to public space. Here, this ultimately meant defining public space as a shopping mall.

Architecture in the Rebuilt City

The story of 9/11 is a story of terrorism, but it is also a story of architecture. The towers were icons of modernist style, their two-ness and immense size mediating their banality. In the immediate aftermath of the destruction of the twin towers, they were the source of enormous nostalgia, and calls were made by politicians and architects alike to rebuild them, taller and bigger than before, testimony to the ways that the loss of buildings themselves was seen as both tragic and emasculating. Architecture is a form of storytelling, and many successful architects are themselves highly skilled storytellers. Architecture has been a primary force for nationalist symbol making, and a crucial economic engine in the project of renewal. It has also been a masculinist project of the assertion of power. In the context of 9/11, architecture has been a means through which loss and affect have been given form and through which a nation, a city, and a profession have grieved. Architecture was thus burdened in this context with both the task of renewal and demands for symbolism. The fraught political battles that have produced the buildings at Ground Zero ultimately emerged from a conflict between architecture as symbolism and narrative and architecture as functionalism in the service of capitalism.

Initially, the symbolic role of architecture was a key factor in the attack of 9/11 and the designation of the World Trade Center as a target. While the attacks took place at several sites, with national targets like the Pentagon and the US Capitol as their goal, the singling out of the World Trade Center towers as a key target was clearly aimed at their iconicity as American capital and the potential spectacular nature of their possible destruction. The terrorists who targeted the twin towers of the World Trade Center did so because of the way they read the architecture and scale of those buildings as symbols not only of global US capitalism but of the US as empire. It was the architectural profile and scale of the buildings, rather than the actual companies within them, that made them a target. One could argue, for instance, that if the terrorists had really wanted to strike at American capitalism, they would have hit the Goldman Sachs building a few blocks to the north, but that building does not distinguish itself in the same symbolic way in the skyline. Eric Darton, who wrote a "biography" of the World Trade Center, argues that there is a "kindred spirit" between the architect and the terrorist that we may be reluctant to see, that the skyscraper architect and the skyscraper terrorist share the capacity to see buildings as abstract forms rather than sites of human habitation. He writes, "To attempt creation or destruction on such an immense scale requires both bombers and master-builders to view living processes in general, and social life in particular, with a high degree of abstraction. Both must undertake a radical distancing of themselves from the flesh and blood experience of mundane existence on the ground."[11] Darton's analysis points to the potentially cold emotional distancing of architecture's embrace of the skyscraper.

Al-Qaeda terrorist Mohamed Atta was a student of architecture who worked as an urban planner. Returning to Egypt from his studies in Germany, he was apparently distressed by the destruction of urban "renewal" obliterating neighborhoods in Cairo, and he then went back to Germany to join the jihad. Atta's architecture thesis makes the argument that vertical modern buildings are anti-Islamic and must be demolished to restore souks and dense horizontal neighborhoods (he focused on the Syrian city of Aleppo, a city that has since been effectively destroyed).[12] Darton writes, "Bluntly put, the Port Authority of New York and New Jersey hired Minoru Yamasaki to erect their towers. A generation later, Osama bin Laden (we presume) contracted Atta to unbuild them."[13]

Twin towers of the World Trade Center in the Manhattan skyline. Photo: Robert Harding/Alamy Stock Photo.

Darton's equation of architectural vision and the cold vision of terrorist destruction is provocative, pointing to the broader question of how that "high level of abstraction" in the design of mega-buildings like skyscrapers makes them dehumanizing structures. In arguing that "the verticalizing and leveling of the WTC constituted enactments of polarized daydreams of domination," he points to how the anti-humanistic vision of packing so many people into that vertical space parallels calculating how to destroy it: "Package fifty thousand people in a ten million square foot office block accounting for weight and windloads and, as Yamasaki did, proclaim it a symbol of world peace. Sure, no problem. And on the other end: calculate the structural properties of the target, the projectile's velocity on impact, the necessary payload of jet fuel. No problem. You just do the mathematics."[14]

With the towers' destruction as equally symbolic as their original modernist architectural evocation of capitalism, it is not surprising that the imaginings of the rebuilt site have demanded symbolism. When earlier plans were commissioned by various factions in the first years, the perceived banality of functional plans such as those by Beyer Binder Bell, commissioned by the Lower Manhattan Development Corporation (LMDC) in July 2002, was seen as their worst offense. Symbolism was defined as renewal, banality as trivializing the event through normalization. Yet as construction at the site nears completion (with a performing arts center still in progress and one building on hold in 2021), the initial imaginings of lower Manhattan, in many official and informal design proposals, however fanciful and impractical many were, have long been lost within the machinations of political and real estate power, to produce a cityscape of banal glass towers hovering over a strange looking transit hub and a memorial plaza. Banality has, in fact, ruled, as the late architecture critic Ada Louise Huxtable noted with wise foresight just one week after 9/11, in an essay titled "Don't Expect Anything Uplifting from the Pols and Realtors Now Pondering the WTC Site," that there would be an earnest process, with a compromise, ending in a "properly pious, meaningless gesture that everyone can buy without loss of face or obvious shame."[15]

The story of the political drama of the rebuilding of downtown has been told in numerous books, including Lynne Sagalyn's nine-hundred-page tome *Power at Ground Zero*, with all the drama of the intersecting worlds of city-state-national politics and of the extraordinary power of real estate developers to shape the urban landscape of New York City.[16] Sagalyn's book chronicles endless political maneuvering, high stakes negotiations over budgets and funding, and power battles that were waged for almost two decades. This is a story in which any discourse of the public and any concepts of public space were given polite "listening" forums and then shuttled into drawers. These domains were also highly gendered; all the key players in politics, architecture, and real estate are men.[17] The women who had any impact on the site were largely in the domain of memorialization—Anita Contini, charged with organizing the memorial competition and process; Alice Greenfield, director of the 9/11 museum; and artist Maya Lin, who was an influential memorial jury member.

One World Trade Center, view from the river. Architect: SOM. Photo courtesy SOM © James Ewing/OTTO.

The rebuilding of downtown, despite its influx of significant public funding, has effectively been a corporate enterprise, and at virtually every turn, the overdetermination of the site and its recuperative narratives of resilience and renewal have been deployed in the service of this corporate vision. The building of tall office buildings and the opening of vast shopping malls, which under normal circumstances would be understood in purely economic terms, have often been narrated in relation to Ground Zero as a response to terrorism. Within the Port Authority, which owns the site, a sense of mission was fueled not only to honor the eighty-four employees from the agency who died but also to reestablish its own reputation, in the words of its former executive director, Christopher O. Ward, "to reestablish itself as a great and majestic builder."[18]

The entrance to One World Observatory, for instance, begins with an underground exhibition—including fake bedrock—about the building of the tower that tells the story as one of dedication, patriotism, and renewal narrated by construction workers as a mission, more than a job. In September 2016, when state comptroller Thomas DiNapoli issued a report on the economic revival of downtown, he stated, "The terrorists clearly did not win. If their message was that downtown Manhattan would be devastated, that it would be a place that people would be afraid to come to visit or to live, you know, just the opposite [happened].... It's a way to say to terrorists, 'You thought you could knock us down but we pick ourselves up and we come back stronger than ever.'"[19] Such characterizations of the rebuilt city are revealing in their mix of discourses, ascribing patriotic motives to economic processes of urban renewal, and smoothing over the brokering, political maneuverings, and architectural posturing to give the rebuilding process a veneer of national and moral values.

The Skyscraper, Real Estate, and the Changing Skyline

The rebuilding of downtown must be situated in the larger context of New York City's dramatic economic changes since the 1990s, when a number of factors contributed to increased gentrification and shifting urban demographics. In the almost two decades since 9/11, New York City has undergone an intense explosion of building that, since 2010 especially, has reshaped the skylines of Manhattan, Brooklyn, and Queens. As I have noted, real estate developers have always had considerable power in New York City, yet that power has grown proportionally in recent decades in relation to the power of housing advocates and city government, accelerated by a confluence of global finance trends that aided the high-end real estate boom. Samuel Stein refers to this financial dynamic, of which New York City is the primary example, as the "real estate state, a government by developers, for developers." In this context, he writes, "land is a commodity and so is everything atop it; property rights are sacred and should never be impinged; a healthy real estate market is the measure of a healthy city; growth is good—in fact, growth is god."[20]

Throughout this building boom, and in the broader global context, the skyscraper continues to have a powerful symbolism that builds on its modernist origins but also moves into new forms of capital with the rise of the "supertall" skyscraper in emerging cities. Defined as taller than a thousand feet, the supertall skyscraper has become a global phenomenon. As architecture critic Paul Goldberger has noted, skyscraper office towers above a height of seventy floors have always been vanity projects, since they are not economically viable because the engineering needed to raise people above that height negates additional revenue.[21] The United States had largely ceded the mega-skyscraper contests to Asia and the Middle East before 9/11. From the building of the Petronas Towers in Kuala Lumpur in 1996, for instance, to the Burj Khalifa in Dubai in 2010, supertall towers have increasingly been used as urban or national brands, which, Stephen Graham writes, are built by "super-rich national elites as attempts to quickly manufacture sites and cities that matter, and that have pulling power, within the intense globalisation of leisure, tourism, finance, business, and real estate."[22] Aihwa Ong notes that the frenzied building of supertall buildings in Asia and the Middle East has aimed to attract speculative capital and to signify confident sovereignty, a kind of branded sovereignty through architecture.[23] The building of symbolically mega-skyscrapers has thus been a means toward using architecture as nation branding in the context of globalization. As Graham makes clear, "The symbolic function of the iconic skyscraper in the contemporary metropolis is to define the presence of the city on the world stage."[24]

Since the mid-2000s, supertall skyscrapers have proliferated in New York; in 2020, there were eight completed buildings with seventeen either proposed or under construction.[25] Technology has been a key factor here, as advances in engineering and design—stronger concrete, more efficient elevators, and computer-modeling design—have allowed developers to find new loopholes in out-of-date laws.[26] These are, unlike the New York skyscrapers of the past, largely residential towers catering to a high-end market.

After 9/11, with its graphic images of people leaping to their deaths from tall buildings, there was a haunting sense that architecture had killed. It remains a bitter truth that most people at the World Trade Center towers died precisely *because of the buildings*, because evacuating the towers was time consuming and difficult. In the wake of the shock, there was little urge to build tall towers in New York City. Goldberger writes, "In the months following September 11, despite the proclivity of architects to conceive of new forms that skyscrapers might take, it was common to hear that very tall buildings were dinosaurs, not just at Ground Zero but everywhere. They had come to symbolize fear as much as romance, danger as much as excitement, and in any event who could afford them?"[27]

Yet this feeling was fleeting at best, because of the shift in economic forces that began increasingly in the 2000s to make real estate the ideal place for global elites to park their capital anonymously outside the countries where they earned, stole, and pilfered it. As Oliver Bullough writes in his book *Moneyland*, global elites and kleptocrats use handlers and legal havens that enable these transactions—islands like Nevis in the Caribbean and Jersey in the UK, and states like Delaware and Nevada—to move legal and illegal capital on a global scale that allows them to choose what laws they will live under, what he describes as effectively a country for elites with multiple passports, numerous secretive LLC shell companies, and vast amounts of high-end real estate functioning as a "safe deposit box" for assets.[28] Along with London and Miami, New York City has been a primary location for the global wealthy to legally hide its legal and illegal capital, using shell companies, which mask actual ownership, in high-end real estate. In 2015, the *New York Times* published an investigative report on the hidden ownership of the high-priced condos in the Time-Warner Center at Columbus Circle and found the largely unoccupied apartments were held by a rash of former officials and magnates from Russia, Colombia, Malaysia, China, Kazakhstan, and Mexico, many of whom were under investigation. The authors Louise Story and Stephanie Saul write:

> Vast sums are flowing unchecked around the world as never before—whether motivated by corruption, tax avoidance or investment strategy, and enabled by an ever-more-borderless economy and a proliferation of ways to move and hide assets. . . . This flood of capital has created colonies of the foreign super-rich, with the attendant resentments and controversies about class inequality made tangible in the glass and steel towers reordering urban landscapes.[29]

Story and Saul note that at the time, about $8 billion was spent each year for New York City residences that individually cost more than $5 million, and those numbers continued to grow, enabled not only by the systems that mask capital and also by tax breaks and a city government that is effectively ruled by the real estate lobby. Former mayor Michael Bloomberg famously said, as he left office, "If we could get every billionaire around the world to move here, it would be a godsend."[30]

This influx of suspect high-end capital not only creates neighborhoods in which there are few tax-paying residents; it has also proliferated into a rash of tall towers that have effectively reshaped the Manhattan skyline. These towers are tall and thin, with developers using a variety of legal loopholes to build higher, and because they are selling apartments that cover the entire floor, they avoid the efficiency problems of moving large numbers of people via elevators. They are, by design, inhabited by small numbers of residents who are often never there. The higher the condo, the greater the view—in particular views over Central Park, which is then recast as a private park for the view of the elite—and the higher the price; these have also spurred debates about how these Midtown towers are casting shadows on the public and the beloved park itself.[31] As Goldberger writes in an essay titled "Too Rich, Too Tall, Too Thin?," the designs of these buildings are based purely on the new marketplace for buildings that are tall with views of the park and one residence per floor.[32] The first two towers, One57, designed by French architect Christian de Portzamparc and completed in 2014, and 432 Park, designed by Rafael Viñoly and completed in 2015, are nearly as tall or taller than the Chrysler Building and the Empire State Building, and both sold their top penthouses for prices near $100 million.[33] Like One World Trade Center, those towers are selling a god's eye view, above the street or overlooking Central Park or New York Harbor. As condominiums, they are also selling privacy, since the elite old-money apartment buildings in New York are largely co-ops, which subject potential buyers to rigorous and prolonged screenings and are known for refusing entry to many.

Ironically, the Patriot Act was a key factor in this boom of high-end condo investment by foreign capital in the US—thus making clear its direct lineage from 9/11. As Franklin Foer writes in the *Atlantic*, the Patriot Act made an unprecedented move to restrict banks from handling money-laundered and suspicious funds that might be used for terrorism, yet the real estate lobby managed to create an elaborate loophole that allowed for that illicit foreign capital to be used without scrutiny in the purchase of real estate, and this added fuel to the already overblown high-end real estate market.[34]

Architects, specifically celebrity architects, or starchitects, have been important to the branding of these high-priced condo towers. Buyers of these apartments are not simply parking money; they are also purchasing the cultural capital that comes from a brand-name architect, such as Viñoly, Robert A. M. Stern, and Jean Nouvel. The profession of architecture has thus been deeply implicated in what had come to be seen, by 2020, as an urban landscape of staggering inequality, one laid bare in brutal fashion in the COVID-19 global pandemic and the subsequent devastation of the global economy and its impact on cities like New York.

Architecture as a profession thus straddles the worlds of public interest and private finance in ways that are often unexamined within the profession. Debates about the ethics of the profession tend to erupt at specific intervals when its complicity with forces of inequality are rendered visible. For instance, when immediately after the election of Donald Trump in 2016 Robert Ivey, the CEO of the American Institute for Architects, which has eighty-nine thousand members, wrote an open letter pledging his organization's desire to cooperate with the new administration on infrastructure projects—"We stand ready to work with him"—he was roundly criticized for an uncritical stance toward the real estate developer president. Sorkin wrote in response, "Trump's well-documented history of racial discrimination, tenant harassment, stiffing creditors (including architects), evasive bankruptcies, predilection for projects of low social value—such as casinos—and his calculated evasion of the taxes that might support our common realm are of a piece with his larger nativist, sexist, and racist political project."[35] As architect Marlon Blackwell noted at the time, while infrastructure can mean roads and public buildings, it can also mean walls and detention centers.

The profession, through such organizations as the AIA, has affirmed its commitments to sustainability, diversity, human rights, and other values, yet by its very nature, it is about the collaboration with structures of power.[36] As I will discuss in chapter 5, architectural firms such as the MASS Design Group, the nonprofit firm that designed the National Memorial for Peace and Justice, explicitly reject this role of architecture.

The question of the profession of architecture's ethics was particularly highlighted by the ascendency of a real estate developer to the position of president, from a real-estate-dominated city like New York. As Reinhold Martin writes, "Under capitalism, property is the most enchanted thing there is. In this light, developers of property—real estate developers—are conjurers, makers of meaning; they are neoliberal capitalism's shamans, priests, rabbis, imams."[37] The role of the architects in this context is to provide cultural and social capital to these real estate conjurers, to gloss their profit making with the veneer of style and culture, without the constraints of considerations of urban planning, neighborhoods, homes, and urban life.

The building of the supertall condos in the 2010s came to symbolize the increased context of inequality in the city, with the global super-rich living in Midtown condos and complexes like Hudson Yards, while large populations of city residents struggled to make a living in the context of overpriced rents. These disparities would become shockingly manifest when the COVID-19 crisis hit in spring 2020 and the wealthy quickly vacated the city while tens of thousands of workers living in cramped dwellings in Queens, Brooklyn, and the Bronx died.

One World Trade Center

While it is an office building and not a condo tower, the building of One World Trade Center can be situated into this reshaping of the Manhattan skyline. The story of the design of One World Trade Center is emblematic of the complex relationship between the New York real estate industry and the world of architectural branding. As the primary building to replace the destroyed twin towers, it was built to be an icon. Iconicity was not only the aim of the design; it was also a demand made on the building's architectural design by politicians, design professionals, and the public at large. Before its design was even begun, the building was mandated as a symbol, and what that symbol would evoke—resilience, renewal, national strength, a response to terrorism, and so on—would be understood to come primarily from its height and its capacity to be seen from a distance, anchoring lower Manhattan as the twin towers had done.

A key player in its construction and architectural realization was real estate developer Larry Silverstein, who acquired the lease for the

One World Trade Center. Photo by author.

building with tragic timing in July 2001 and whose posturing, battles with insurance companies, and misguided mission to rebuild the same amount of office space have been crucial factors in the site's outcomes. As New York subsequently acquired a serious office glut, especially with the building of Hudson Yards in west Midtown and then the effects of the pandemic, it is clear that the machinations of New York politics and real estate mean that there has effectively been no urban planning in the rebuilding process. One of the consequences of this overbuilding, which was predicted by many but which the city was unable to rein in, is that all of the new buildings at Ground Zero have large numbers of vacancies despite having anchor tenants, and Silverstein has wrangled additional large public subsidies to keep building (building two, designed by Norman Foster, is on hold at the time of this writing). The problem of vacant offices was already evident at the time the global pandemic hit, which not only ground the economy to a halt but also prompted many businesses to reconsider their need for expensive office space. In addition, the vast amount of public funds spent to fuel this rebuilding and overbuilding is astonishing at a moment when the city is having a crisis of underfunded infrastructure. The Port Authority's essential mandate is infrastructure not real estate, and it has consistently been advised to divest itself of its real estate and focus on its failing infrastructure.[38]

The hyperbole surrounding the One World Trade Center building and its symbolic mandate has thus allowed for what is essentially a private office building to be paid for by public funds. Judith Dupré's coffee-table book, *One World Trade Center: Biography of the Building*, for instance, describes the rebuilding of the World Trade Center complex as "one of the most profound collaborations in human history," noting that all the people she interviewed for the book told her that "this was the greatest project of their lives."[39] The primary narrative that emerges from accounts of the building of One World Trade Center is resilience even more than renewal, coding the very act of rebuilding as one that affirms all of the professions involved, from architecture to engineering to construction to security, endowing each with the symbolic weight of national renewal. As architecture critic Sarah Williams Goldhagen writes, "One WTC is a project fraught with the agony of meaning."[40]

The building's symbolic burden was most profoundly embodied in the tower's original name, the Freedom Tower, which it was given by New York governor George Pataki in 2003.[41] When Daniel Libeskind won the competition in 2002 to design the master plan for the site, he proposed a tall, delicate, tapering tower surrounded by a spiral of lower buildings and cultural centers. The tallest tower was immediately enshrined by Libeskind in patriotic symbolism and designated at 1,776 feet to echo US independence.

In retrospect, Libeskind's design was a dramatically different kind of symbol from the building that was eventually built. Libeskind's tapered tower is delicate, without the bulky presence of One World Trade Center, ending in a single tall antenna, attached by walkways to a lower office tower. It included "vertical world gardens" interspersed with office levels, including different types of landscape in each: tundra, taiga, deciduous, savannah, desert, tropical. This particular vision of the building never made it beyond the conceptual stage and is exemplary of the fanciful early stage of many architectural designs before consultants, engineers, and security professionals get involved. In this case, while Libeskind had had a storied career as a conceptual architect with several museum buildings under his name, he had never built a tall skyscraper. He was masterful at selling the design concept, but the fact that he had no experience with a structure this size became fodder in the negotiations going forward and was used to effectively sideline him in the building process after his master plan was chosen in 2002 to great public embrace. Silverstein was brutal in his assessment of Libeskind's inappropriateness for the position, despite the architect's public and political support: "He's never designed a high-rise in his life. Tell me, if you were needing neurosurgery, would you go to a general practitioner who has never done any kind of operating in his life?"[42]

The design of the Freedom Tower would undergo many iterations in the first few years of the project. It was effectively taken over by the political entities governing the site (the Lower Manhattan Development Corporation, the Port Authority, Silverstein) and assigned to well-respected architect David Childs of the highly successful architecture firm Skidmore Owings Merrill (SOM). Childs had already designed the much-praised Seven World Trade Center building for Silverstein

Properties. Initially, there was an attempt for Libeskind and Childs to collaborate on the design, and over two years, the building evolved from various idealistic and utopian designs, starting with Libeskind's initial gardens and moving to SOM's 2003 design of a torqued tapered tower with wind turbines in an open-air structure topped by antennas. As the architects continued an awkward collaboration of sorts, increasingly strange hybrids were produced, with one particularly Frankensteinian version in 2003 that featured Libeskind's tapered spire attached to Childs's open-air structure, before Libeskind was basically written out of the process; according to architecture critic Martin Filler, Childs "edged him out of the commission with Machiavellian dispatch."[43] By 2005, the building was again radically redesigned—as were many structures of Ground Zero—because of security and financial concerns to have a clunky top with an antenna within a radome structure. In the final design, the radome was eliminated for cost reasons; the result is an antenna that seems to squat on the building's clunky top. Around this time, New York realtor and reality TV star Donald Trump held a press conference to attack the Freedom Tower and propose his own design of two towers that resembled the original towers, but "taller and better."[44]

The building is defined by its prismatic form of eight intersecting triangular surfaces, four of which peak at the top, the other four at the base. This is the building's most evocative feature. David Childs has stated that he aimed to evoke the profile of the original World Trade Center towers with the new element of twisting their square boxy form and that he was inspired by the obelisk of the Washington Monument. The building is thus intended to be both a play off the original towers and, in his words, a "new interpretation of the Washington Monument." As Dupré writes, Child's design "recasts Washington's monument as a massive crystal, an illusion created by a curtain wall composed of thousands of glass windows." Childs himself describes it as "a stick of butter cut with a hot knife."[45] This means that the building's reflective surfaces can evocatively and dramatically change throughout the day. Yet this tapered prismatic effect is truncated at the top, ending in a leveled top with little elegance. Even the Washington Monument is tapered in its crown. As once critic notes, it looks like a "giant air freshener with an inverted Tilt-a-Whirl stuck on top."[46]

The fundamental battle that produced the final building, embodied in the battle between Libeskind and Childs, was of architecture as metaphor and symbolism (effectively, architecture as narrative) versus architecture as modernist functionalism, from Libeskind's narrative architecture of 1,776 feet to Childs's more subtle reference to a national monument. Occasionally, this meant that the disputes over the financing of the building took the form of the argument that it was the government's duty to pay for symbolism, not the obligation of the real estate industry. At one point in the negotiations, Silverstein argued that his obligation was only to build an office tower and that the state should pay for the expense of symbolic elements such as the radome.[47]

Similarly, the demise of the Freedom Tower name was a decision that defined the building within business rather national terms. Steve Cuozzo, the tabloid *New York Post* real estate reporter, writes, "At a stroke, it [the name change] signifies that the tormented project has finally emerged from its politically poisoned origins and endlessly protracted planning into the real world of development and commercial leasing."[48] The Freedom Tower name had become an albatross, too much of a reminder of the building's potential as a future target, though the construction and iron workers, for whom the project's symbolism gave meaning to their work, continued to use the Freedom Tower name. In the world of real estate, a name burdened with a narrative of the past is unsellable. In March 2009, the Port Authority announced that the name Freedom Tower would be replaced by One World Trade Center, which in real estate parlance is a "signature address," whereas, according to Dupré, "Freedom Tower was a political message."[49] As the building has been occupied by such companies as Condé Nast, it has been normalized as a business address, away from its symbolic moniker.

One of the few features from Libeskind's original plan that survived the redesign process was his designation of the building's height as a metaphoric 1,776 feet. In the early moment of raw emotion and grief during which Libeskind's master plan was chosen, this was a kitschy patriotic gesture at national symbolism; the building's height in feet is undetectable, of course, to those looking at it, and both the aesthetic detail and its symbolism must be explained. This gesture remains as empty now as when it was when it was first suggested. For the building to qualify for the (somewhat meaningless) title of the tallest building in the Western Hemisphere, it was extended from its actual height of 1,368 feet to 1,776 feet by its antenna. Crucial in the negotiation over the awarding of that title, which had been held by the Willis (Sears) Tower in Chicago and had to be approved by the Height Committee of the Council on Tall Buildings and Urban Habitat, was whether the structure extending its height to 1,776 feet was a spire or an antenna. Apparently, Childs made a persuasive appeal to the building's symbolism, comparing the spire to the torch of the Statue of Liberty. Here, Libeskind's original vision was still at play, as he often staged his master plan with the Statue of Liberty as a reference point. Nevertheless, the spire of the building gives the building an unsymbolic crown and is largely understood as a cheap way to qualify for height. As *New York Times* architecture critic Michael Kimmelman notes, "Counting the antenna is like counting relish at a hot dog eating contest."[50]

One might well wonder why the height of the building mattered so much. The answer lay in the symbolism of the building's scale, which was meant to project national power, resilience, and masculine prowess—a kind of f-you to al-Qaeda in the form of architecture. As I have noted, very tall skyscrapers do not make sense economically as buildings, thus symbolism is their key selling feature.[51] Symbolism is thus often marshaled as the key feature of the building's uniqueness. As one Port Authority official stated, "It's like building the Statue of Liberty."[52] Dupré writes, in a text exemplary of this hyperbole, "One World Trade Center occupies a realm beyond mere measurement.... This tower aspires to a higher order, where what is most important is intangible. Remembrance, resolve, faith in the future... dedicated to freedom, the tower will stand as tall as each individual believes it can."[53]

This level of overdetermination inevitably means that the building will not achieve its intended iconic status. Goldhagen writes, "Everyone had every right to expect a major civic icon.... As a civic icon and public monument, what One WTC mostly represents is a gross betrayal of public trust. In no way is it remarkable. No heart will soar at its prospect. The base is horrendously clunky, the overall composition disjointed and incoherent. It crashes into rather than meets the ground." Goldhagen makes clear the ways that the private-public partnerships involved in the building compromised the design, giving various entities and Silverstein far too much power without public input, time and time again, in a building funded by public money. She ends by noting, "This building should never had become what it is, a failed project by an excellent design firm, and a symbol of American political incompetence, private ignorance, and greed."

Among architecture critics, the building has been largely received as an emblem of banality, an empty symbol of hollowed-out power, what one critic refers to as an "icy stalagmite."[54] Kimmelman wrote when it opened in 2014, "Like the corporate campus and plaza it shares, 1 World Trade speaks volumes about political opportunism, outmoded thinking and upside-down urban priorities. It's what happens when a commercial developer is pretty much handed the keys to the castle. . . . I find myself picturing General MacArthur in aviator sunglasses when I see the building. Its mirrored exterior is opaque, shellacked, monomaniacal."[55]

There is one measure, however, by which the building's iconicity might be measured: its replication into tourist curios and kitsch, as the original twin towers had been. After it had been open a few years, the building began to proliferate on pizza boxes and in tourist goods—snow globes, paperweights, keychains, shot glasses. As *New York Times* reporters David Dunlap and Todd Heisler note, "Using Times Square tchotchke shops as a barometer, the . . . tower is already nearing the apotheosis of kitsch."[56] This is perhaps most meaningful when one considers that the twin towers continue to be an iconic feature in tourist curios almost twenty years after they were destroyed.

Where One World Trade Center really emerges as a symbol of post-9/11 US culture is through its security design and defensive architecture, which is a primary factor in its exorbitant price tag. Since it is presumed to always be a target because of its scale and its location on the site of the twin towers, it was designed to withstand any potential attack that can be imagined within the security parameters of today. The building was redesigned in 2005 in response to security concerns raised by the NYPD, which resulted in its twenty-story concrete base, designed to withstand any potential bombings, which the architect masked with glass panels or "fins." This bunker means there are no storefronts in the building, and in addition, the area surrounding its entrance is essentially cordoned off by security bollards and forbids any street-level activity. As Goldhagen writes, this demand for high-security design was one of several "inexcusable decisions" leading to the final design, with "the insistence by New York City's police department that this supertall tower be built to security specifications resembling those of a U.S. embassy on foreign soil." She continues, this "projects cowardice, not strength; as one architect involved in its design told me, we might as well live underground."[57] Here we see scale as a form of defense, and defense as an inevitable outcome of massive scale. It is as if the site were caught up in its own spiraling set of meanings that feed on each other. In de Certeau's terms, there are no pedestrian speech acts of the street here, with adjacent streets designed to be empty of the bustle of urban life. One could say it is Jane Jacobs's nightmare. As Nicolai Ouroussoff writes, "If this is a potentially fascinating work of architecture, it is, sadly, fascinating in the way that Albert Speer's architectural nightmares were fascinating: as expressions of the values of a particular time and era. The Freedom Tower embodies, in its way, a world shaped by fear."[58] Even David Childs appeared to question the security project, stating, "Do you design for a small bomb, dirty bomb, small aircraft? Yes, if a plane flew into the new building the building would respond differently [than] the twin towers.... But the place to solve these problems is at airports, not in buildings, or all we'd have would be concrete towers."[59]

One World Trade Center is essentially a very large office building. It has a dramatic lobby space and spacious office floors with spectacular views. The decision of Condé Nast publishers to move from their Midtown offices down to One World Trade Center in 2014 as its anchor tenant, with a twenty-five-year lease at $2 billion and significant tax breaks, was followed with great attention in the press (Condé Nast has since considerably shrunk its footprint in the building). Like the original twin towers, the building was always in danger of falling short of full occupancy, even before the economic crisis, and so from the beginning, the Port Authority pledged to house departments there (it also has offices in Four World Trade Center), and the federal government houses the General Services Administration, the Federal Emergency Management Agency, and the US Customs and Border Patrol in the building. Condé Nast's highly favorable terms to anchor the building means, according to Joe Nocera, that "a company that publishes high-end magazines aimed at rich people will be getting an enormous government subsidy for the

Fortified base of One World Trade Center. Photo by author.

Security bollards near One World Trade Center. Photo by author.

foreseeable future."⁶⁰ Nocera points out that the Port Authority, which had pledged not to raise tolls on the Hudson River bridges and tunnels because of the building, did just that, and that politicians and even the press were tiptoeing around criticizing the building because of its overwrought symbolism. The Port Authority had actually sold the idea of the tolls by threatening to slow work on the building, which angered the construction unions who applied their political muscle to the politicians. The Condé Nast deal also had the effect of bringing an entire ecosystem of related businesses to the neighborhood, including nail salons and blow bars, all of which needed to be situated within a few blocks, literally the distance walkable in high heels.⁶¹ The urban landscape thus evolves from the large scale to the dictates of something as small as a shoe heel.

One World Trade Center is now the primary building in a group of World Trade Center buildings, which began with the building of Seven World Trade Center north of the complex in 2006, a shimmering glass tower of fifty-two floors designed by David Childs and SOM, and the construction of Three and Four World Trade Center to the east of the memorial and museum. Designed by Japanese architect Fumihiko Maki, building four is a seventy-two-story glass tower, completed in 2013, with stepped levels, described by the architect as "a 'minimalist' tower that achieves an appropriate presence, quiet but with dignity, and a 'podium' that becomes a catalyst for activating the surrounding urban streetscape as part of the revitalization of lower Manhattan."⁶² Building three, completed in 2018 and designed by British architect Richard Rogers's firm, Rogers Stirk Harbour + Partners, is an eighty-floor glass tower with a K-frame design along its edge. Building two was built up to street level and then delayed because Silverstein was unable to lock in an anchor tenant. The tower was originally designed by British architect Norman Foster (Foster + Partners) with a slanted four-column top and then was redesigned into a series of stepped boxes by Bjarke Ingels (BIG) when several media companies, including News Corporation and 21st Century Fox, were planning to move there. When that deal fell through, Silverstein then reverted back to Foster for a revised design in 2021.

The real estate and architecture press largely followed the building of this complex of buildings as a horse race for tenant acquisition, following the story of deals with tenants such as Spotify, Uber, BMI, and

One World Trade Center at dusk, with memorial and museum pavilion. Architect: SOM. Photo courtesy SOM © James Ewing/OTTO.

MediaMath. With the global economic crisis of 2020, however, this overbuilding of office space in tall corporate glass towers appears to have been, as many predicted starting as early as 2001, a misguided view of the urban landscape of New York in the twenty-first century. While downtown was being developed by Silverstein, the Hudson Yards complex was adding significant numbers of offices in west Midtown. That the downtown office space has been filled with newer companies of the tech-app-share economy, the kinds of companies that did not even exist in 2001, rather than more traditional finance companies, demonstrates the shifting terrain of lower Manhattan, where proximity to Hoboken/Jersey City and Brooklyn are selling points for a young demographic of workers. Yet these are also companies for whom the crisis of the pandemic shutdown also means a rethinking of the role of office space in general and the rise of the virtual office. The rebuilding of downtown was thus planned for an economy that predated the twin towers fall and then woefully overbuilt for the post-pandemic shrinkage of the retail and office space.

The complex of now strangely numbered World Trade Center buildings (no five or six are likely) represents not only a failed project of architecture, with a banal set of glass towers ringing the memorial complex, and a failed set of economics, with empty office spaces in a neighborhood that has a strong need for residential spaces, but also a shameful example of real estate maneuvering at the expense of public funds and public space. Silverstein, who before September 11 had been considered to be what Martin Filler calls "something of a bottom-feeder among the big deal *machers* of the New York real estate establishment," is painted in the various histories of the rebuilding process as a creature of greed glossed through a narrative of patriotism.[63] These buildings have been heavily subsidized by public funds from the federal government, the Port Authority, New York State, and New York City, effectively all of it taxpayer dollars, a significant portion of the $25 billion deployed to rebuild Ground Zero that, aside from the memorial and museum, have provided little more than office buildings.

And of course, a New York real estate developer with no prior government experience was elected president of the nation in the midst of this rebuilding process. Silverstein's playbook bears a strong resemblance to Trump's long career of leveraging public funds and tax breaks for personal profit.⁶⁴ Reinhold Martin makes the comparison of Silverstein and Trump explicit. Defining the "master builder who restores meaning to the desolate landscapes of imperial decline" as assigned by neoliberalism to the role of the real estate developer, he writes:

> At Ground Zero, it was the lessee of the World Trade Center, Larry Silverstein, a relatively minor New York player whose unrelenting effort to turn tragedy into profit by "rebuilding" a sacred site was recast as an epic struggle with public authorities, insurance companies, and potential tenants. On the national stage, it was another minor player in New York real estate who cast himself as an artist—or better, an architect—charged with rebuilding the nation as sacred ground: "Make America Great Again."⁶⁵

Martin's characterization of the developer as "conjurer" makes this comparison to Trump the politician apt. The romanticization of the real estate developer as the ultimate dealmaker undergirds the powerful role they have played undermining the role of the public in the urban landscape of cities like New York.

The Shopping Mall Cathedral

Of all the structures built at Ground Zero, the one that has produced the most virulent debates about cost and value is the transportation hub, designed by Spanish architect Santiago Calatrava, with its most famous space, the Oculus. While it is not a particularly large structure above ground, the Calatrava transportation hub consists of a substantial underground station for the PATH trains to New Jersey with the large cathedral-like atrium of the Oculus connecting to several subways lines under an above-ground structure of arching white winged forms. The structure was assigned early on to Calatrava, who is known for building inspirational structures, and it was largely praised initially for its symbolism of hope and renewal. Indeed, the unveiling of the commission and design in January 2004 was rapturous if not ecstatic. The exterior building of the Oculus is designed by Calatrava to resemble a "bird in flight," and at the ceremony, the architect's young daughter released two doves (actually, Nassau County homing pigeons masquerading as doves). The Port Authority had commissioned Calatrava to build a transportation hub, a project clearly within its mission as an agency, but what it was really purchasing was a symbolic structure. The building would become so overdetermined that it was eventually freighted with the meanings of the entire site, including the sense of vast funds wasted and architectural visions failed. At the unveiling of the design, hopes were high that it would provide the necessary uplift and renewal for the Ground Zero rebuilding process. In the *New York Times*, architecture critic Herbert Muschamp referred to the ceremony as an "exorcism" and proclaimed, "It will cast out the defeatist attitude that has clogged New York's architectural arteries since the destruction of the old Pennsylvania Station," and Michael Kimmelman wrote, "NYC once again prepared for architectural adventure."[66] The normally more cynical Ada Louise Huxtable proclaimed that "his soaring bird is spot on for New York, where tragic circumstances and an unparalleled opportunity require a symbolic act of aesthetic daring."[67]

The story of the Calatrava structure, later more often referred to as a "boondoggle," can be encapsulated by a comparison of this rapturous unveiling to the lack of a ceremony when the building finally opened twelve years later and $2 billion over budget. In February 2016, Patrick J. Foye, executive director of the Port Authority, cancelled plans for an opening-day ceremony because the structure had become a "symbol of excess." As *New York Times* reporter David Dunlap quipped, the opening "won't even have the homing pigeons."[68]

The transportation hub largely comprises a massive underground space that connects the PATH trains from New Jersey (which go to Hoboken, Jersey City, and Newark) to numerous NYC subway lines (the E/A/C, R, 2/3, 4/5, and J/Z trains) and a series of underground walkways to One World Trade Center, and the Brookfield Place complex of buildings by the Hudson River, formerly known as the World Financial Center. Its central feature is the Oculus, a skeletal structure of interlocking wings that forms the cathedral ceiling for a large and spectacular atrium inside. This is nominally a site of transit, where subway and train riders traverse the space en route to offices. The lower level PATH train lobby is large and spills upward to the Oculus and the passageways, with the subway entrances at the opposite end. Yet the atrium space of the Oculus is also primarily a shopping mall, connected to several multi-level shopping malls in buildings three and four. It is for this reason that

World Trade Center transportation hub, by Santiago Calatrava. Photo by author.

arguments about the outrageous costs of the complex tend to take on a moral tone. Kimmelman writes that "the project's cost soared toward a head-slapping, unconscionable $4 billion in public money for what, in effect, is the 18th-busiest subway stop in New York City, tucked inside a shopping mall, down the block from another shopping center."[69] He would later remark, "I can't think of a recent project that did more to squander public faith or sour New Yorkers on the value of architecture."[70]

There is no doubt that the Oculus is an unusual structure on the exterior, standing out from the surrounding buildings, and an awe-inspiring one on the interior. Its cathedral-like interior space is visually impressive and a primary tourist destination. In Calatrava's repertoire, however, the building is not unique. Its forms are quite reminiscent of his designs for the Milwaukee Art Museum and his Lyon train station. Calatrava has said that he was inspired to emulate (not imitate) the civic monumentality of Grand Central Station, but the bird in flight is a well-worn motif of his oeuvre.

That it is symbolic is clear, but what its symbolism is supposed to mean has been the source of debate. Calatrava has often stated that he is inspired, as was famous Spanish architect Antoni Gaudí, whom he admires, by the organic geometric forms of nature.[71] The reference of the Oculus to a bird in flight, like the dove being released from a child's hand, is meant to evoke a phoenix rising from the ashes of Ground Zero. Goldhagen writes, "In drawing his guiding principles and images from nature, Calatrava has chosen misguided principles on which to ground contemporary architecture. Why exactly should a subway station look like a bird?" She refers to this symbolism of transportation-equals-flight as a "one-liner."[72]

It is unlikely that most viewers, unless told, would see doves in the skeletal forms of the building. Indeed, the Oculus could take the prize for the building that has inspired the most clever metaphors: "a kitschy jeu d'esprit," "a sharp-edged stegosaurus," the "Calatrasaurus," "shrapnel," "a vulture-picked carcass," "a curved fish skeleton," or an appropriately American metaphor, "a turkey skeleton picked clean at Thanksgiving."[73] Kimmelman writes, "I no longer know what the hub is supposed to mean, symbolically, with its now-thickened rubs, hunkered torso and angry snouts on either end, weirdly compressing the entrances from the street. It's like a Pokémon."[74] And as Dave Schilling in the *Guardian* writes of this "heavenly monstrosity":

> When viewing it in the right light, one could be forgiven for thinking an angel had crashed to Earth and landed facedown on the concrete. . . . It resembles an exposed ribcage from the outside and a refurbished set from Logan's Run or Conquest of the Planet of the Apes on the inside. It's so white, futuristic and ethereal that you might find yourself thinking you had died and St Peter was waiting to ring you up at Banana Republic.[75]

On the exterior, standing next to the memorial plaza and museum pavilion and now dwarfed by the surrounding towers three and four, the Oculus does not read monumental; rather, it looks diminutive—in part because its central atrium is actually two stories below ground. It even seems dwarfed by the vast pools of the memorial. For years, when its computer renditions imagined it within the rebuilt Ground Zero, it appeared to hold its own within the site, but now, its size seems strangely out of whack with its fellow buildings. The architect has stated that he sees the scale of the building on its exterior as "an intermediary scale between the scale of the towers and your own scale, that of your body," to "humanize the overall context of gigantic towers."[76]

The aesthetic of the Oculus interior is derived from the dazzling whiteness of the space, with the patterns of its "ribs" of white steel bringing in light. It is filled with what Goldberger calls "oceans of white marble," thus the quintessential opposite of the New York subway from which commuters emerge, which is gritty and tiled in a nineteenth-century modernism. Indeed, Goldberger has praised it as "a genuine people's cathedral," stating, "This is the first time in half a century that New York City has built a truly sumptuous interior space for the benefit of the public."[77] Calatrava imagined the Oculus atrium as an interior "piazza for New York," where people would gather and sit with a coffee, yet the lack of cafés and the relentless use of the space for brand-marketing displays has negated this use.[78] The aesthetic of whiteness, clean lines, and a biomorphic structure gives the space a futuristic tech aesthetic, which is affirmed by the fact that the shopping mall includes an Apple store on the ground level that is so perfectly in concert with the atrium space aesthetic that it doesn't even need a sign identifying it.

Calatrava often talks idealistically about the structure in terms of the public that he sees it serving as a transportation hub. The station, as he narrates it, is not conceived as a site of commerce but as a public space for the commuters:

> I wanted to create places that deliver the people the sense of comfort and also deliver the sense of security. This person who is coming to New York to work hard in one day may be living in a very modest house, and working also in a very modest job. This person is for me very important . . . because finally this is a public work, this thing is here for you.[79]

Tourists taking photos of Oculus. Photo by author.

In his terms, then, the majestic cathedral space is intended to provide an uplift for the ordinary worker who gets off the PATH train or subway and walks through the space.

Calatrava is renowned as an architect who is also an engineer, a key feature of his profile, along with his apparent charisma, that makes him appealing as an architect of municipal infrastructure projects, many of which have shared the problems of cost overrun and structural issues. His grandiose architectural visions, which have often included moving parts at least in the conceptual phase of design, are symbolic gestures that bring enormous engineering problems, and have often, as is the case with his Milwaukee Art Museum design, accumulated additional costs after the buildings are built. As with the Oculus, the museum's very similar wing-like structure was designed to open and close and was the source of tremendous cost overruns.[80] The battles over the Hub included Calatrava's demand that the space not have interior columns and that the feature of the winged-shaped roof be designed to open and close.[81] This was one of the key symbolic elements of Daniel Libeskind's original master plan, which included a "wedge of light" where (until it was deemed impossible) the light would come into the space on the morning of September 11 anniversaries. Calatrava paid tribute to this concept by positioning the building at an angle to the memorial and the street grid and designed the bird-in-flight roof to open on the anniversaries of September 11.[82] Eventually, the engineering challenges and costs of the opening and closing of the roof became too much, and it was eliminated by the Port Authority. Moving parts in buildings, for the sake of symbolism rather than function, turn out to be a kind of costly folly that rarely make it to realization. In this sense, Calatrava aligns his design with the ethos of Libeskind's original notions of architecture as narrative reenactment. Calatrava has often described the project in terms of uplift and renewal. He states that the goal was to "deliver something optimistic looking to the future where so much sadness and depression was there."[83] He states, "It is not a memorial to death; it is a memorial to life."[84]

This raises broader issues of about symbolism in architecture and how the building is burdened by its association with 9/11 memory. Why design a train station with an expensive feature that would operate for an anniversary ceremony each year of a terrorist attack? Here, both the symbolic memorial intent and the moving parts necessary to produce that symbolism eventually collided with the limits of the project. As Filler writes, "Fish gotta swim, birds gotta fly, but buildings do not have to move, at least not in the literal and often costly Calatrava manner."[85] The compromise design feature was a skylight that would open on the anniversary of 9/11, although this too has been subject to leaks requiring expensive repairs.[86] In addition, commuters complained about the actual train station of the complex being less functional than it should be, with slippery and narrow (though aesthetically pleasing) staircases and too narrow platforms.[87]

Oculus. Photo by author.

Inevitably, in the debates about the cost overruns of the hub, which became a huge public embarrassment for the Port Authority, and about the concern that it was "architecture for architecture's sake," criticisms of the building would compare its extraordinary costs comparison to the need for a new Penn Station in Midtown. The PATH station services approximately forty thousand commuters daily, and the poorly designed and overcrowded Penn Station, where Amtrak, New Jersey Transit, and the Long Island Railroad converge, normally services 650,000 commuters each day.[88] On January 1, 2021, the new Moynihan Train Hall was opened as an expansion of Penn Station into the large classical post office building next door; the public nature of the Moynihan Hall design prompted immediate comparison to the Oculus transportation hub, with critics praising the Moynihan Hall as a highly functional train hall rather than a shopping mall.[89]

Normally, train stations are filled with low-end stores and shops that cater to commuters, like sandwich shops, drugstores, sock shops, and magazine stands, as well as bars and cheap restaurants. The shopping mall at the Oculus, by contrast, which is run by the large global mall company Unibail-Rodamco-Westfield (formerly Westfield Corporation) and which connects to several multistoried malls in buildings three and four, is filled with upscale shops, including a branch of the Italian food store Eataly, pricey global chains, and, with its Freedom Wine Store, the occasional reminder of 9/11. One can move through the entire space without ever leaving the complex, which is unusual in New York. These features of the shopping interior make clear that the primary constituency of the mall are the tourists who normally come by the tens of thousands to visit the memorial and the museum and One World Observatory. The mall thus cannot survive by catering to the commuters who rush through it; it must appeal, through its spectacular space, to tourists. As Alan Brake writes, "Calatrava's task is to draw as many of those people down to the shopping concourses below as possible, converting tourists into consumers."[90] In the overall complex, the street level is primarily occupied by tourists, while the everyday people who work and commute there are effectively shuttled underground—one can enter the Condé Nast offices directly from the underground walkway—in Calatrava's dazzlingly white passages. Commuters do not tend to traverse the memorial plaza on their way to work. It is not conducive to that kind of everyday activity, and perhaps it feels disrespectful to rush through it on the clock.

This convergence in the Oculus of commuting, consumerism, tourism, and commemoration demonstrates the ways in which it can be seen as the emblematic structure at Ground Zero, one whose symbolism unites the different meanings and activities of the site. As Alexandra Efimenko writes, "The WTC Hub facilitates a certain type of urban subjectivity. While supporting the circulation of people, information—through the digital screens inside—and material goods as part of the local regional, and even global networks, it simultaneously attempts at

Underground walkway between Oculus and One World Trade Center. Photo by author.

becoming a zen space with its own symbolic dimension, where transcendence is a possible urban experience. This subjectivity allows the practices of commemoration, consumption, and commuting to coexist."[91] Ironically, it could be argued that it is the hub, rather than the memorial, that provides the symbolism to unite the site as one of memory, renewal, *and* consumerism.

It thus makes sense that the atrium of the Oculus, with its cathedral-like, awe-inspiring structure, graces not the train station part of the complex but the shopping mall. This has been the source of much criticism, in particular when it is seen as a waste of public funds to build a spectacular shopping mall rather than a spectacular train station. If the 9/11 memorial is steeped in the time frame of 9/11, drawing visitors back to the past, the Oculus can be said to project the future precisely because it is about the return of consumption to the site. Shopping represents renewal here. Shopping means that life goes on.[92] The cathedral-like structure also gives that consumerism religious overtones. Calatrava himself often uses the language of religion to talk about the building, stating that it communicates "a sense of man's vulnerability, while maintaining a link to a higher order."[93] The structure's religious modes facilitate and smooth over these activities at a site where, initially, there was a fear that commercialism would encroach upon "sacred ground." Reinhold Martin calls the Oculus the most "sacred" structure at Ground Zero in its synthesis of these secular-religious tensions: "Its massive, top-lit nave with a see-through structural ribcage barely sublimates the architecture of the Gothic cathedral . . . in an orgy of consumerist branding. This apotheosis of kitsch reveals the aesthetic and political program for the entire site, which is to generate a surfeit of theological 'meaning' in order that business might proceed as usual."[94]

The sacred overtones of the architecture inevitably spill over into kitsch. It is no accident that Libeskind and Calatrava were two of the primary architects to appeal to the power brokers of the site, because they share a bold capacity as architectural storytellers for narrative architecture, often referred to as architecture parlante, which the traumatic events of 9/11 seemed to demand. They are also both architects who have been accused of designing kitsch elements that appeal to cheap sentimentality. The kitsch elements of simplistic symbolism in their work—Libeskind's 1,776 height stipulation, Calatrava's "bird in flight," and their shared project of creating architecture that would bring in light for the anniversary of 9/11—is the kind of kitsch that sells itself with the cultural capital of high-end architecture. As Filler notes of Calatrava, "The seemingly advanced (though in fact retrograde) aspects of his architecture disguise its underlying sentimentality, and make it palatable to patrons of a certain sophistication who would reject more pronounced expressions of kitsch."[95] As such, it may be that unlike the heavily fortified One WTC, the more kitschy Oculus emerges as the civic icon at the site, a building that is more appealing to the public. Goldhagen writes that in his long career of turning infrastructural projects into civic icons, Calatrava has participated in recognizing how "in democratic societies, such icons can play an under-recognized and sustaining social and political role by promoting people's awareness that they are members of a community and a polity."[96] In the neoliberal economy in which the privatized and heavily securitized spaces of Ground Zero have emerged, it makes unfortunate sense that the civic icon would in fact be a shopping-mall cathedral.

Tourists move seamlessly between the 9/11 memorial and the museum (where they have presumably visited the gift shop) and the nearby entrance to the Oculus, where they are greeted by the spectacular vista and are invited to shop. Throughout these experiences, they are, of course, actively participating in picture taking and social media sharing in a world that has been increasingly shaped by digital media since 2001. The Oculus, with its spectacular vistas and balconies for viewing is a perfect location for Instagram—even though it was designed before the existence of Facebook and Instagram. Indeed, the profession of architecture itself has been increasingly influenced by the rise of Instagram culture and social media design consultants now advise on making designs "shareable."[97] Calatrava was ahead of Instagram culture in that many of his most famous designs (of bridges, museums, etc.) seem designed to be photographed, their functionality subsumed into stunning structures of cables, arches, and platforms. Reflecting back on the hypermediated experience of One World Observatory, with which I began this chapter, we can see how the rebuilding of Ground Zero reveals the dramatic reshaping of urban life through digital technology that has taken place not only since the twin towers were first built in the 1970s but even since 2001, a reminder that smartphones, Facebook, Instagram, and Twitter all emerged since 9/11. We could say, then, that the Oculus complex is built more for picture taking and tourism than even for shopping. According to the *New Yorker*, in the first year and a half that it was open, two people fell from its balconies, one woman by accident who died and one man who attempted suicide and survived.[98]

So the question remains, Who is this space for and how is the public served by this rebuilding of Ground Zero, a rebuilding that came largely out of public funds? Ultimately, architecture has played a key role here in the rebuilding of the city as a neoliberal triumph, in which a shopping mall constitutes public space and even the experience of memory and mourning has a price tag, all within a high-end securitized urban context. There is very little space here that might qualify as public space, and the presence of ubiquitous security bollards surrounding the memorial plaza and on the surrounding streets normalizes as a slick, surveilled space devoid of the messiness of urban life. As Sorkin writes, this evokes "a soulless and sinister police state Modernism, all slick surfaces pared of originality and eccentricity, designed for the efficient movement of crowds, overseen by a ubiquitous apparatus of surveillance and control, which becomes a validating part of the 'experience.'"[99]

This brings us back to the question of how cities rebuild and renew themselves in the wake of violence. In the many years since the destruction of 9/11, the struggle to mark the site of Ground Zero as national, significant, and as a symbol of resilience and renewal at the same time that it produces vast amounts of office space, shopping venues, and transportation infrastructure, has placed particular burdens on architecture. Yet as the rebuilding of Ground Zero has demonstrated, visions of renewal have been squandered in the pursuit of "business as usual." Whether facilitated by nationalism and patriotism or by a sense of sacredness, the structures at the site of Ground Zero ultimately affirm the power of real estate developers and consumer culture. This is, the site appears to say, what a renewed America looks like.

4

Visibility and Erasure

Memory and the Global War on Terror

The *Fallen Heroes Project*, created by Michael Reagan, a Vietnam veteran, produces drawn portraits of soldiers—American, British, Canadian, and Polish—who died in the Iraq War and the War in Afghanistan.[1] Reagan, who has been making portrait drawings for years, began to draw images of Iraq and Afghanistan war dead at the request of families, and as the project became well known, they began to regularly send him photographs to draw from. Reagan provides these images for free for the families of those who have died in the post-9/11 wars. Families report that it is the drawn portrait rather than the photograph that really conveys a sense of the presence of their lost ones. As one family, Tony and Naomi Lucente, wrote to him:

> I opened our gift from you and what I saw was absolutely breathtaking. We haven't seen our son since his viewing on Nov. 25th, 2005, the night before his funeral. Last night, we saw our son. Your portrait of JT brought a room full of people to tears. Tears of sadness, and somehow, tears of joy. Joy is not something that we have felt much of lately, but last night, we saw our son, and he was finally back home with us.[2]

Several testimonies state this feeling that the drawn portrait seems to make the dead seem present in ways that the original photograph does not.

Perhaps even more intriguingly, Reagan has produced a number of images that form virtual portraits, so to speak. In this image, Michael Carey is paired in the image with his daughter, Mia, who was born several weeks before he died. In another image, two brothers, Kevin and Jeffrey Graham, who died separately, are paired in combat gear in a single portrait, an image that constructs a time when both brothers are imagined at war together. There are many portraits of men with infant children. The portraits that Reagan creates of pairings of children and parents who have never met in real life, could, of course, be assembled in Photoshop. The time-space created by the drawn portrait evokes something different, however. It is not a fake; it is, rather, an imagined encounter, the drawing of the powerful desire to see the new life—the life of this child—conquer death, the desire for a redemptive and comforting narrative of reunion out of war and after death. The drawing itself creates a hopeful sense of presence. Given that many of the letters thanking Reagan for the portraits speak a religious language about seeing their loved ones again someday, these virtual portraits can also be seen as projecting into the future a reuniting of family members after death. There is also a relentlessness to the rows and rows of images on the website and in posters; so many of the dead appear so young, and many are depicted in drawings from photographs of happier moments of prior innocence, unknowing of what would follow.

There are many aspects to the Fallen Heroes Project that encapsulate the issues of memory that have emerged from the post-9/11 wars in Iraq and Afghanistan, or what has come to be known as the "global war on terror." This is a memorialization of the soldiers who were sent to fight these wars, many of them young, and, at least in the US, from a volunteer army and National Guard troops. It is a project that uses visual representations to mediate that loss, to provide some comfort to the families who have lost loved ones. As with the dead of 9/11, families are the primary social unit that is invoked in this loss. The project is also about drawing, an activity that involves spending time creating an image of the dead. In the many art projects that emerged around memorialization and the wars in Iraq and Afghanistan, art media forms that involve labor, such as drawing and tattooing, have been prevalent. Many of these works eschew photography for older visual technologies, such as drawing.

This brings us to a second image: the empty bedroom of Marine Corporal Christopher G. Scherer in East Northport, New York. Scherer was killed by a sniper in Anbar Province, Iraq, in July 2007 at the age of twenty-one. This photograph was taken by Ashley Gilbertson, a photojournalist who had photographed the war in Iraq and then began photographing the preserved bedrooms of dead soldiers, from US and coalition forces, who died in the wars in Iraq and Afghanistan.[3] In this

Drawing of Private First Class Michael Carey with his daughter, by Michael Reagan. Courtesy Fallen Heroes Project

Drawing of brothers Cadet Kevin Graham and Second Lieutenant Jeffrey Graham, by Michael Reagan. Courtesy Fallen Heroes Project.

image, the paraphernalia of a teenage life speaks to a kind of liminal adulthood, somewhere still close to childhood. Gilbertson's project shows us the rooms of these young men and women that the families have chosen to leave untouched—teddy bears on the bed, shoes lined up on the floor, high school paraphernalia on the shelves, and clothes in laundry baskets; one image has a dog lying on the bed, another room is filled with plants. In many cases, these are rooms left with the doors closed, the families never entering the space, and it sometimes took months for Gilbertson to convince families to allow him to photograph them. These rooms are shrines and spaces of mourning in which the absence of the dead is rendered present. These are also spaces of arrested time. The rooms are reminders that many of the American dead from the Iraq War were very young, practically children, dying at the ages of nineteen, twenty, twenty-one.

In these homes, the dead will always be young, not yet gone to war. In the stories Gilbertson tells, many of the families talk about leaving things intact because it allows them feel as though their son or daughter could just walk back in at any moment. If the Fallen Heroes image conjures a virtual presence for the dead via drawing, the Gilbertson photographs speak of a festering absence that comes from the time arrested in these rooms, haunting the rest of the house. Both the drawings and the empty bedrooms are ways to mediate grief, to attempt to keep the deep level of loss at bay, either through religious narratives of reunion or through the preserved room that anticipates the return of the absent one.

These bedrooms are aligned in many ways with the museum and memorial strategies, discussed in earlier chapters, that aim to mediate the absence of the dead by rendering them present with photographs, audio, objects, and through naming. Gilbertson narrates in the book that this project was a response to his own traumatic experience of war. He had gone to take a photograph of an insurgent who lay dead in the minaret of a mosque in Falluja, as proof that the mosques were being used for warfare in violation of the Geneva Conventions, and the captain made him take a squad of Marines with him; one of them, Lance Corporal Billy Miller, went up the stairs first and was shot dead. Journalist Dexter Filkins was with Gilbertson and wrote about the incident as a reporter.[4] Gilbertson was so traumatized by this experience and felt such guilt that he went searching for a way to photograph absence: "War takes people

Bedrooms of the Fallen, by Ashley Gilbertson. Marine Corporal Christopher G. Scherer, twenty-one, was killed by a sniper on July 21, 2007, in Karmah, Iraq. He was from East Northport, New York. His bedroom was photographed in February 2009. Ashley Gilbertson/VII/Redux.

away from those who love them. I came home. So did Dominguez. Billy Miller didn't. I needed to photograph his absence."[5]

These images speak to the dynamics of erasure and visibility in the memorialization of those killed in the post-9/11 wars in Iraq and Afghanistan. The post-9/11 wars, also referred to as the long war and the global war on terror, have been defined as wars that are difficult to end. As the withdrawal of US troops inevitably gave rise to new violence, it exposes the trauma that comes from the understanding that lives were lost in vain. In other words, the disengagement of the US in two highly unstable contexts is equal to conceding defeat, to admitting that those deaths were futile, in defiance of affirmative national narratives of US military dominance and global power.

The wars in Iraq and Afghanistan have posed very particular problems for memorialization, as these two images reveal. While US society designates war dead as those who deserve memorialization—and one could say that in this light, those who died on 9/11 have been folded into that category of war dead—it is very difficult for any society to memorialize a war that is not yet over. The "forever" war of the global war on terror has been defined in ways that give it no discernable end, and the US involvement in the wars in Iraq and Afghanistan, which dragged on for almost two decades, was deeply difficult to wind down because of the destabilization in the region to which the wars contributed. In addition to this narrative of the forever war, the wars have also been framed as ones of erasure. The costs of the wars, both human and economic, have been largely erased from public view and public discourse since the early first years. The role of the US veterans of the post-9/11 wars has been complex. There are many veterans who continue to suffer debilitating injuries, including a high level of brain injuries and PTSD, and many who have been lost to suicide, who have effectively been erased from public view. Yet at the same time, increasing numbers of veterans are now holding public office across the political spectrum and participating in public protests. In this chapter, I analyze how memory projects and memorial proposals about the post-9/11 wars respond to these dynamics of erasure and absence, and the role of veterans as figures of memory. These memory projects, many of which are unrealized, act as a kind of countervisual force to the proliferation of 9/11 memorials, telling a much more conflicted story of grief, regret, complicity, and sorrow.

The Long War

The post-9/11 wars in Iraq and Afghanistan dragged on for almost two decades. In 2021, 2,500 US troops remain in Iraq, and US troops were withdrawn from Afghanistan by the twentieth anniversary of 9/11. The costs of these wars have been incalculably high—over seven thousand US troops killed in Iraq, Afghanistan, and Pakistan, over fifty-two thousand wounded, many of them severely, and as of this date, a total of $6.4 trillion spent for the US war on terror. Given the high numbers of military contractors in these wars, the actual numbers of casualties is much higher, with possibly eight thousand military contractors killed in the Middle East in the post-9/11 period.[6] The estimates of Iraqi civilians officially hover above two hundred thousand, with an estimate of 335,000 civilians killed in the war on terror, but with estimates as high as six hundred thousand dead and more than eight million displaced throughout the region.[7] In 2020, the Brown University Costs of War project estimated that at least thirty-seven million people had been displaced by America's war on terror.[8] These numbers have been difficult to calculate and are contested, as part of a broader erasure of the costs of war in which political interests in the US and in the region have had a stake in not counting the dead and those affected. The politicized question of counting has thus been a key theme of the memory projects about these wars.

The wars that followed in the wake of 9/11 were initially termed the "long war" by the war's architects. As Nikhil Pal Singh writes, it was secretary of defense Donald Rumsfeld who predicted, post-9/11, that this would be a "long war" lasting generations, comparing it to the Cold War.[9] The long war was, by definition, a war for which, by implication, an ending could not be imagined in the present. As Greg Grandin wrote in 2019, "The United States is now into the eighteenth year of a war that it will never win. Soldiers who fought in Afghanistan and Iraq in the early 2000s are now seeing their children enlist."[10]

Throughout US history, wars of aggression have often been narrated as wars of national security and protection. While the war in Afghanistan was defined as a response to the terrorist attacks of 9/11, the war in Iraq was sold to the US public as a war in the national interest, on the basis of false claims of Iraq building "weapons of mass destruction" that would threaten the US. On the eve of the invasion of Iraq, Americans felt under threat; they bought duct tape and obsessed about securing their homes, when it was people in Baghdad who were the ones threatened.[11] The broader imperial aims of the Iraq War, of protecting and expanding US interests in oil in the region, were veiled by the false beliefs, cynically sold to the US public, that Iraq was responsible for 9/11 and that Saddam Hussein himself was a threat to the United States.

The long war has been prolonged by many factors, including extraordinary ignorance on behalf of the architects of war about the countries and regions they were invading, resulting in inept strategies and the rise of new anti-American insurgent groups such as ISIS. Cities such as Falluja, which were won at great cost, were then lost again and fought for twice over. The wars have also been prolonged by massive corruption within the military-industrial complex and the private profit making of the war machine, what Heidi Peltier calls the "camo economy," in which the military uses its commercialization as a camouflage to hide the true cost of war. These wars are massively profitable for this military-industrial war machine, which has also deep ties to political power in the US.[12]

Early in the wake of 9/11, the Bush administration began to call the post-9/11 wars the "war on terror," an epithet that expanded over time to become the "global war on terror," the very name of which implies an open-ended project without end. How could a war on terror itself ever be won? Use of the term *war on terror* enabled it to be expansive, to include, on the basis of flimsy evidence, Saddam Hussein's regime in Iraq, which engaged in brutal acts of state terrorism but had nothing to do with the 9/11 attacks. It also was expansive enough to include conflicts in Yemen, Pakistan, and Syria, which followed from the post-9/11 wars. Obama came into office in 2008 vowing to end these wars and was largely stymied in his efforts by Congress, in particular his effort to close the prison in Guantánamo Bay, Cuba, furthering the narrative of the war that will not end. In a 2013 speech at the National Defense University at Fort McNair in Washington, DC, President Obama rejected the term *global war on terror* and explicitly aimed to resituate the US actions as a targeted response to specific threats: "Beyond Afghanistan, we must define our effort not as a boundless 'global war on terror,' but rather as a series of persistent, targeted efforts to dismantle specific networks of violent extremists that threaten America."[13] In this speech, in which Obama both defended and promised to scale down the drone war and in which he outlined yet again his attempts to close Guantánamo, he was able to declare US involvement in Iraq to be over. This was, however, prior to his administration's redeployment of troops in response to the rise of ISIS.

Despite the Obama administration's rejection of the term, the terminology of global war on terror/terrorism has resurfaced in memorial efforts around the post-9/11 wars. Yet the never-ending quality of the long war and the global war on terror poses many problems for memorialization. Memorialization has been understood throughout history to be a process that begins when conflicts, wars, and tragic events have reached some definable end. This is the reason that colonial and imperial wars such as the Spanish-American War have tended to go un-memorialized, since their end point was only defined by the further conflict of decolonization. The political stakes in the memory of wars, however, do not begin when they are over; they begin with the first loss of the war. In other words, the urge to memorialize begins when loss is first experienced. Let us remember that calls for a memorial for the victims of

9/11 began the next day, long before any understanding of what kind of conflict it was and before the number of dead could be established. Questions of time frame are thus crucial to the meaning of memorialization; to memorialize a war that is ongoing is, almost inherently, to make a political statement about the costs of war.

This question of the time frame of memorialization has also been encoded into US law. In response to the memory boom and the dramatic increase of memorials proposed for the National Mall, Congress enacted the Commemorative Works Act in 1986, which established a timeline for memorialization, explicitly designating that ten years must have passed after the official end of a war before it could be memorialized on the National Mall. As Kirk Savage notes:

> Today, we have a fully professionalized, volunteer military that moves relentlessly from one part of the world to another, from one operation to another, relying increasingly on elite forces and unmanned weapons. The Commemorative Works Act does not even have a frame of reference for this institutionalized warfare, with its never-ending actions against shifting and elusive adversaries. Our military has become in many ways its own world—an extension of a national security apparatus that remains largely hidden but hovers in a permanent state of emergency over many aspects of our lives. The old ideal of the citizen-soldier that underpinned our war memorials, even the tribute to the American dead in Vietnam, has been eclipsed, apparently forever.[14]

Precisely because they seem without a discernable end, the post-9/11 wars do not fit the criteria of the Commemorative Works Act. Despite this impediment, advocates for a memorial to the war on terror on the National Mall succeeded in convincing Congress to let their project move forward. The Global War on Terrorism Memorial, which was approved by Congress in 2017, was given an exemption to the rule of ten years after a war's end. As US representative Tom McClintock argued:

> The Commemorative Works Act requires that a war be ended for at least 10 years before planning can commence on a national memorial. There is good reason for this requirement: it gives history the insight to place the war in an historic context and to begin to fully appreciate its full signifi-

cance to our country and future generations. But the war on terrorism has been fought in a decidedly different way than our past wars. We are now approaching the 16th anniversary of the attack on New York and Washington. The veterans who sacrificed so much to keep that war away from our shores deserve some tangible and lasting tribute to their patriotism and altruism while they, their families, and their fellow countrymen can know it.[15]

While the debate over the memorial acknowledged that this memorialization was being approved for a war that was not over, it also responded to the fact that the losses of the war at that point had begun more than a decade and a half before. As I noted, the desire to memorialize is spurred on by loss, not by a sense that a conflict is over.

The Erasure of the Post-9/11 Wars

A key factor of prolonging the long war was the ways that the costs of the war, both human and economic, remained largely out of view of the US public, whose initial support gradually transformed into a muted opposition to and fatigue with the wars. As the wars dragged on through the 2010s, with troop surges and drone warfare under the Obama administration, many aspects of the costs of war remained largely invisible. While some veterans of the war have become more publicly visible as they have pursued elected office or as part of movements such as Veterans for Peace, it remains a stunning feature of these wars that the struggles of these veterans have been mostly absent from public view. These wars have been fought by a volunteer army and National Guard troops, many of them from small towns like those that Gilbertson photographed. Philip Gourevitch writes that after the end of the draft with the Vietnam War, "the military became the business of small, self-selecting subset of the nation, whose charge it is to fight so that the rest of us should never know war. . . . Military families have endured every conceivable strain and anguish. But for the vast majority of us, these wars are not just overseas, they are completely foreign: they do not hit us where we live."[16] One of the most pernicious aspects of the structure of these wars, in their dependence on the limited pool of volunteer troops, Andrew Bacevich writes, is that many were sent on multiple combat tours: "A year in the war zone followed by a year at home followed by orders back to war—for active duty soldiers, this became a new normal." The troops "kept going back again and again to wars they could not win," resulting in rampant debilitating emotional and psychological problems. Bacevich notes that this strain on the US military meant that Army leaders increasingly called up National Guard troops, in basic violation of their terms of service, which designated that "the nation would call upon them only in extreme emergencies." He states that the final bill for all the veteran disability claims of the post 9/11 wars, the long wars, will likely approach $1 trillion.[17]

Erasure implies, of course, a kind of invisibility, an erasure from view. It is worth situating this erasure within the broader visual economy of the wars. The post-9/11 wars in Afghanistan and Iraq, in particular in their early years, were wars that Americans consumed through images. The news coverage of these wars, like that of the 1991 Gulf War before them, was filled with images of spectacular destruction, the "shock and awe" of the 2003 bombing of Baghdad in the beginning of the war on Iraq, the dramatic destruction of statues of Saddam Hussein, and the images of soldiers against the spectacular landscape of mountains in Afghanistan. Photojournalists were embedded by the military with particular troops, and the photographs generated by the wars focused on US troops at war yet also were complicit in the media focus on the techno-war, with its emphasis on the spectacle of the air war. The image archive of the post-9/11 wars also includes the images of torture at Abu Ghraib in 2004 and the rupture of their public circulation.

This image archive is vast, including many thousands of images posted on the web by US soldiers and veterans.[18] It is an archive of both image proliferation and image suppression. Thus, the visual economy of the war included the domination of images of war machines, the deliberate erasure of the costs of war through censorship and restrictions on journalists, and the unchecked sharing of images by US soldiers on emerging digital and social media venues. The visual economy of the war has been one of contradiction—on one hand indicative of the new digital and global circulation of images, decentralized, out of the control of nations and government entities, such as the circulation of the images of Abu Ghraib and numerous websites where US soldiers uploaded a range of images, from images of everyday life in war to graphic images of the dead; and on the other hand extremely retrograde, with effective and consistent censorship.

One of the most glaring and shocking examples of this image censorship was the banning by the military of photographs of the coffins of dead American soldiers who are brought "home" to Dover Air Force base. The Pentagon created its own archive of images of the war dead coffins, but it refused to release these images until it was forced to by two Freedom of Information Act suits.[19] In releasing the second group of images in 2005, which were immediately placed on the websites of a nonprofit organization, the cleverly named National Security Archive, and subsequently published in many major newspapers, the military chose to black out (or redact) the faces of the soldiers who were carrying the coffins, screening out any expression—in effect, any register of loss—they may have had. The absurdity of this practice is multilevel; the deliberate attempt to render the images unusable conveys in visual terms a shame about the war dead. The ban was only finally lifted in March 2009.[20]

The government censuring of the official act of bringing back and honoring the dead demonstrates the degree to which there has been a need to mask not only the war's carnage in Iraq and Afghanistan, a need with which the media was entirely complicit, but also to erase from view of US citizens the costs of the war, both economic and human, a war that was sold on the basis that it would constitute a quick and easy revenge that would require no sacrifice. Thus, *any* image of mourning became coded as an image that exposed the sacrifice of the war. John Bodnar argues that we see two polar forms of patriotism at play in the post-9/11 wars, what he sees as a "tug of war between a patriotism that is empathetic, willing to recognize the torment it can bring and acknowledge the pain of others, and one that is war-based or redemptive and reluctant to come to terms with the suffering it might provoke." He writes, "In the immediate aftermath of 9/11, war-based patriotism commanded a higher ground than its empathetic cousin."[21] Yet, he argues, eventually "many Americans were simply unwilling to embrace a patriotism enmeshed in militarism, consumed with the pursuit of enemies and indifferent to the evidence of trauma all around them." Within this framework, the redacted image erased not only the sacrifice of the dead but also the therapeutic labor of sacrifice of the soldiers carrying the coffins, at a moment when war patriotism dominated empathetic patriotism.

Censored honor guard with coffins of US war dead. National Security Archive.

The erasure of the costs of war can be situated within a broader context of a changing context of image circulation. The era in which the post-9/11 wars have been waged can be defined by a particular set of disruptive shifts in visual production and consumption. We can chart this through the rise of YouTube culture starting in 2005, the integration of images into smart mobile phones in 2007, and the emergence of Facebook in 2006 and Instagram in 2010, all very recent technologies that came into being since the wars began, all of which have disrupted media industries, information networks, and photographic practices. In this context, digital media produces key values of linkages, networks, navigability, viral circulation, and aggregation. Because in the age of Google there is so much information and there are so many images, it is the linkage, the aggregation, the search mechanism, and the practices of curation that define visual modes. In the midst of so many images, it is that which is most viral, the most in circulation, that is the most valued.

This context of network aggregation/linkage/viral circulation defines contemporary image culture within the values of linkage rather than within the values of visibility. In this networked culture, the simple assertion of *visibility as a political mode* came to be seen as out of currency.

Yet this politics of visibility, as a kind of strategy of countervisuality, has emerged in memory projects about the wars, in the form of counting. Nicholas Mirzoeff writes of the "right to look" as a key strategy of countervisuality, a challenge to the authority of visuality, through which power is organized in visual domains and complexes (defined by Mirzoeff as the plantation complex, the imperial complex, and the military-industrial complex).[22] In analyzing the countervisual strategies of memory and art projects about the post-9/11 wars, I want to point to the strategy of the right to be counted. The refusal of the war machine to count the dead thus produced counting as a key practice of artistic and memory projects that have refused the erasure of the war dead and the wounded of the post-9/11 wars.

These artistic projects aim to memorialize the dead of the post-9/11 wars, from the US war dead to the hundreds of thousands who have died in the Middle East, and to render visible the status of the wounded US veterans. These works deploy strategies that aim to break through the power structures of visuality that have defined the wars in order to render visible the costs of these wars to the nation and to the world. These countervisual strategies thus aim by extension to redefine the story of 9/11 in relation to all that followed in its wake.

The Politics of Visibility: Counting and Countervisuality

The visual economy of the post-911 wars, with their contradictions of viral images, censorship, spectacle, and erasure, have produced a broad range of artistic responses, with many antiwar art projects by US and European artists and artists in Iraq and its diasporas being produced in the post-9/11 era. There have been a number of exhibitions of artistic works in response to the post 9/11 wars, with the exhibition *Memorial to the Iraq War* at the Institute of Contemporary Arts in London in 2007, the *Age of Terror: Art Since 9/11* exhibit at the Imperial War Museum in London, and *Theater of Operations: The Gulf Wars, 1991–2011*, at the Museum of Modern Art/PS 1 in New York in 2019–20. Many of the works in these exhibitions were visceral protest art works, aimed at exposing the lies of the wars. For instance, Sam Durant's work *Proposal for Iraq War Memorial* (2007) displayed images of piles of burned-out cars, rubble, and the ruins of war in front of the US Capitol, the British

Parliament, 10 Downing Street, and the White House. These exhibitions also included works by Iraqi artists, both in Iraq and in exile, and Afghani artists in exile, that aimed to address the wars and the destruction of Iraq. Many of the Iraqi art works deployed the aesthetic strategy of the *dafatir*, paintings within notebook structures (*daftar* is Arabic for notebook) that generated testimonies, both in words and images, of the destruction of Baghdad, for instance. As Nada Shabout writes, "*Dafatir* are essentially books by Iraqi artists that have come to signify visual art production during the Gulf Wars, sanctions, and invasion of Iraq. . . . During a time of instability and fear, these *dafatir* allowed Iraqi artists a voice, performing the act of writing and representation as equally personal and historical interventions by artists from the inside."[23] In his *Homage to al-Mutanabbi Street* (2007), Ghassan Ghaib deploys painting and text to mourn the destruction of Baghdad's historical book market. Al Mutanabbi Street was filled with book-making shops and was targeted with car bombings following the 2003 invasion. The destroyed book, here wrapped in barbed wire, embodies the broader destruction of culture that resulted from the US invasion, treating the cultural remains of the book as a kind of corporeal remains, seemingly bloodied and bound, at once held together and unable to open.

In the early years of the post-9/11 wars, many antiwar projects and responses to the wars, in particular the war in Iraq, aimed to counter the erasure of the costs of war by memorializing the dead, initially the dead of the US and coalition troops and then the dead in Afghanistan and Iraq. In the early years of the Iraq war, these first cataloguings of the dead took the form of rows of crosses at several sites in California. On the beach in Santa Barbara, a group put up an increasing number of crosses every Sunday, at first for the war in Iraq and then for Afghanistan. Begun by Stephen Sherrill and eventually run by the Veterans for Peace, it would eventually be called Arlington West. Every week, volunteers would come and erect the crosses in a designated area, until the numbers became too numerous and they decided to write the total on a front cross and to continue to fill the area with crosses. This project eventually expanded to a weekly display of crosses on the beach in Santa Monica. It also attempted to visualize the Iraqi dead, with a sign that read, "If we were to honor the Iraqi dead, it would cover the entire beach." These displays of crosses were intended to interject the

Homage to al-Mutanabbi Street 1 (2007), by Ghassan Ghaib. Courtesy Ghassan Ghaib.

reality of the cost of war into the everyday lives of the US public who had acquiesced to the wars and found them easy to ignore. The contradictions between the somber crosses and the carefree leisure activities of the beach were intended to be jarring, a "cemetery in the sand."[24] The Arlington West projects would often include flag-draped coffins that, precisely because images of them had been banned by the Pentagon, had become antiwar symbols of the erasure of the dead.

Arlington West memorial, Santa Monica, California. Photo: Larry Brownstein/Alamy Stock Photo.

In Lafayette, California, near the Bay Area, local peace advocates Jeff Heaton, Louise Clark, and Lynn MacMichael put up a series of crosses and other religious symbols starting in 2006 on a hillside owned by Clark that faces on a major freeway (they first attempted it in 2003 and the crosses were constantly taken down). Focused at first on the Iraq War dead, and then expanded to include Americans killed in Afghanistan, the display was initially attacked as a highly visible antiwar statement, labeled unpatriotic, anti-military, and un-American, and was subject to a city council debate.[25] The negative response to the field of crosses was revealing and surprising. Why would honoring the dead be controversial? In Bodnar's terms, the empathetic patriotism in evidence at the memorial, in honoring the dead, was incompatible with the discourse of

People attend a vigil in Lafayette, California, May 25, 2009, where there are 4,990 crosses to soldiers killed in Iraq. Photo: UPI Photo/Terry Schmitt/Alamy Stock Photo.

war patriotism, into which any narrative of sacrifice can appear to be a critique of the war project.

The controversy over such simple displays was notable given that most of those making them were enormously careful not to take political stands about the wars. Erika Doss notes that these memorials were usually framed not as antiwar memorials but as displays of gratitude to those who died. This reveals the degree to which the public had acquiesced to the administration's narrative of the war in Iraq in particular as one that would involve no sacrifice, and these framings were also part of a broader attempt to not replicate the rejection of veterans and the dead that had characterized the Vietnam War, a narrative that haunted the responses to veterans of the post-9/11 wars. As Doss notes, these projects were often explicitly defined as "Iraq War dead memorials" not "*war* memorials," as if appreciation for the sacrifice of the troops could be separated from the war itself. The problem with gratitude, she writes, is its affirmation of war itself: "War memorials weld feelings of gratitude with national imperatives, cultivating affective modes of citizenship and patriotism and persuading publics of the necessity of war itself."[26]

In emphasizing support for peace in a general sense, however, some of these memorial projects were explicitly antiwar. The memorial project Eyes Wide Open, created by the American Friends Service Committee, a Quaker social justice organization, was defined as "an exhibition on the human cost" of the wars in Iraq and Afghanistan, which consisted of a pair of polished black military boots for each solider who had died and shoes representing Iraqi war dead, which toured the country. The image of boots representing the dead is a well-worn though potent symbol; the visual power of this project is through the repetition of the boots, endlessly laid out in a room or a landscape, that visually make present the multitude of the dead. Similarly, the Dog Tag Memorial Garden in North Church in Boston displays rows and rows of dog tags to memorialize soldiers who have died in Iraq and Afghanistan. Each of these displays is in many ways very conventional, deploying well-worn symbols (crosses, empty boots) to evoke the numbers of the dead. It is precisely in their familiarity and their variation that they are evocative—the crosses and boots, so uniform yet, on inspection, so unique.

The practice of cataloguing and rendering visible the bodies of the dead is one that can engage antiwar narratives and narratives of wartime sacrifice simultaneously. Thus, the naming involved in memorials is an aesthetic trope that allows for many different political engagements. The naming of the individual can be simultaneously an antiwar statement about loss and the recognition of an individual that deploys concepts of sacrifice for the nation and patriotism. Just as the names on the Vietnam Veterans Memorial in Washington, DC, have been understood as existing within an antiheroic and antiwar aesthetic, the naming on that memorial also allows it to be the site for pro-military gestures honoring sacrifice. Similarly, Arlington West and the Lafayette Crosses have been the subject of remembrances that are decidedly about affirming the meaning of these deaths as lost in defending and protecting the American public, thus enfolding the Iraq war into the narrative of 9/11

Eyes Wide Open exhibit commemorates Iraq War deaths. Photo: Jim West/Alamy Stock Photo.

without question. Such displays also succeeded in small ways in visualizing the human and national costs of war. The *Eyes Wide Open* exhibit included at one point a *Cost of War* exhibition, which included banners displaying the financial costs of the wars, with such phrases as "One day of the Iraq War = $720 million. How would you spend it?"[27]

These grassroots efforts at memorialization can be seen on a continuum with works that have attempted to memorialize the wars in Iraq and Afghanistan in the art world context. Even though the grassroots projects and these art works have different audiences and valuation, their aesthetic strategies share the aim of countervisuality in relation to the war's erasure. British artist Steve McQueen's work *Queen and Country*, which is now in the collection of the Imperial War Museum in London, consists of a large cabinet containing 160 uncut sheets of postage stamps bearing the faces of British soldiers who died in the Iraq War. McQueen continued to add faces to the work after he conceived it in 2007 and collaborated with the families of the dead to choose the images. The work plays with the dynamics of visibility and invisibility. As Mark Godfrey writes, "McQueen makes visible the faces of the dead ... but the cabinet's structure means that these faces remain invisible until the viewer decides to pull each drawer out; each viewer is thus made responsible for deciding whether to make each dead soldier appear." Each face has a small profile of the Queen above it, Godfrey notes, "the nominal figure for whom the soldiers died."[28] McQueen's work succeeds in rendering the war dead visible within what could be considered traditional codes of honoring—the official-looking cabinet, the stamp as a form of memorial and honoring, the honoring of soldiers. However, this rendering visible of the dead was deemed by the authorities, in this case the Royal Mail service, to be outside traditional codes of honoring, despite the support of families for his campaign to officially make these postage stamps.

Traditional codes of honoring are recoded in many of these works. Jane Hammond's work *Fallen* (2004–12) can be seen as deploying the conventional notion of a fallen soldier and transforming it into a mournful memorial for US soldiers who have been killed in the Iraq War.[29] Hammond scanned fall leaves and then inscribed each with the name of one soldier. In each display of the work, she arranges the leaves on a low rectangular pedestal to look like a casual pile of fall leaves, in

Queen and Country (2007–10), by Steve McQueen.
Oak cabinet containing a series of 160 facsimile postage sheets bearing portrait heads of soldiers who lost their lives in the conflict in Iraq between 2003 and 2009, 260 x 140 x 190 cm, 102 3/8 x 55 1/8 x 74 3/4 in. Exhibition View, 'Steve McQueen', 16 March—1 September 2013, Schaulager, Muenchenstein/ Basel 2013. © Steve McQueen. Courtesy the artist, Thomas Dane Gallery and Marian Goodman Gallery. Commissioned by Imperial War Museum and Manchester International Festival. Photo: Tom Bisig, Basel.

Installation view of *Fallen* at the FLAG Art Foundation. *Fallen* (2004–12). Color ink jet print, printed from digital file recto and verso, on archival paper, cut, with matt medium, Jade glue, fiberglass strand, sumi ink, and additional handwork in acrylic paint and gouache. Dimensions variable. Whitney Museum of American Art, New York.[31]

Detail from *Fallen* at the FLAG Art Foundation. *Fallen* (2004–12).

a riot of color that evokes abstract expressionism. The work has the potential to convey a normalization of the deaths of war as being somehow as natural and organic as the seasons and the life cycle of decay and passage. The notion of the fallen conveys the sense of bodies falling in battle as naturally as leaves falling from tress. Yet in its evocation of the arbitrariness of those fallen (leaves, people), the work provides a tension with this narrative. It is never clear which names will be visible in its arrangement—apparently, one woman who had recently lost her son came upon the work and immediately saw his name on a leaf. Because of how the leaves are layered, in each display many names are hidden.[30] Since it is arbitrary which names will be rendered visible, the work engages directly with questions of erasure. Hammond continued to add names and leaves to the work for eight years in a laborious process that involved scanning both sides of a leaf and then writing the name of a soldier on it. Like many of the other artists working on these memory projects, Hammond was characterized as having trouble keeping up with the numbers of the dead, and she continued to work on adding names until 2012, five years after the work was acquired by the Whitney Museum of American Art. Hammond's work can be seen as both aestheticizing the counting of the dead and problematizing the very aims to catalogue and add to the continuing list of those who died. As such, it both counters the erasure of the dead and demands that we see that erasure.

The problem of the catalogue of the dead is the primary theme in Emily Prince's artwork, *American Servicemen and Women Who Have Died in Iraq and Afghanistan (But Not Including the Wounded, Nor the Iraqis nor the Afghanis)* (2004-12). This work engages through its very self-conscious title with the problems of cataloguing, counting, and attempting to make visible the dead from this war; its tally is 5,213 portraits. This is crucial to its effect, with the implication of the endlessly expandable parenthetic list of its title. To make this work, Prince created individual hand-drawn portraits of each of the American soldiers who have died. She started with the individual portraits of the American war dead posted on a military website by their families. She then redrew each of those photographs, using different colors to indicate race, which she posted on a wall in different forms, sometimes with the images set out in a map of the US with the portraits clustered at the hometowns of the dead or chronologically as depicted here. The drawings have a

American Servicemen and Women Who Have Died in Iraq and Afghanistan (But Not Including the Wounded, Nor the Iraqis nor the Afghanis) (2004–12), by Emily Prince, on exhibit at Saatchi Gallery, London, January 7, 2010. Photo: Reuters/Kevin Coombs/Alamy Stock Photo.

deliberately crude style, evoking the sense that they are more about the labor of remembrance than about aesthetic rendering.

This work is about spending time reflecting on the dead. Prince deliberately took time to draw a replica of a photograph for each person killed and to imply that for each one, there are a multitude who are absent. When working on this piece, she stated that she was always behind in trying to keep up with the numbers. Her ongoing labor was thus integral to the work, and its ever-unfinished nature is key to its memorial effect. This theme of the labor of counting the dead emerges in many of these art projects and points not only to the powerful effects of the weight of erasure but also to the need, again and again, to attempt to render the dead visible; rendering the dead visible is thus a continuous task. This is the *labor* of remembering, in which works like *Fallen* and the Prince work are not so much about a final work of art as they are about signifying the work of memorialization. This is reminiscent of the AIDS Memorial Quilt, whose meaning is in part about its evocation of the time spent in its creation. Prince's work foregrounds this labor precisely in her choice of a time-consuming medium (drawing) replicating an instant one (photography). Here, the comparisons to the Fallen Heroes project are worth noting, as the families value those portraits more than photographs in part because of the labor that artist Michael Reagan puts into creating them.

Prince's work signals not only the problems of cataloguing the dead but also the problem of memorializing only the American war dead—the title of the work shows its ironic self-critique of its own earnestness in its parenthesis *(But Not Including the Wounded, Nor the Iraqis nor the Afghanis)*. A debate about body counts has been a key aspect of activist engagements and nonprofit efforts in relation to the post-9/11 wars, in particular to the war in Iraq. Counting, rendering visible, is thus a simple act that aims to expose the broader strategy of the wars in Iraq and Afghanistan as masking the true cost of war. One can see this erasure clearly instantiated in the very uncertainty that surrounds the actual count of Iraqi dead, ranging from two hundred thousand to six hundred thousand and the enormous efforts by organizations to establish their numbers. The Iraq war dead remain a structuring absence to these projects that aim to memorialize the American war dead, as Prince's work notes.

One project that uses design to engage with the erasure of Iraqi civilians is the virtual exhibition and memorial site iraqimemorial.org, which was created by artist Joseph DeLappe in 2007. DeLappe has stated that his initial motivation was to counter the online publication of the 5,201 proposals for the World Trade Center Memorial Competition in fall 2003 with a mirror call for proposals to memorialize the many more Iraqi civilians who had died. He states, "How do we respond as artists (is it possible to respond)—to the deaths of Iraqi civilians that are occurring as the result of the actions of our government?"[32] Here, DeLappe is directly responding to the valuing of the deaths of those who died on 9/11 with a recognition of the hundreds of thousands of Iraqi war dead who followed in their wake, demanding that we also see them as grievable lives, in Judith Butler's terms.

The proposals, which numbered over 180, were commented on by a jury, with selections exhibited several times. They run the gamut in aesthetic styles from realism to abstraction. Many are about evoking the landscape of Iraq and imagining what a memorial would look like there. As DeLappe and David Simpson write, memorials "take time and money and, above all, peacetime, time to look back and to declare an end to violence. None of these conditions pertains in Iraq. . . . At least for the foreseeable future there are unlikely to be any international competitions for building memorials to the Iraqi dead. Their names will go largely unrecorded in a place where record keeping itself is a scarce luxury."[33] These works are thus a reminder that memorialization is a privileged activity, one which, as we saw in the case of New York, can come at very high expense. It also means that these proposals, like the unbuilt proposals for Ground Zero, have a flexible creativity set apart from the difficulties of actually building and financing a memorial.

Many proposals explicitly imagine Baghdad as a site of memory. Peter Janssen and Ward Janssen's *The Circle* depicts a circle whose circumference is 27.5 kilometers long—which represents one millimeter for each Iraqi citizen—that is drawn around the center of Baghdad, demarcated by a thin copper wire. The artists write, "Anyone entering or leaving the city central areas will always have to cross the circle and might for a short moment reflect on those compatriots who did not survive the Iraq tragedies but also on his or her 27,500,000 fellow citizens, fellow mourners." Athanasia Karaloannoglou's proposal, *Marked for Life*, imagines the rivers in Baghdad turned red by underwater lighting on March 19, the anniversary of the 2003 invasion of Baghdad. The work evokes the rivers running red with blood, as a geography literally embodying those who died.

Other proposals imagine the Iraqi dead passing like haunting figures within the landscape of the United States. Michael Magrath's proposal *Lot's Tribe*, which he installed in Seattle in 2006, consists of three life-sized figures based on Associated Press images of Iraqi citizens: a squatting blindfolded boy with his hands tied behind him, a father holding his lifeless son, and a seated figure with his face contorted in pain. Magrath defines the work as a "memorial for the post-9/11 world."[34] The figures

Lot's Tribe: Pieta (2006), by Michael Magrath. Materials: salt, 9/11/2006. Courtesy Michael Magrath.

are created out of salt, a reference to the biblical story of Lot's wife, who turned back to look at Sodom and was transformed into salt, and so are intended to become worn and to eventually fade away; when realized in Seattle, they slowly disintegrated over several months. Magrath states that he was responding to the way that people in the US became used to turning away from images, numb and distant to their depictions of suffering, but that "sculpture has an entirely other, critically untapped potential in this discussion. It is harder to shrug off. Present in space and time with the viewer, it literally won't get out of the way." The work's disintegration conveys the transitory nature of life, of mortality, and functions as a critique of the permanence of the monument, now a key factor in the debates about taking monuments down.

Also transitory is Iraqi artist Nadia Awad's proposal, *This War*, which consists of thousands of life-size figures of detainees, civilians, and children who have been mutilated by the war, constructed of the reeds from southern Iraq, their heads covered in white sheets. These are floated silently down the Potomac River, in her words, "wafting past Capitol Hill in quiet confrontation with the architects of the War." The proposal allows one to imagine the thousands of figures continuously floating past like ghosts, haunting those who thought they could wage war without consequences. As DeLappe and Simpson write, "Think of the silence, the lack of explicit accusation or designation, the mystery of who these figures represent, the gradual recognition of associations—reeds, marshes, Iraqi rivers, Sumerian funeral rituals—that would lead some beholders to make a connection to the war in the Middle East."[35] The work evokes the power of the silent accusation and the sense of nature—the reeds, the river—in contrast to the edifices of government.

This War, by Nadia Awad. Courtesy Nadia Awad.

Many of the Iraqi memorial proposals engage very intentionally with the question of counting the dead and the sense that the Iraqi dead have not been counted or been made present. In their digital *U.S./Iraq War Memorial,* John Craig Freeman and Mark Skwarek designed a phone app that inserts US and Iraqi coffins into any photographs of the user's home environment. Elise Engler's *Collateral Damage* uses small pencil-drawn silhouettes to depict civilian casualties. A second project, titled *Collateral Damage,* by Joshua Berger, simply uses *x*'s to tally the dead. Prince Varguese Thomas's work *Body Count* consists of piles of pennies to represent the individual lives lost that then accumulate into piles and piles. The project of counting, the sense of the need to render the dead present—the simple act of counting and the simple act of drawing—thus haunts many of these proposals.

The work of Iraqi-born artist Wafaa Bilal takes this project of counting further. Bilal, who grew up under Saddam Hussein's regime and emigrated to the United States in the early 1990s, has made several works in response to the death of his brother, Haji, from a missile fired at a checkpoint in 2004. Among them is *Shoot an Iraqi* (2008), an interactive web-based installation in which viewers were invited to shoot paintballs at him over the period of a month. For his 2010 performance *and Counting . . . ,* he had his back tattooed with a borderless map of Iraq covered with one dot for each Iraqi and American casualty near the cities where they fell. The five thousand dead American soldiers are represented by red dots of permanent, visible ink, and the more than hundred thousand Iraqi casualties are represented by green dots of UV ink, invisible unless displayed under black light. He states:

> I wanted to create that monument, when I could carry it with me. So, at the first glance, on my back, you are going to see the Iraqi cities in Arabic and the 5,000 dots that represent American death. And there are different circumstances when you have a UV light. You are going to see the 100,000 dots come to life. And that is examining the issue of Iraqi death not being visible, not being acknowledged. And the number, it's so high we cannot even comprehend.[36]

Bilal's work deploys inscription as a form of counting, tattooing, wounding his own body as a performative gesture of memorialization.

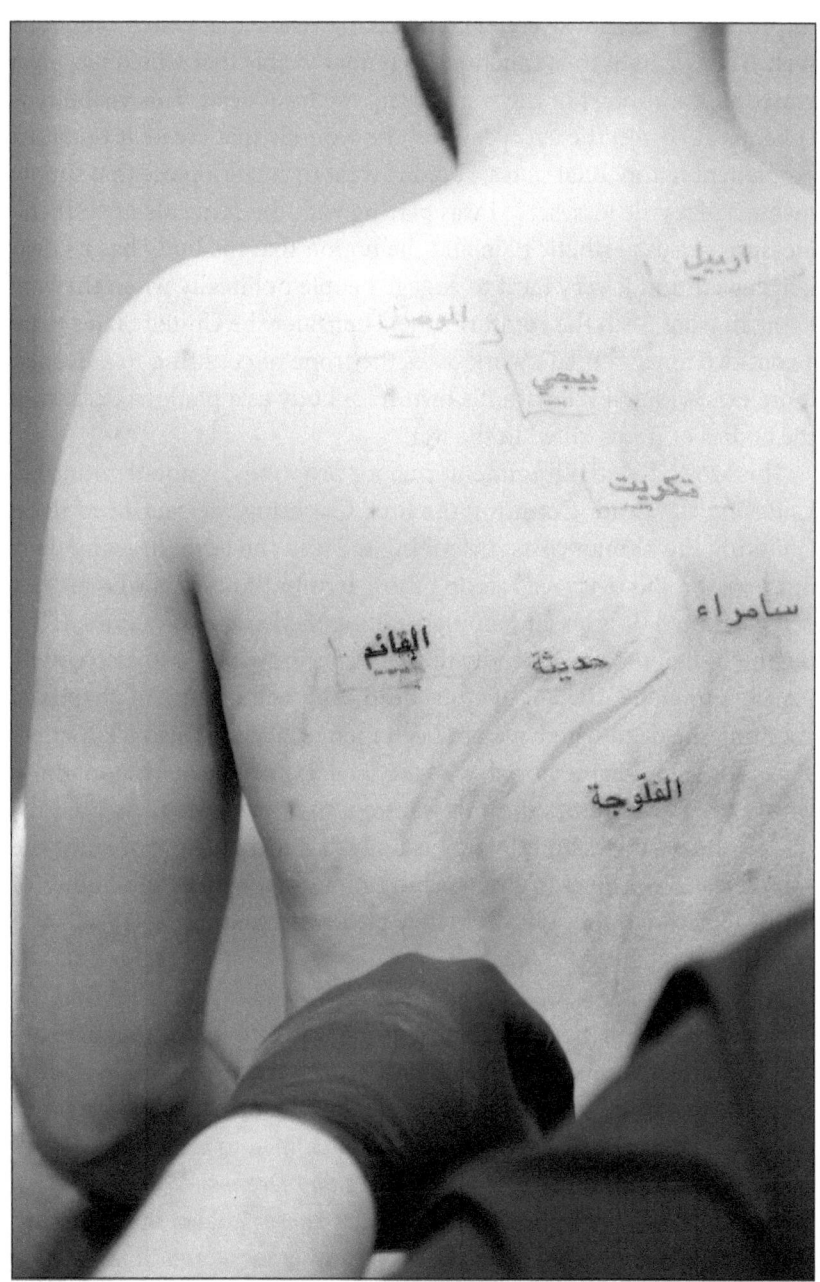

and Counting . . . (2010), by Wafaa Bilal. Photo: Brad Farwell.

Its primary trope, however, is about making visible that which cannot be seen. The UV light thus functions to render visible that which has been erased in the context of the war in Iraq, the Iraqi dead. This visibility is ephemeral, lost in the everyday, but the wounds that create it remain a permanent tattoo. Bilal states, "I didn't want to create a piece that simply memorializes the losses. . . . I was playing with the concepts of aesthetic pleasure versus aesthetic pain and the notion that the body has its own language. I find it very hard to engage people politically when they are living in what I call the comfort zone. I consider the United States to be a comfort zone."[37] Bilal's work takes the trope of counting to a deeper, more existential, level, with his own Iraqi body as a platform, carrying the bodies of Iraqis killed in the war.

This work, like the iraqimemorial.org proposals, is about counting. Counting the dead. Counting the loss. Counting the sacrificed lives. Counting the human costs. Inscribing them in the flesh, drawing their images over and over. And noting those tens of thousands who are not being counted. It is about naming—noting the legacies of names, tallying the individuality evoked by the very specific name, and also counting the unnamed, the anonymous dead. As I will discuss in chapter 5, counting the dead who have not been memorialized is also a key strategy of the lynching memorial, with the same explicit need to count those whom the perpetrators did not want counted or named. As Bilal inscribes the numbers literally on his body as a form of corporeality, the soil collection project of the lynching memorial evokes the bodies of the dead through the soil where they bled, with rows of jars of soil as a counting of the dead.

As the post-9/11 wars dragged on as never-ending conflicts, and the US strategy turned increasingly to a drone war with its own set of invisible victims, several artists have made works about drones, including James Bridle, who paints large drone shadows in urban landscapes, and DeLappe, who created a series of works that aimed to render the drones and their victims visible. DeLappe's *The 1,000 Drones—A Participatory Memorial* (2014, 2017) borrows from the Japanese ritual of one thousand cranes, in which people create paper origami cranes, often in a wish for peace. Here, DeLappe had participants create small paper drones, modeled on General Atomics' MQ-1 Predator drone, and write the name of a civilian drone casualty on the wings, working from a list of known

1,000 Drones—A Participatory Memorial, by Joseph DeLappe, at the Sonoma Valley Museum of Art, 2017. Photo by Robert Holmes.

victims of drone strikes in Pakistan and Yemen. The project took several months in its realization, thus, like many of the works I discussed earlier, it is about taking time to remember and about the labor of using one's hands to create the memory of someone the maker did not know. As DeLappe writes, "Through the act of participating in this work of creative remembrance, the intention is for we, as Americans, to recognize and remember those innocents killed in our ongoing Global War on Terror."[38] In all these works, we can see that it is a radical act to mourn a stranger.

The Wounded Veteran

The post-9/11 wars have produced 2.7 million veterans within the United States, with a proportionately high level of veterans who were wounded and who suffer from posttraumatic stress syndrome and brain injuries.[39] With advancements in battlefield medicine, many more gravely wounded veterans survived the wars than in past conflicts, thus creating a context in which the ratio of wounded veterans to war dead was dramatically changed.[40] As Kirk Savage writes:

> The constant threat of improvised explosives, combined with remarkable advances in medical technology, has produced one of the most profound changes in professional warfare: ever higher rations of the wounded to the dead. In Vietnam, the ratio was not yet three to one; in Iraq, it is almost eight to one. Many of these troops are permanently disabled, human memorials to the costs of war, but largely out of sight of the general public.[41]

The suicide rate among US veterans of the Iraq War and the War in Afghanistan has also been extremely high, the numbers now exceeding those killed, with an average of six thousand veterans committing suicide each year from 2006 to 2019.[42] Close to one million veterans have qualified for some kind of officially recognized disability.[43] As Savage notes, the United States thus has within it a large population of veterans whose wounds and scars function as "human memorials to the costs of war."

The veterans of the post-9/11 wars span the political spectrum from what Bodnar terms war patriotism to antiwar activism. There have been a visible number of veterans who have been elected to political office, some of whom are disabled. Notable among these is Illinois senator Tammy Duckworth, who was a helicopter pilot in Iraq and lost both legs when her helicopter was shot down and who is a vocal presence on the national stage. Attacked by right-wing commentator Tucker Carlson in July 2020 for recommending that there be a review of existing monuments, she wrote a scathing *New York Times* opinion piece, stating, "They should know, though, that attacks from self-serving, insecure men who can't tell the difference between true patriotism and hateful nationalism will never diminish my love for this country—or my willingness to sacrifice for it so they don't have to. These titanium legs don't buckle."[44] Duckworth is an example of a wounded veteran who deploys her position to argue for patriotism that involves sacrifice.

There has been significant analysis about the fact that many veterans of the post-9/11 wars have also become part of alt-right movements and that in the attack on the US Capitol on January 6, 2021, there were some war veterans in positions of leadership. Within the right-wing and white-supremacist groups that converged in that event, those with military training, weapons, and skills are highly valued.

By contrast, in ways that echo the involvement of Vietnam veterans in the antiwar movement against the Vietnam War, many veterans of the post-9/11 wars have become active in organizations like Veterans for Peace and what Lisa Leitz terms the military peace movement. As I noted earlier, Veterans for Peace was the primary organization behind the Arlington West displays of crosses, and a small proportion of veterans were actively involved in antiwar protests and activities. According to Leitz, "Despite the constraints of military culture, between ten and fifteen thousand members of the American military community joined anti-Iraq War protests."[45] Leitz notes that the peace movement lost steam after the 2008 financial crisis and the apparent winding down of the war in 2011, but its resurgence would later prompt the visible participation of numerous veterans in the Standing Rock Indian Reservation protests against the Dakota Access pipeline, with highly visible contingents of veterans, including many who were Native American, at protests in 2016 and through December 2017.[46] Veterans have also been visibly present at the Black Lives Matter protests, explicitly identifying themselves as veterans in support of the protests in summer 2020. In many of these contexts, these veterans put forward a kind of moral authority that comes from those who have served.

For many members of the military peace movement, according to Leitz, an embrace of antiwar activities was understood as a higher form of patriotism; they "not only asserted that protest supported the military but claimed that protest made the country better." They deployed their "insider-outsider identities in order to suggest that they alone had the legitimacy in the debates over the wars in Iraq and Afghanistan."[47] Patriotism is thus deployed strategically to argue against the project of war from within. We could take this further to argue that these veterans, most of whom went voluntarily to war with a set of ideals, are emblematic in their realization of the falsehood of the wars, one that they experienced at a deep personal level and often at significant cost. Several of the veteran peace organizations make this point explicit. About Face: Veterans against the War, which incorporated Iraq Veterans against the War, a group that advocated withdrawal from Iraq and reparations to the Iraqi people, states, "We are Post-9/11 service members and veterans organizing to end a foreign policy of permanent war and the use of military weapons, tactics, and values in communities across the country. As people intimately familiar with the inner workings of the world's largest military, we use our knowledge and experiences to expose the truth about these conflicts overseas and the growing militarization in the United States."[48] In 2020, About Face was active in encouraging National Guard troops to refuse to help the suppression of protests for racial justice. In many ways, these veterans' political actions can be seen as contributing to the end of the post-9/11 era.

In other words, the veterans of the peace movement deploy a moral position within national identity—those who were willing to personally sacrifice for the nation—to critique the project of the long war, the post-9/11 wars, and effectively the project of American empire. (It can be said that many of the high profile veterans in political office also put forward a moral position of those who have served, in this case as a means of affirming the nation.) Many of the stories told of the trauma of the war are stories not only of the chaos of the conflict and the terror of constant attack but also of the traumatic memories of the terroristic actions of the troops themselves, of the killing of civilians and the violence of their own actions and brutal violations of human rights. In the 2006 documentary *The Ground Truth*, veterans talk about how they were recruited into the Army with promises of opportunities and benefits, trained to be emotionless efficient war machines, and are haunted by the memories of the killings and deaths of civilians, only to return home to a context in which many are unable to get treatment for PTSD.[49] By 2019, the majority of veterans and the US public felt that the post-9/11 wars had not been worth fighting, and a narrative of futility over the losses of the war and of the wars as "failures" grew increasingly pervasive.[50] This was in sharp contrast to the post-9/11 fervor and confidence and the national unity with which the wars had begun.

A number of documentary photographers have created images that aim to visualize the memories and experience of wounded and disabled veterans of the post-9/11 wars. In artist-photographer Jennifer Karady's long-term project *Soldiers' Stories from Iraq and Afghanistan*, she stages photographs that aim to depict the emotional content of traumatic memories of veterans. She interviews the veterans extensively and then restages the incident, often using their family members as figures within the frame—she insists on purely analog images, with no digital manipulation. Karady states that she is interested in the "emotional truth" of the memories: "I am not trying to represent realistically, what happened and what did it look like, I am more interested in what it felt like."[51] Karady describes the images as being about the slow process of the transition back to being a civilian, and the staging of the images evokes the disconnect between the memories of war and the domestic landscape. Many of the veterans narrate PTSD stories of how a flash of a light, the sound of a truck hitting a pothole, and other everyday activities will activate their memories involuntarily, leaving them disoriented about where they are and feeling a heightened sense of danger. Several of them tell stories of the gruesome killing of civilians. In this image, former sergeant Mike Moriarty is haunted by a scene in which his truck hit and killed a woman whose body was then run over by a convoy of trucks and his horror when he tries to move her dismembered body. Many of Karady's images are dreamlike, almost fantastic, such as one in which a former airline radar technician hovers over a domestic scene and a woman sits up in a bedroom in a demolished house. They convey the surreal sense in which traumatic memories of war invade domestic life.

Soldiers' Stories from Iraq and Afghanistan, by Jennifer Karady.
Former Sergeant Mike Moriarty, New Hampshire Army National Guard, veteran of Operation Iraqi Freedom, with wife, Randi, and children, Matthew and Kenley; Keene, NH, June 2007. 48" x 48" Chromogenic Color Print. Courtesy Jennifer Karady.

The presence of the wounded veteran in US culture, whether as patriotic figure of sacrifice or as the painful reminder of the injuries and brutality of war, constitutes a kind of human memorial in US culture, as Savage notes. The veterans and their injuries are present forms of cultural memory, potentially implicitly embodying critiques of war, but they are also subject to forms of incorporation and disavowal about wars that are now largely understood as futile and failures. Rebecca Adelman writes that the US public is often entreated to respond to US soldiers and veterans through tropes of gratitude, affection, and admiration, thus to respond to the war itself in an affective range that precludes anger. She notes that there were a significant number of projects that organized to give "thanks" to soldiers, with groups called Hugs for our Soldiers and A Million Thanks, sending notes of thanks and care packages.[52] David Finkel's much-praised book (and subsequent film version) *Thank You for Your Service* critiques, through its cynical title, this easy sentiment.[53] Adelman goes further to note that the proliferation of videos of veterans reunited with their dogs, whether dogs they left at home or dogs they encountered in war, functions as a stand-in for the imagined emotions of the US public.[54] The wounded and disabled veteran is a disruptive figure within national culture, because they embody the sacrifice that these wars were not supposed to have. These forms of public feeling, from abstract thank-you messages to videos of homecomings, effectively work to contain this disruptive quality.

What this reveals is a broader disavowal in public discourse of the destructive effects of the post-9/11 wars on US culture, one mediated by erasure, gratitude, and the continued belief that the sacrifice was worth it. We can see this disavowal in the two images with which I began this chapter, Michael Reagan's drawn portrait of Michael Carey and his never-known daughter, Mia, for whom he is the never-known father, and Christopher Scherer's empty bedroom, untouched, preserved, arrested in time. The first image poignantly mediates grief in its construction of the fantasy of an imagined encounter; the drawing is both a means to make Michael Carey, long dead, present and co-present with his child Mia. This image is also about the labor of remembering, the time it takes to draw. But it is a recuperative image that disavows loss, imagining a relationship that was never able to exist. The empty bedroom is also emblematic of loss, but it is also about the hidden, the closed door, a compartmentalization of loss. It participates in another kind of erasure and an inability to integrate loss into the present. If the bedroom is never changed, then the prewar Scherer can be imagined to always be on the verge of emerging whole and alive. Thus, these images reveal a kind of disavowal of loss and the sacrifices that have come from the post-9/11 wars.

A disavowal of the failed project of the post-9/11 wars is most strangely and problematically rendered in the project by former president George W. Bush, *Portraits of Courage*, in which Bush, taking up painting in his post-presidential life, chose to paint portraits of almost one hundred wounded veterans, which traveled as an exhibition and was published as a book. Subtitled *A Commander in Chief's Tribute to America's Warriors*, the 2017 coffee-table book features individual portraits, as well as a group mural, of veterans, mostly focused on their faces, along with descriptions of their postwar difficulties and injuries. Many of them have prosthetics and traumatic brain injuries, and all appear to have suffered from PTSD, yet the stories are narrated as ones of triumph and renewal, in which many of them found recovery through activities like mountain-bike riding. Bush came to know many of them through his participation in the Bush Institute W100k mountain-bike rides and Warrior Open golf tournament.

The stories told by these wounded veterans are not stories of war so much as stories of the recovery from war, of difficulties returning home, of painful and lengthy physical and emotional recoveries from often horrific injuries. Bush narrates his relationships with these veterans, whose portraits he painted from photographs not with sittings, as one of respect if not awe at how they triumphed over these difficulties. Unlike other engagements with veterans and the war dead, however, this project is explicitly about a commander in chief interpreting the experiences of these men and women. As such, the project not only functions as a rehabilitation of Bush, the former president and architect of that war, but also situates Bush as a person recovering from the war as well. Bush himself has referred to the project as "therapeutic," and several of the veterans depicted in the project have stated that they see it as a kind of art therapy for the former president, recovering from the "moral injury" of sending troops to war.[55]

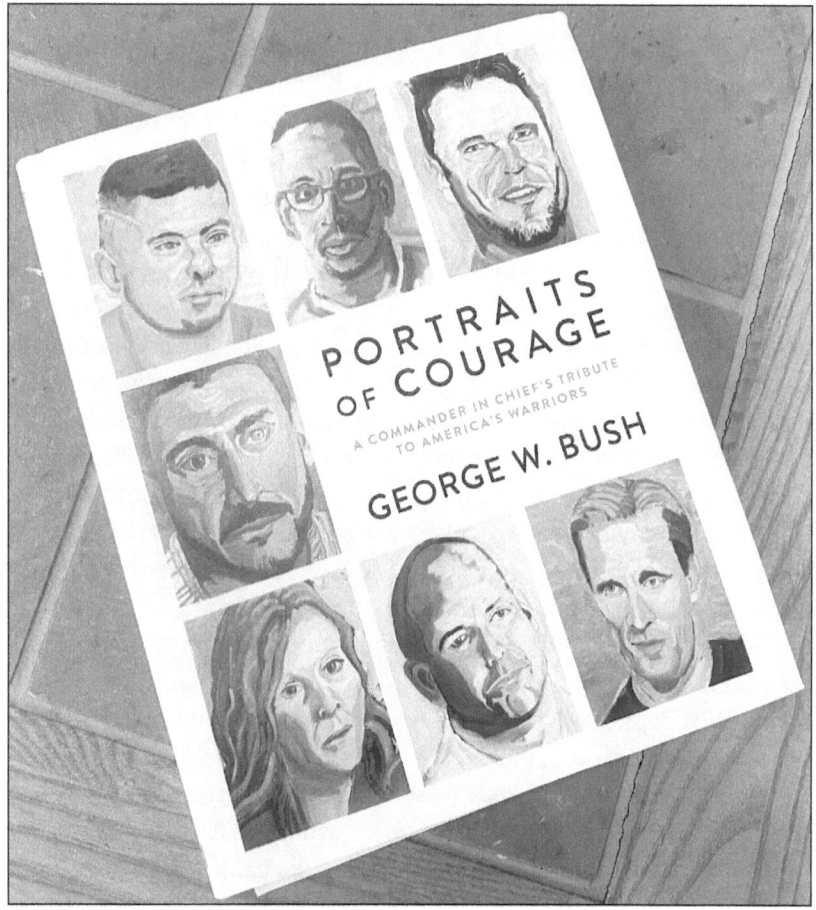

Portraits of Courage coffee-table book by George W. Bush.

On one hand, *Portraits of Courage* is explicitly about the difficulties and wounds of the veterans of the post-9/11 wars. On the other hand, it is about the erasure of Bush's responsibility for the wars. As Robin Wagner-Pacifici writes, "With roles that oscillate between concerned observer, witness to post-war history, sympathetic benefactor, Commander-in-Chief and (semi)official portraitist, Bush's visual and textual representational projects forestall a clear narrative of responsibility for the conditions in which the wounded veterans find themselves."[56] At no point is there any expression of remorse, on his part or on the part of the veterans; indeed, the trope of "I would do it again" is often invoked. Their triumph over these injuries, which is the central theme of the book, is depicted by and deployed by Bush as one that he can foster and support. Here, we could say, the veterans are being used to create a benign and even comforting portrayal of Bush as an empathetic and even artistic man, a portrayal that erases the image of Bush as the cocky, uninformed, and bellicose leader who along with his vice president, Dick Cheney, led the nation into two long and enormously destructive wars. Bush the perpetrator is thus replaced by Bush the victim. In these images, we can also see the primary symbolic role played by wounded veterans as mediating between war and civilian life, between being perpetrators and victims, and as a moral force that manifests within their bodies the hideousness and brutality of war.

This brings us to one last image: Nina Berman's well-known portrait of former Marine sergeant Ty Ziegel in *Marine Wedding*. Ziegel was seriously wounded by a suicide bomb in 2004 and underwent fifty operations. Berman produced a series of photographs on his marriage to his high school sweetheart, Renee, in 2006 (the couple separated a year later, and Ziegel died of an overdose in 2012).[57] Berman has been systematically photographing the wounded veterans of the Iraq War in her book *Purple Hearts*, producing images that aim to allow these men to retain their dignity as they pose with their injuries starkly visible. This wedding photograph gains its power from the startling contrast of the conventions of the marine wedding and the painful disfiguration of Ty's face, erased of expression, cobbled together from skin grafts, barely appearing human. Berman has stated that though she had seen many wounded veterans, she was shocked when she first saw the extent of Ziegel's injuries, yet he was probably the least self-conscious person she had ever met.[58] The bride's apparent emotional disconnect adds weight to the image, but what we really see is the distortion of the mythic Marine tableau, the monstrous impact of the war on simple manhood, the trappings of military symbols, and marital unity. As Suzannah Biernoff writes, "Valor, heroism, patriotism, courage: these concepts assume visible form, and do their cultural work, when they are personified and embodied. Mutilated or disabled, the veteran's body can connote the hollowness of corruption of these ideals."[59] One of the key aspects of these injuries is also how they mute and transform facial expression.

Marine Wedding (2006), by Nina Berman. Nina Berman/NOOR/Redux.

Marine Wedding won several prizes and was exhibited in several art exhibitions, including the 2007 Whitney Biennial. It received significant attention and was the source of debate about what it meant to depict someone with such extensive and visible injuries and for such an image to be shown in an art context. Berman states, "What other people bring to the picture is extraordinary. I got linked to by everyone from pro-war sites to antiwar sites to sites dedicated to love and Valentine's Day."[60] The Berman photograph is both a devastating portrait of the injuries suffered by one young man, Ty Ziegel, and an image of the devastation of the war itself. The war, instigated by a nation in a moment of unchecked power, a war so misguided not only in its intent but in how it was fought, has taken the American soldier and rendered him unrecognizable. He stands in for the monstrousness of the nation at war, turned now against itself.

National Memory

The Global War on Terrorism Memorial is now the subject of a congressional bill about its potential location on the National Mall. With the many phases of approval and fundraising that the Global War on Terrorism Memorial Foundation will need to go through before it can even proceed with a design competition, it is likely to be years before the project is realized.[61] There are currently a number of small memorials to the post-9/11 wars, including the Gulf War Memorial in Cumberland, Maryland, and the Global War on Terrorism Memorial at the National Infantry Museum in Columbus/Fort Benning, Georgia. This memorial lists more than seven thousand names of the US dead (what it terms "soldiers, sailors, airmen, and marines") and includes a thirteen-foot piece of steel from the North Tower of the World Trade Center along with a number of bronze statues of an infantry group and a medal of honor recipient who sacrificed his life for them at age nineteen.[62] Also underway is the National Desert Storm and Desert Shield War Memorial, approved for the mall in 2017, whose strangest feature is its being named after the military operation. Questions of naming reveal the fact that these are undeclared imperial wars of aggression, all part of the long war of the US in the Middle East. The official memorialization of the post-9/11 wars thus enters into the context of debate about the proliferation of war memorials on the National Mall since the opening of the Vietnam

Veterans Memorial in 1982. By 2021, a World War I memorial had opened near the mall, and there were still numerous memorials in progress on the mall and elsewhere in DC, including a memorial to African Americans who fought in the American Revolution and a memorial to Native American veterans. The sense that the National Mall, ostensibly a site of national pride and affirmation, is being inundated with memorials from constituencies across the political spectrum has often ignited debates about this excess of memorialization.

There has also been a parallel debate among veterans of the wars in Afghanistan and Iraq about whether or not it was too soon to have a memorial, with some veterans emphasizing that money should go toward improved services for veterans rather than toward building a memorial. The specter of the World War II memorial, built in 2004, after many veterans had died, is often invoked by politicians in these debates, with the argument that the memorial should go forward before veterans begin to die. The section of Arlington National Cemetery where the war dead of Afghanistan and Iraq are buried has functioned in some ways as a memorial, a place to go to recognize the dead. Arguing for the approval of the memorial, Republican representative Mike Gallagher, one of the sponsors of the bill, stated, "We're not saying 'Mission accomplished, there's nothing to see here.' Indeed the opposite. We are reminding everyone of the enormous costs of these wars."[63] Michael "Rod" Rodriguez, executive director of the Global War on Terror Memorial Foundation, takes the position that memorializing an unresolved war radically alters notions of what a memorial is. "We're pursuing the position of thought leader in this space. It will be the first national memorial in Washington authorized for an ongoing war."[64]

Given the emergence of veteran groups that have taken a stand on ongoing forms of oppression in US society, there have also been arguments for a radically different way of thinking about the memory of the global war on terror. In arguing against the memorial, veteran Chris Yeazel writes:

> If it's possible to pass legislation that waives the waiting period for construction of a war memorial, this should be done for legislation that honors the sacrifices made by interpreters who risked their lives to support American troops deployed to their home countries.... Or protects access

to clean drinking water in places like Flint or Standing Rock. Or perhaps veterans of these ongoing conflict could help pressure elected officials into providing clearly defined and realistically achievable strategic objects that could conclude America's longest war, or focus on the herculean tasks of rebuilding the lives, and entire nations, ravaged by these wars. Or demand accountability, transparency, and sanity be applied to military actions to be considered in an uncertain future.[65]

It remains to be seen how the memorial project will play out, but this emphasis on the costs of war and the subjectivity of many of these veterans, many of them injured and aware that the wars were futile, infuses the process. It is important to remember that these veterans served in a volunteer army and were pulled from National Guard regiments, sent on multiple deployments, and exposed to horrific violence. Numbers of them joined protests in summer 2020 to stand against the deployment of federal officers against protestors, to demand that they honor the Constitution. Those who came out to protest in Portland, Oregon, to create the Wall of Vets (along with the Wall of Moms and the Wall of Dads) were responding to the video footage of US Navy Veteran Chris David being beaten with a baton and pepper sprayed by DHS agents.[66] In January 2021, when it became known that some veterans participated in the assault on the Capitol, veteran David Smith was so upset that he organized a group of veterans to clean up the mess on the mall that the crowd had left behind, removing neo-Nazi and alt-right stickers and Trump paraphernalia.[67] Smith created an organization in June 2020 called Continue to Serve that aims to engage veterans in community service and social justice activism. He takes a moral position based on the fact that he and other veterans fought for the nation: "We want this country we fought for to be the place it's meant to be."

Kirk Savage wonders if the injured veteran will become the primary symbol of the post-9/11 wars: if new memorials go forward, "the realities of injury and trauma may emerge front and center. Traditionally, American war memorials avoid the wounded and idealize their soldiers. . . . Perhaps in the future, the figure of the disabled soldier will become a new icon for monument designers." Even more radical, he notes, would be to have the heart and wherewithal to honor "the countless Afghani and Iraqi civilians dead, wounded and orphaned, caught in the crossfire of our global war on terror. . . . We share with them the fundamental human cost of war."⁶⁸ This concept of the shared costs of war is, in fact, a radical one, and one that does not often emerge in the context of memorialization.

Finally, the troubled relationship between 9/11 memory, with the excessive memorialization of the 9/11 terrorist attacks, and the wars that followed in its wake raises the specter of terrorism's impact on US national identity. As I noted at the outset, terrorism has been narrativized in US culture as a foreign threat visited upon the US from elsewhere. The global war on terror defines that "terror" as a foreign one, attacking the American way of life and "our freedom." Yet this global war *on* terror is also itself a campaign *of* terror, with systematic violations of human rights that have terrorized whole populations in the Middle East and killed hundreds of thousands. In 2004, when the photographs of US soldiers torturing inmates at the prison in Abu Ghraib came to light and increased stories about atrocities committed by soldiers circulated, the fact that the US was engaging in forms of terrorism itself made the war an increasingly difficult project for unconditional public support. If many veterans now question these wars, it is often this sense of the pervasiveness of terroristic practices, the lasting effects of horrific injuries, the disconnect between the professed reasons for waging these wars and the actual brutal experience of them on the ground that prompts their deeper questioning.

Rethinking what terror means in national identity, and in its role in shaping the post-9/11 era, thus means refusing to participate in the split between the foreign and the domestic, one that enables the nation to wage wars with broad public acquiescence and thus with no impunity. It means demanding a recognition of the connections between oppression of US citizens at home with the brutal actions of US-led wars of aggression, asking that both be seen within a framework of human rights. Commentators have long pointed out that the torture in Abu Ghraib and Guantánamo was by people who had been trained in the US prison system, a system of mass incarceration for Blacks, and, as Singh points out, at Abu Ghraib, "the stacking and arrangement of bodies and celebratory photographs of naked, tortured, and sexually abused prisoners was reminiscent of a lynching party."⁶⁹ He writes, "Perhaps the active disconnect between the foreign and the domestic is where we must look if we are to understand the evolution of empire in the US global age."[70] The emergence of long existing right-wing militant groups into the public domain with the activation of those groups to invade the Capitol in January 2021 allowed for domestic terrorism to be seen in new ways by the American public. That the terrorism inflicted by Americans on Americans became the dominant threat by the end of the Trump administration, which had enabled and abetted their rise, signaled a dramatic shift in how terrorism is understood in relation to the nation.

To connect the Iraqi civilians, the victims of lynching, and the injured veterans with the 9/11 dead, to demand that they are all seen as grievable lives, is a challenge that much of this memory work aims to confront, deploying memory as a form of social change. Terrorism, as I will explore in the next chapter, is neither a recent nor an imported phenomenon in the United States. It has been a foundational aspect of the nation, beginning with the genocidal wars against Native Americans, and has been enacted over centuries of racial terror against Blacks, Latinos, Asian Americans, and other nonwhites. In the next chapter, I address how the memorial and museum to the victims of lynching, in Montgomery, Alabama, aim to rethink the story of the United States and terrorism and how memory can be activated to rescript national identity.

5

The Memory of Racial Terror

The Legacy Museum and the National Memorial for Peace and Justice

In a central corridor of the National Memorial for Peace and Justice, which opened in Montgomery, Alabama, in April 2018 as a memorial to 4,400 Blacks who were lynched between 1877 and 1950, there is a small listing of some of the names with the "reasons" why they were lynched:

> Warren Powell, 14, was lynched in East Point, Georgia, in 1889 for "frightening" a white girl.
> William Stephens and Jefferson Cole were lynched in Delta County, Texas, in 1895 after they refused to abandon their land to white people.
> David Walker, his wife, and their four children were lynched in Hickman, Kentucky, in 1908 after Mr. Walker was accused of using inappropriate language with a white woman.
> A Black man was lynched in Millersburg, Ohio, in 1892 for "standing around" in a white neighborhood.
> Jesse Thornton was lynched in Luverne, Alabama, in 1940 for addressing a white police officer without the title "mister."
> Henry Patterson was lynched in Labelle, Florida, in 1926 for asking a white woman for a drink of water.
> Elizabeth Lawrence was lynched in Birmingham, Alabama, in 1933 for reprimanding white children who threw rocks at her.

This list of petty excuses, which so powerfully distills the banality of lynching's horror, makes utterly clear that these acts had nothing to do with crime—except insofar as the "crime" was participating in everyday behavior while Black, of owning businesses and demanding rights while Black, of living while Black. Research done by the Equal Justice Initiative

Listing of lynchings at the National Memorial for Peace and Justice. Photo by author.

(EJI) showed that there were several common motivations for lynchings: a widely distorted fear of interracial sex, a desire for a public spectacle, a response to allegations of crime as terrorist violence, and as retribution against sharecroppers, ministers, and community leaders who resisted mistreatment. Many of these lynchings were motivated, as these statements make clear, by minor social transgressions or by the assertion of basic rights.[1] The resonance is unmistakable with contemporary incidents of white people calling the police and the police harassing and killing Blacks who are participating in everyday activities such as driving, jogging, birdwatching, and having a barbeque, brought to particular public attention in 2020 through social media.

It is fitting that the National Memorial for Peace and Justice, known also as the lynching memorial, with its accompanying Legacy Museum, which addresses the history of slavery and lynching as legacies to contemporary mass incarceration, is the last significant memory project of the post-9/11 era. As I will argue in this chapter, the lynching memorial and museum constitute radical engagements with national memory as forms of memory activism, and shift the relationship of memory to national identity in ways that signal the end of the post-9/11 era and the beginning of a new era to follow. If the post-9/11 era began with the obsessive proliferation of 9/11 memorials and the construction of the 9/11 museum, almost all of which deployed memory as a form of national unity, that era ends with a memorial and museum that demand a rewriting of the national narrative to demonstrate how racism and terrorism has been integral to the national fabric.

The 9/11 memorial/museum and the EJI memorial/museum can thus be seen to straddle opposing ends of the spectrum of American memorialization and nationalism. Yet both memorialize victims of terrorism: victims of Islamic fundamentalist terrorism in one, Black victims of domestic racial terrorism in the other. While those who died on 9/11 were memorialized ten to thirteen years after their deaths in a national memorial, even though at the time that was thought to be overdue, the National Memorial for Peace and Justice reaches back 150 years, explicitly defining this as a repressed memory of those who have never been properly named and mourned. The 9/11 memorial and museum ultimately affirm the narrative of American innocence, for its victims and the nation, whereas the lynching memorial and museum reject the narrative of innocence and establish complicity to violence. Thus, while the 9/11 memorial and museum can be said to affirm the nation, the Legacy Museum and the National Memorial of Peace and Justice take the nation to task and ask it to change. It is their shared goal to memorialize victims of *terrorism* that reveals the very radical coincidence of these two memorials' being completed in a relatively short period of time.

While figures such as Ida B. Wells, W. E. B. Du Bois, and others used the term *terrorism* to describe racial violence against Blacks, and many civil rights organizations such as the NAACP have worked to define lynching as terrorism, this understanding has not produced a broader public engagement with the idea of lynching as state-sanctioned terrorism.[2] The long road to define racial violence as racial terrorism was taken up by Bryan Stevenson, who founded EJI in 1989 as a nonprofit that pursues legal advocacy in Alabama and beyond for death row inmates and those wrongfully accused or receiving excessive sentences. EJI deliberately uses the term *racial terror lynchings*. Working in the heart of the racist and unjust criminal justice system of Alabama, one of the worst states for legal representation, with inhumane prison conditions and high rates of incarceration for Blacks, including teenagers, EJI and Stevenson came to understand that their legal project could only go so far without a broader change in the culture and its telling of history. They began producing historical reports on the slave trade and the history of lynching, and they conceived the idea of a memorial. Stevenson, working with fellow attorney Sia Sanneh and a team, began looking at the processes that have taken place in Germany in relation to Holocaust memory, in South Africa after Apartheid, and in Rwanda after the massacres and began to understand that in the United States, there was a need for truth and reconciliation to deal with the legacy of slavery, lynching, and racial injustice. The dominant US narrative—that slavery was an evil of a bygone past, that Confederate monuments are merely about heritage, that the civil rights movement ushered in legal equality for all, that an African American president signaled a largely postracial moment, and that white extremist violence today is an aberration rather than a norm—needed to be challenged, rejected, and revised with the histories of racial violence and terrorism that it masks. In defining racial terrorism as a form of state-sanctioned terrorism, these projects also engaged with questions of human rights, long absent from US memorialization—and glaringly absent from the 9/11 museum. Erika Doss has written that in US history, terrorism has been reduced to the narrative of demonic foreigners or evil misfits, like Timothy McVeigh, allowing it to appear to remain outside of everyday American life.[3] Conversely, the Legacy Museum defines the trajectory of white on Black racial violence from slavery to lynching to segregation to mass incarceration not only as terrorism but as foundational to the nation's origins. Terrorism alters everyday life through fear. It constitutes an unmaking of the world. Lynching in particular was a truly effective practice to this end.

Historically, the actual effects of racial violence *as terrorism* have been under-told. This is not simply about lynchings, but about families who fled the threat of lynching or who lived with the fear of lynching as a terrorizing force in daily life. The Great Migration of six million Blacks out of the South beginning in the early twentieth century was an exodus away from racial terrorism and the threat of violent death.[4] Indeed, many historians have argued that the name Great Migration is a misnomer that makes it appear that Blacks voluntarily left the South to migrate elsewhere, when the terms *forced exodus* and *refugees* would be more accurate.[5] Moreover, understanding lynching as terrorism requires turning the story on the ordinary people, on those families having to flee, and then just as importantly, on the white crowds who watched those lynchings, including white families, to show that they were engaging in terrorism when they celebrated torture and murder as a public spectacle. This demands a consideration of how terrorism has been at the heart of the nation's story, that white supremacy was incorporated into the nation's founding and has enabled centuries of white resistance to racial change that haunts the country's major institutions and social structure, from the educational system to housing and human welfare, economic access and opportunity, and criminal justice. In other words, this means recognizing that the "American way of life," so often defended against foreign terrorism, has been and continues to be itself one of racial terror. The January 6, 2021, assault on the US Capitol by supporters of President Trump and white supremacists signaled a shift from the post-9/11 era based on fear of foreign terrorism to a new era in which domestic terrorism is recognized as a threat to such a degree that it was mentioned by President Biden in his inaugural speech.

The shared project of memorializing victims of terrorism connects the 9/11 memorial and the National Memorial for Peace and Justice. Bryan Stevenson has noted that in the wake of 9/11, when he would speak about his work, "Old people of color come up to me sometimes and say, 'Mr. Stevenson, I get so angry when I hear someone on TV talking about how they're dealing with domestic terrorism for the first time in our nation's history after 9/11. You need to make them stop saying that, because that's not true.'"[6] The excessive memorialization of 9/11 victims of terrorism on US soil thus exposed the erasure of the history of lynching as one of racial terrorism. Yet it is significant that the memorial in Alabama is framed in terms of peace and justice, signaling in its name the injunction to move beyond the violence of lynching to encompass the entirety of social justice. In comparison to the National September 11 Memorial and Museum in New York, which names the violent event, the name of this memorial is aspirational.

EJI's Community Remembrance Project

Beginning in 2010, Stevenson and EJI began a project of cataloging all the lynchings that took place between 1875 and 1950 in twelve southern states, with a broad network of researchers and volunteers scouring newspapers and archives. Building on the work of the NAACP and other organizations, they were convinced that the numbers of lynchings had not been adequately counted.[7] They eventually amassed an archive of over 4,400 lynchings in thirty-five states reaching as far as Oklahoma and New York; they would later go on to archive an additional two thousand lynchings during Reconstruction, 1865 to 1876, and lynchings after 1950, as well as lynchings of Mexican Americans and Mexicans along the border. In their oral histories, they also documented "near-lynchings" where people described packing up and moving in a day, fleeing as exiles after a threatening encounter. They use the term *racial terror lynchings* specifically for those lynchings that were committed outside any criminal justice process, excluding lynchings or mob killings that were committed after a trial had taken place. They also distinguished them from mob killings of non-minorities. According to EJI's *Lynching in America* report, racial terror lynchings "were carried out with impunity, sometimes in broad daylight, often 'on the courthouse lawn.'"[8] As Stevenson notes, "The aim was to maintain white supremacy and political and economic racial subordination."[9]

EJI also began a Community Remembrance Project in 2013 that aimed initially to intervene in the local context of Montgomery and its proliferation of Confederate monuments and then more broadly throughout the South. Montgomery includes a towering statue of Jefferson Davis by the State Capitol building; there are fifty-nine markers and monuments to the Confederacy within the city limits, and both local high schools, which are majority Black, are named after Confederate general Robert E. Lee and Confederacy president Jefferson Davis. As Stevenson states regularly, "This landscape is littered with the iconography of the Confederacy." Rather than advocate to have the monuments removed,

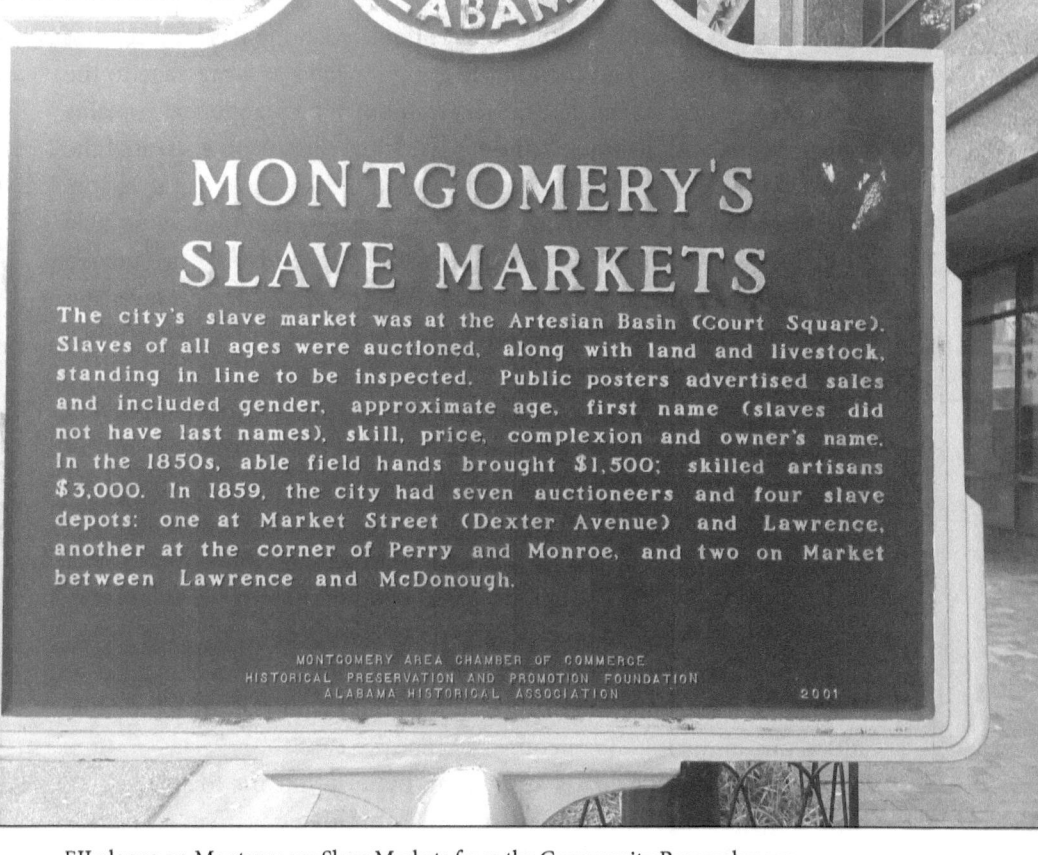

EJI plaque on Montgomery Slave Markets from the Community Remembrance Project. Photo by author.

EJI began to advocate for the insertion into the cityscape of Montgomery and throughout the South of a parallel history of slavery and racial violence. This began very simply with the erection of plaques throughout the downtown area that told the story of Montgomery's history as a major slave port, where enslaved people were brought in by ship on the river, warehoused, and sold. According to Stevenson, in 1860, three-quarters of the population of Montgomery were enslaved people.[10]

The historical plaques of the Community Remembrance Project aim to tell both a history of violence and a history of Black people's accomplishments that produced that violence. One example is the story of Anthony Crawford, a prosperous Black farmer in Abbeville, South

Carolina, who was lynched in 1916 in a dispute over the price of his cotton; he was taken out by a mob of three hundred, hung from a tree, shot two hundred times, and then left to hang for days as a message to the Black community. At the dedication ceremony for a plaque that explains Crawford's accomplishments and his lynching, Stevenson entreated the crowd, which included many descendants of Crawford whose ancestors fled the region in the aftermath, to see the plaque as the "most honorable place" in Abbeville, where the "bruises and cuts and scars are turned into medals of honor" and to proclaim, "We are here."[11] Here, Stevenson engages in an rhetorical move to turn this horrific act of violence into a statement of empowerment and redemption of Black achievement.

EJI also undertook one of its most extraordinary projects, the Soil Collection Project, in which volunteers collect dirt from the sites of these documented lynchings and place them in jars with the name of the victim and the date and place of the lynching. Eventually, an exhibition design for the rows of jars for the Community Soil Collection Project was created by MASS Design group, who would design the memorial. Initially, the idea was to incorporate the soil with concrete in the markers of the memorial; this evolved into the use of Corten steel instead. A large box of the soil is incorporated into the memorial, which people added dirt to during the opening ceremony.

This collection of dirt is a powerful material means to situate this history within the landscape. The soil is highly evocative—it ranges widely in color, from dark red hues to different shades of brown from light to dark. It reminds us that these bodies were not given proper rituals of burial. I noted in chapter 1 that those who died on 9/11 in New York were the focus of an enormous and expensive DNA identification process. Remarkably, in the Soil Collection Project, participants often invoke DNA as a code for the potential trace of the victim in the dirt. One of the volunteers, Anthony Ray Hinton, who was released through EJI's advocacy after thirty years on death row for a crime he did not commit, speaks to the dead man, Joe Souls, when he gathers the dirt: "I came here today to hope that I can get your DNA and take it to a place where you will be respected, and not leave your DNA on this roadside in Montgomery, Alabama."[12]

The jars of soil are on display in the museum and at the memorial pavilion next to the memorial, and their identical glass forms give them

EJI Soil Collection Project. Photo: Equal Justice Initiative/Human Pictures.

an exhibitionary aesthetic, creating beautiful displays. Their variation is remarkable enough to evoke not only the individuals killed but also the landscape and the geography of the South. The soil is alive; some jars seem to have organic material growing in them. As Stevenson notes:

> When I see the jar it tells its own story. There's a variation in color, down on the Gulf Coast, where it's sandy and light, in the Black Belt where it's dark and rich and in the northern part where the clay is red. There is this geographic story but there is also a story about our history. There is sweat in the soil, the sweat of enslaved people; there are the tears of people who suffered when they were being brutalized and lynched; there's the blood of these victims. But there is also hope in that soil.[13]

The soil is evocative of the fact that the bodies of victims of lynchings were usually left on display for days as a form of terrorism; thus, the soil in the jars is narrated as the blood-soaked ground beneath hanging bodies. It is also a reminder of the crucial struggles over land—and the soil to grow crops in—that were central to racial repression in the South, even to this day in battles of Black farmers to retain their farms in the South. The history of Blacks' relationship to the land and the soil of the South is one of dispossession.[14] The post–Civil War reconstruction era promised "forty acres and a mule" to the newly freed Blacks, defining freedom as access to the land and the capacity to farm one's own land, a promise unfulfilled. The Great Migration was also a move away from agrarian life to industrial cities, and so the land, and in particular the land of the South, has held a particular important symbolism in Black literature and culture. In a certain sense, the jars of soil are claiming a different kind of ownership over the land, to say that the dirt is owned by those whose sweat and blood saturated it. This would explain the constant reiteration of the soil containing DNA, that it signifies a claiming of the land through the comingling of body and dirt. The dirt itself also stands as a kind of testimony of nature, signifying that the categories of race and the ideology of white supremacy are not natural.

The gathering of the dirt is also about ritual and speaking to the dead. In this sense, it is a multiply reparative process. The activity of digging the dirt together, a shared experience, has been narrativized by Stephenson and others as a way to come together through the labor of digging; he tells one story in particular of a white man who joined a Black woman who was digging and then brought the dirt with her back to EJI. The EJI website and the Legacy Museum display several videos of the process by which volunteers collected the dirt, and many of them depict moments when the volunteers feel compelled, as Hinton did, to speak to the dead. In one scene, former magistrate judge Vanzetta McPherson, digging the dirt for John Temple, who was lynched in Montgomery, prays, "Our father in heaven, we pause so very briefly this morning to remember and to mourn a man who we did not know, but in so many ways a man we *do* know. We pray that the sacrifice that he so involuntarily made strengthens us, edifies us, and helps us to move forward in a way that will prevent this ever from occurring again." She ends by saying, "For all I know, some of the very dirt we dug was there. What if this dirt could talk? I thought that digging on that soil was a poignant way to connect to the time, the event, and, most importantly, the man."

In this sense, the soil project redefines the dirt as a witness, a material form of memorialization that has held the memory of these lynchings through the years that they were "forgotten" at the sites where they took place. The soil project declares that the memory of those lynchings has been there, in the dirt, all along; by gathering the dirt and naming it, the project honors the *soil as memory*.[15] Here, too, we see the radical act of mourning a stranger, and in her words, saying we know him, we recognize him.

The Legacy Museum: From Enslavement to Mass Incarceration

The 2018 opening of the Legacy Museum and National Memorial for Peace and Justice was the culmination of EJI's remembrance projects. Both have received an extraordinary amount of attention and succeeded in bringing large numbers of visitors into Montgomery in the years since, to date at least 750,000. Montgomery was already one of several sites of civil rights movement tourism, regularly featured on tours that go through Birmingham, Selma, and Montgomery, given its important role in the history of the civil rights movement, with the Montgomery Bus Boycott in 1955–56, which was instigated by Rosa Parks's arrest for refusing to give up her seat for a white man. Tourist destinations in the city include the Rosa Parks Museum, the Dexter Avenue King Memorial Baptist Church, where Martin Luther King Jr. preached, the Freedom Rides Museum, and the Civil Rights Memorial Center at the Southern Poverty Law Center, which has the Civil Rights Memorial, designed by Maya Lin. (There is also the Hank Williams Museum right next to EJI as well as the nearby First White House of the Confederacy, which was occupied by Jefferson Davis.) In their location in Montgomery between these contrasting sites, Lori Pierce and Kaily Heitz write, "the museum and memorial are actually perfectly situated as an ongoing reminder of the sometimes deadly paradoxes that hold the country in a constant state of suspended racial tension."[16]

Stevenson is often asked why he didn't want to do these memory projects in Washington, DC, given that it is a *national* memorial and museum, not a local one. He has stated that he wanted people to make the journey to Montgomery, that his intent was to change the identity of Montgomery as well as the nation. Former mayor Todd Strange told the *New Yorker* in 2016, "We certainly appreciate the fact that it's going to lead to a big influx of people who want to come and gain some understanding. Those are good, clean tourist dollars."[17] (In 2019, Montgomery elected mayor Steven Reed, who is Black and a former judge.) Stevenson made a strategic decision to not use public funds for the museum and the memorial in order to stay below the radar; they were paid for by private donations, for the relatively low sum of $15 million for the memorial and $8 million for the museum (as compared to the $1 billion for the 9/11 memorial and museum in New York).

The Legacy Museum was first housed in a former warehouse for enslaved people situated in the downtown area and in October 2021 was moved to a larger museum building nearby. The museum begins by situating visitors physically within this local history of the slave trade through direct address. A painted wall that greets visitors on arrival reads, "You are standing on a site where enslaved people were warehoused." Montgomery was a crucial and active port in the slave trade; at one point in the mid-nineteenth century, enslaved people held in these warehouses numbered in the hundreds each day.

The Legacy Museum has as its primary argument that, as Stevenson often states, slavery in the United States did not end with the Emancipation Proclamation; rather, it evolved, and its racial oppression can be traced through several subsequent eras, of lynching, segregation, and finally, to the mass incarceration of Blacks in the present day. Rather than simply narrate a history, the museum makes an argument; as one commentator notes, the exhibit is structured "like a great legal argument" that "relies on both emotion and an accumulation of evidence."[18] Stevenson's persuasive rhetoric, legal reasoning, and racial philosophy suffuse all aspects of the project. The museum's narration reveals a powerful belief that representing this history will have an enlightening effect on visitors and the national conversation about race.[19] It is Stevenson's life story of working in the trenches of the Alabama criminal justice system, one that is told in his best-selling 2015 book *Just Mercy* and in the film based on the book in 2019, that provides the intellectual argument of the exhibition and also its refusal to sugarcoat.[20] As Phillip Kennicott writes in the *Washington Post*, "Stevenson's long exposure to the inequities and cruelty of the criminal justice system also has made him quietly and intellectually uncompromising. More than anything else, he decided from the beginning not to let anyone off easy when it came to telling this story."²¹

Storytelling is a crucial strategy in the law as well as in memorialization. Sanneh explains that EJI's work on the memorial and museum was shaped by their experiences as lawyers making arguments in court to people, such as judges, who represent a range of potential positions: "Doing capital cases in Alabama and the Deep South, we have never had the luxury of being able to speak to an audience of our choosing, of like-minded people. One of the things that I have learned as a lawyer is if you present your argument to Bryan to practice, you are going to be pushed about what the story is that you are telling."²² She emphasizes that as lawyers, they translated their strategies of legal narrative persuasion derived from arguing in small courtrooms around the country to the realm of design: "How do we use architecture and art and landscape design and font size and color to move people so that they come in with a set of thoughts on the history of enslavement and they leave with new perspectives?"

The museum's narrative trajectory is segmented into four eras—Era 1: Slavery in America; Era 2: Racial Terror; Era 3: Segregation Forever; Era 4: Mass Incarceration. The museum intends to have visitors arrive at its final section understanding the "legacies"—hence the museum's name—handed down over the decades from slavery to present-day mass incarceration.²³ In this sense, the museum is, in the words of Jake Barton, whose firm Local Projects designed the exhibition (as well as the digital projects in 9/11 museum), an "activist museum" that has as its primary aim not simply to tell a history but to make an argument about the present and, in its most ambitious aim, to transform visitors into those who will act. Part of how the museum achieves this is to refuse in many ways to tell a story of uplift. This is a response to the more common narratives about the long struggles of civil rights, in which the history of slavery is told as a prelude to the triumphs of the civil rights movement, culminating in the election of the first Black president. As Alison Landsberg writes, "To dismantle the widely accepted triumphalist narrative that moves from slavery to abolition to Civil Rights, the visitor is asked to see *what has remained constant* throughout these four periods instead of what has changed."²⁴ Landsberg argues that the museum's focus on the present as the primary temporal moment for its narrative means that it is effectively rejecting the conventional notion of the history museum, which is that history is in the past and separate from the present. For these reasons, Landsberg argues that the Legacy Museum is a memory museum rather than a history museum, because history "has not been successful at fueling political change, for advancing social justice around race." Memory, she argues, can be deployed in the museum to actively encourage visitors to see present-day racial violence as existing on a continuum with histories of slavery and lynching. She states, "Memory with its porous temporal boundaries tends to collapse the division between past and present. To *remember* enslavement, racially motivated violence, and dispossession would be to feel its ongoing presence in the present and in so doing to open debate about who we are as a nation." In this strategy, the museum emphatically rejects the narratives of American exceptionalism and innocence. Thus, the tenacity of the narrative of racial uplift, which affirms the nation as one of moral authority that eventually does the right thing, is aligned with the equally tenacious narrative of American innocence.

The Legacy Museum tactically situates visitors in relation to the present through a series of technological strategies that aim to blur distinctions between past and present. Upon entry into the museum, visitors descend down a ramp that takes them to a series of dark cells, like the cells where enslaved people were warehoused in this actual building before they were auctioned. Here, ghost-like figures on life-size video screens come to life, moving from a hazy view into focus, as if they were holograms, when one leans toward the wooden bars of the cell, and they begin to talk directly to the visitor. One woman pleads, "Help me find my children!" Several sing hymns. Two children call out, "Momma! Have you seen our momma?" There is a significant amount of artifice here that asks viewers to engage in a different mode than many museum displays, though their words are derived from actual enslaved people's narratives. Although the figures are clearly played by actors, their form of direct address to the visitor is a confrontation—one feels obligated to stay through their speaking, not to turn away. The aim here is to create empathy by inserting contemporary visitors into a time frame of the past, asking us, What would you do if confronted with an actual enslaved person pleading for help? From the beginning, then, the museum display situates the past explicitly within the present and signals that

Legacy Museum Slavery Evolved Wall. Photo: Equal Justice Initiative.

it will demand that visitors engage at the level of complicity with the exhibition content. Here, too, we can see a contrast to the 9/11 museum, which effectively situates visitors into the subject position of 9/11 victims and does not provide the possibility of engaging with complicity.

At this point, the museum also signals that it will create different kinds of subject positions for visitors according to race and nationality. White visitors' responses to the animated figures are likely to incorporate a sense of guilt, discomfort, and empathy, whereas for African American visitors these displays speak to much more specific legacies of pain and the deep familial memories of violence. One key question this raises is whether the museum lets off the hook those US visitors not from the South, since its discussion of slavery and lynching outside the South is minimal.

Like other museums, the Legacy Museum situates visitors as witnesses, although its strategy is not to situate visitors as witnesses to history but rather to set them up as witnesses to the past as present. The reenactments set this tone from the beginning, and then in the exhibition section on slavery, there is documentary evidence—notices of slave auctions, testimonies from enslaved people, and photographs—including photographic reenactments of potential historical images. Barton, who directed the exhibition design, notes that the existing canon of photographs of enslaved people is sparse, because enslaved people were not seen as people worthy enough to be photographed, with those few images used to the point of being cliché; there is also some evidence that the documentary images of enslaved people that appear bucolic were staged. He explains that the use of reenacted images in the warehouse pens and the restaging of photographs in the museum aims to "shock you with the personness" of the enslaved people.[25]

The museum exhibition narrates the trajectory of slavery, lynching, segregation, and mass incarceration through an onslaught of information and media, with a timeline extending across the walls and floor on the left and corresponding exhibitions on the right, including multiple interactive video screens with deep historical information, art work and sculptures, videos by artists such as Molly Crabapple, whose watercolor images are painted before the camera, documentary photographs and videos, posters and signs, and various displays that allow visitors to make choices on content. One digital screen of lynching photographs is coded as difficult content and gives viewers a warning before they touch to begin viewing. The museum's displays trace several narratives through each of the eras, with a focus not only on the brutality, deprivation, and dehumanization but also on the trauma of family separations as a routine act of slave auctions and as a key aspect of mass incarceration.

Each era is, in effect, rescripted and narrated differently from its more conventional historical narrative. As Landsberg notes, slavery here is recoded as "kidnapping," a characterization that disavows the legality of the slave trade: "By highlighting 'kidnapping' as central to the slave trade, the museum underscores slavery's illegality, its criminality; such a framing works to denaturalize, or call into question the very idea of a 'slave trade,' a formulation that would seem to normalize and legitimize the sale of human bodies."[26] Similarly, lynching is recoded as racial terror, emphasizing the terrorization of all Blacks not only in the wake of lynching but also in the contemporary experience of terrorism, one that, because of 9/11, most visitors to the museum will have experienced from

Legacy Museum exhibit on segregation. Photo: Equal Justice Initiative/Human Pictures.

the subject position of potential victims or those under threat from terrorism. As the exhibition moves into the more well-known history of segregation, defined here as white supremacy by law, and the civil rights movement, it presents the struggle and nonviolent protests, including an in-depth and uplifting film about the Montgomery Bus Boycott, which emphasizes the complexity of the organizing infrastructure that sustained it. Unlike most civil rights museums, however, it downplays any upbeat message regarding civil rights success, juxtaposing these positive depictions with a large wall of racist Jim Crow signs and photographs that capture white hatred in the anti-desegregation school protests, advertisements, and videos of racist speeches from members of the White Citizen's Councils and major elected officials. What hasn't changed, as Landsberg notes, is the narrative. This refusal to highlight a story of racial progress is also a refusal to engage with the narrative that the nation has lived up to its values and retained its innocence.

The museum's final section, Mass Incarceration, brings the atrocities of white supremacy full circle and is potentially its most devastating. Here, the presentness of the crisis is rendered with urgency. The exhibition emphasizes the cruelty of family separation, as a continuum from slavery, with a large, devastating photograph of a teenager in tears, his head pressed against his mother's chest after he has been sentenced to the death penalty. It presents the injustices of the criminal justice system and the brutal conditions of US prisons, with conscripted labor and overcrowding, the cruelties of juvenile detention, all forms of stripping human rights. One wall displays a selection of heartbreaking letters from incarcerated men and women to the lawyers of EJI, describing appalling injustices and pleading for help. Reading these letters is wrenching, and they remind visitors of EJI's immediate and ongoing role as an organization of legal intervention. In the words of Nicole Fleetwood, prisons are evidence of what she sees as the aim of the "settler state" to "separate people from everyone they love." Just as the policies of slavery actively and deliberately separated families, the carceral system is fundamentally based on keeping prisoners separate from those they love.[27]

Here, interactive technologies are used to render present those who are on death row and incarcerated, to bring their personhood out of the prison and into the museum. Visitors are invited to sit in four replicas of a prison visiting booth, next to a list of rules about allowed behavior as would be posted as in prison visiting room, where they pick up a phone before a still video image of an incarcerated person. Once the phone is picked up, the video is activated and the prisoners begin to narrate their stories in prison and in the courts, speaking directly to the visitor. This is a primary manifestation of what Stevenson defines as the aim of the museum to have people "experience directly" racial oppression. The display is designed to keep visitors from easily moving on—one does not want to hang up on an incarcerated person telling a devastating story of brutality and injustice (there are seven stories, two of which are women).

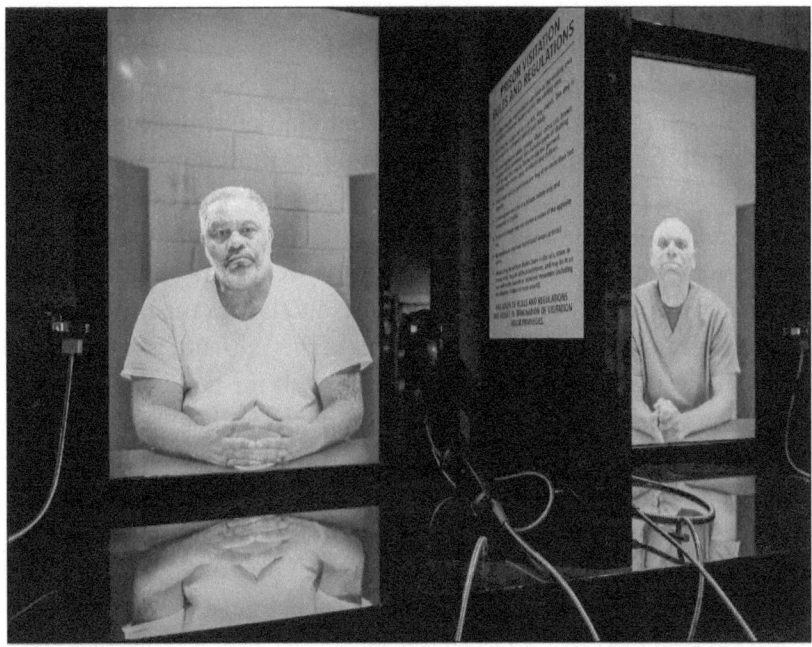

A multimedia exhibit allowing visitors to "speak" to inmates on death row, including Anthony Ray Hinton, left, wrongly convicted of two murders, at the Legacy Museum. Photo: Audra Melton/New York Times/Redux.

These are "simulated" prison visits, with the men and women wearing prison uniforms, but all of these are former incarcerated people that EJI has successfully secured releases for, and some of them were convicted to life sentences as juveniles. When I visited the museum with Katherine Hite in 2019, we learned that one of the people in the video, Kuntrell Jackson, was standing silently nearby, watching people interact with the videos and the exhibition in general. At age fourteen, Jackson had participated in a robbery in which a store clerk was killed by another juvenile, and he was sentenced to life without parole. Jackson's case was won by Stevenson in the Supreme Court, with the ruling that juveniles could not be sentenced to life imprisonment without the possibility of parole. He was subsequently retried and released, and he has been affiliated with EJI and has written a book about his experience.[28] As it details his experiences as a child in prison, his video is particularly difficult to watch. As we spoke with him about the museum, which he clearly feels a strong pride in and connection to, that sense of presence was powerful and something I had never experienced in a museum before. At that point, this was no longer a museum experience. It was a site of advocacy.

In this sense, the museum is a different kind of institution not only from a historical museum but even other memory museums. When Barton calls it an "activist museum," he draws a comparison to the 9/11 museum, a project he also worked on. The 9/11 museum, he notes, "is not trying to make a larger point about the world," it's aiming to tell a particular story, but "Bryan is an activist, and he has made a museum because he is an activist." One of the aims of this museum is to shape the emotional experience of visitors after they exit the building. After the exhibition section on mass incarceration and the wall of letters from incarcerated people pleading for help, the museum has a Reflection Space that displays images of figures who have been important to the fight for racial justice; it then has a long corridor that includes art by such artists as Sanford Biggs, whose bronze sculpture of a brutalized body is dedicated to Michael Brown, who was killed by police in Ferguson, Missouri, in 2014 and whose death sparked the Black Lives Matter movement, and by Hank Willis Thomas, whose sculpture of hands reaching out of holes evoke the hands of people in prison. Here, the museum makes the statement that art is an essential forum for responses to injustice. It also has a number of interactive displays at the end, asking a set of questions: What will you do with what you have learned here? How will you carry the museum's message forward? Through these various forms of political address, from the lifelike enslaved people asking for help to the incarcerated people telling us their stories directly, the Legacy Museum insists that visitors wrestle with and confront stark historical and contemporary realities and the ongoing legacies of racist terror—an experience that can be quite distinct for white versus Black visitors. Visitors to the museum are mostly quiet, faces pained. These interventions at the end of the exhibition, to encourage visitors to reflect and then to act, cannot fully mediate the powerful message of the overall exhibition, which is about the devastating ways in which racial justice has not been achieved and the evolution of slavery into the brutality of systems of policing, incarceration, and criminal justice. In this sense, one of the primary differences between the 9/11 museum and the Legacy Museum, as memory museums, is that, as I noted, the 9/11 museum interpellates

Legacy Museum tote bag.

visitors into a position of empathy with those who died, but not into a position of complicity. At the Legacy Museum, the aim is that the emotional trauma that visitors can feel on exiting the museum is ideally put into service in some form. Whether it achieves this goal is of course difficult to measure.[29] Some commentators, such as Pierce and Heitz, have noted that the museum has little space for recovery, that visitors tend to be exhausted and depleted by the end of the exhibit. This is, they note, different from the newly opened National Museum of African American History and Culture in Washington, DC, which follows exhibitions of the history of slavery and segregation with significant exhibits on African American culture and life.[30]

In the contemporary context of brand culture, the museum's activist aims coexist with the branding of the museum and memorial. The Legacy Museum has a gift shop, one that sells a broad array of books, clothing such as hoodies and T-shirts, coffee mugs, kitchen magnets, and tote bags. It is interesting to note that this store, unlike the 9/11 museum gift shop, has received no criticism for this merchandise. This is because the Legacy Museum merchandise is explicitly political in its messaging, with phrases from Stevenson on its tote bags ("The opposite of poverty is not wealth. The opposite of poverty is justice.") and also because its logo depicts a breaking chain, to signify breaking the chains of slavery and incarceration. Through this kind of marketing, Stevenson himself becomes a brand. Thus, in making its merchandise explicitly about the political aim of EJI, even as it participates in a kind of celebrity making of Stevenson, the museum avoids the critique that it is profiting off of the dead that has haunted the 9/11 consumerism.

The National Memorial for Peace and Justice

The National Memorial for Peace and Justice sits on a hill above the downtown area where the Legacy Museum is situated, about a fifteen-minute walk away. The memorial has been the primary draw of EJI's memory projects and the subject of an enormous amount of positive press attention, in particular when it opened. While there was some anecdotal coverage in the media of negative feelings among locals, and the Alabama governor did not attend the opening ceremonies, the memorial has been largely embraced by visitors.[31] The area of the memorial is an expansive six acres, and across the street from it is the Peace and Justice Memorial Center that houses an auditorium, a wall of the jars of soil, and small exhibitions. While the Legacy Museum has a complex narrative trajectory, the memorial, which is colloquially often called the "lynching memorial," has a simple clarity that has aided in its public embrace. The memorial names over 4,400 victims of lynching who were killed between 1877 and 1950. An additional plaque at

National Memorial for Peace and Justice, view from entrance. Photo: Equal Justice Initiative/Human Pictures.

the Peace and Justice Memorial Center across the street memorializes those lynched in the 1950s, and at the Legacy Pavilion near the museum, opened in 2020, there is a listing of the two thousand people killed between 1865 and 1876.

While the memorial has become quite popular since it opened, it is worth reflecting on how such a memorial is a radical intervention into US memory culture. The memory boom of memorial building in the United States, which began with the Vietnam Veterans Memorial in 1982, has largely been driven by memorializing those dead from wars and terrorism and has for the most part been narrated in national terms (for example, the Korean War Memorial, the World War II Memorial, the Oklahoma City memorial, the 9/11 memorial, and so on). The opening of the National Museum of African American History and Culture in 2016, which preceded the Legacy Museum and lynching memorial as a radical addition to the National Mall in Washington, DC, was a stark reminder of the absence of memorials in Washington to the genocide of Native Americans and to the victims of slavery. The distinction of these different kinds of potential memorials is about the subject positions they make available for viewers, specifically in relation to complicity—that is, the vast majority of the memorials built in the last forty years have not demanded of visitors that they situate themselves in relation to those mourned in any position of guilt or complicity. The lynching memorial demands a reckoning with history for those who visit it and specifically situates viewers in the dual position of mourners and complicit onlookers.

The lynching memorial is also an intervention into the monument culture of the South and the broader national culture of memorials. As I have noted, EJI's educational mission has been as much about intervening into the proliferation of Confederate monuments in the southern landscape as it has been about telling the legacy of lynching. Thus, the lynching memorial is an implicit critique of the Confederate monuments both in terms of political and historical meaning and also in terms of aesthetics. EJI establishes through the memorial the primacy of lynching in the history of racial oppression: "Nothing sustained racial inequality more than lynching. Lynching was racial terrorism."[32]

For the memorial design, EJI partnered with MASS Design Group, a non-profit architecture firm based in Boston and cofounded in 2008 by Michael Murphy and Alan Ricks. Its name stands for "model of architecture serving society," and the firm's stated aim is to build architecture in partnership with local communities "that promotes justice and human dignity." The firm originated when Murphy began working with Paul Farmer, founder of Partners in Health, to build a hospital in Rwanda, and here Murphy came to ascribe to a key set of principles about non-profit architecture working with local labor, sourcing materials locally, and building with dignity and health as primary goals.[33] In many ways, MASS was a potentially symbiotic partner for Stevenson and EJI, given that in its ten years of existence, it had also developed a philosophy around justice and the idea of good design being in service of justice and beauty.[34] One of MASS's primary slogans is, "Architecture is never neutral, it either heals or hurts." Murphy often narrates that it was in designing hospitals in Africa and Haiti that he learned how buildings could sicken and kill people, as he saw when Farmer took him to a hospital in South Africa where patients were exposed in airless corridors to drug-resistant strains of tuberculosis. MASS had also considered issues of memory and design, designing a (not yet built) structure for an archive for the Rwandan post-genocide trials, at the Kitgali Genocide Memorial.

According to Murphy, he saw a mention of the planned lynching memorial in the *New York Times* in 2015 and called Stevenson cold to ask who his architect was. When Stevenson replied that he did not have one and that there was no money at that point for the project, Murphy went to Montgomery to see him.[35]

In many ways, MASS Design Group is, in its philosophy, the polar opposite of the starchitect culture and corporate architecture that rebuilt lower Manhattan. Murphy is explicit in this distinction in his philosophy of architecture:

> Architecture is not just about the huge heroic buildings, it's the everyday decisions which construct our lives, it's the simple decisions from where you source the material to who builds that building to how that building functions to where we walk in our city streets, to the equity of our neighborhoods. These are decisions that must be designed and if we ask the harder questions about what else we can do, we can be making more informed and positive decisions about our built space instead of just letting the private sector build it all.[36]

MASS has been proactive in its global partnerships, helping to train architects in Rwanda, incorporating landscape architecture and garden design, and building local stakeholders in its projects. In their first project, they discovered that there were piles of volcanic stone all over the area that had been cleared by farmers and was considered useless by locals. This stone was eventually used by local workers to create beautiful stone walls for the hospital. This is an example of what MASS calls "lo-fab," or local fabricated design elements. MASS now has over 120 architects and projects throughout Africa (Rwanda, Uganda, Liberia, Kenya, Ethiopia), the US, Vietnam, and Haiti. EJI chose MASS to work with, Sanneh explains, because EJI wanted to be in charge of the design process and not hand it off to a design team. The process with EJI and MASS was thus a highly collaborative one, one that builds on MASS's history of collaboration with local partners.

As is the case with many contemporary memorials, the memorial is designed to take visitors on a journey. Irene Cheng identifies several trends in memorial design over the last few decades of memorials that honor victims rather than heroes, and that are "spatial rather than sculptural," hence designed by architects rather than sculptors. These newer memorials, she notes,

> produce not just encounters with an object but a more comprehensive 'experience' or . . . 'journey,' often correlated with an elevational change, hence the preponderance of ramps in contemporary spatial memorials. These memorials tend to adopt a therapeutic rather than triumphalist tone. Lastly, several of these memorials deploy the tactic of using a field of identical or near-identical objects to represent individual lives lost, thus engaging in a kind of spatialization of quantity.[37]

The lynching memorial deploys many of these strategies to create an experience for visitors that aims to go from confrontation to hope. The entrance into the memorial grounds is intended to give visitors time before they arrive at the actual memorial pavilion, to have a slow transition into the memorial. Visitors enter the complex through a security screening, a reminder that this memorial is not without controversy, and then have a view of the memorial structure up a long path. They are confronted immediately by a sculpture of enslaved people chained together, because, as Sanneh states, they wanted people to think first about slavery when they entered the memorial, not about lynching, and to consider that lynching is impossible to disconnect from slavery. There is then an extended path up to the memorial that is intended to give visitors time to adjust to the context.

The memorial's primary feature is 805 markers made of Corten steel, onto which are inscribed the names of counties where Black people were lynched throughout the United States, with the names of the lynching victims of that county listed underneath. At first, the markers are at eye level, resting on the ground, so that visitors must navigate between them. Gradually, the path begins to descend and the markers to rise so that they are eventually hanging over visitor's heads. As the journey of the memorial continues and the steel markers rise, the design intentionally places viewers in subject positions that create discomfort, a discomfort that they are challenged to make sense of. It is a massive memorial that takes time to walk through. Visitors are, by design, supposed to be overwhelmed by it, to be exhausted by it. This is a memorial about counting, demanding recognition, and taking up space.

Marker at eye level at beginning of memorial walkway. Photo by author.

The markers, which are six feet long, look like stone stelae, like coffins, and like bodies hanging from trees. Since each marker is specific to a county, for some counties, there are many names, listed smaller in order for them to fit. The marker with the largest number of names is for Phillips County, Arkansas, with 245. The memorial includes lynching victims from as far north as New York State and as far west as Oklahoma, but the vast majority of the names are from the Deep South. By design, the Corten steel (which is a favored material of minimalist sculptors such as Richard Serra) will rust in streaks as it ages, giving it a textured and aged quality. As Regina Yang of MASS states

> The materiality and physicality of Corten forged a visceral, emotional connection to the lynchings: a "living material," the steel responds to its physical environment and changes over time. This natural process of weathering would not only leave its mark on the ground beneath, reinforcing the long-lasting legacy of racial terror, but it would also create over 800 unique tonal expressions, reflecting the diversity of Black people in America.[38]

The journey of the memorial experience, as designed by MASS, guides visitors through a narrative sequence inspired by what Stevenson and EJI refer to as the "stages of transformation": identity, discomfort, proximity, transformation, and finally, hope. Murphy sees the journey of the memorial beginning with an experience of a "classical almost familiar building type like the Parthenon or the colonnade of the Vatican but as we enter the ground drops below us and our perception shifts" to the markers themselves.[39] Identity is the first stage, in which visitors enter the memorial and engage with the markers face to face, on an equal ground plane. As the floor descends, the markers remain at a fixed elevation, their hovering creating discomfort for the visitor in the second stage. In the third stage (proximity), with the markers consolidated overhead above an amphitheater, visitors are "invited to sit and pause in close proximity to their discomfort." The transformation of stage four is imagined as visitors walk past a water wall dedicated to all the unknown victims of lynching. As MASS writes:

> At the end of this water wall, the visitor is invited to climb a hill at the center of the memorial, where they rise above the markers for the first

The descending walkway with markers. Photo by author.

time. This hill inverts the experience of lynching, where the living stands at the center of the public square in judgement by the dead. Stevenson has described this as the most hopeful moment in the memorial, where the visitor is called to action.[40]

The design of the National Memorial for Peace and Justice deploys the vocabulary of modernism to embody the presence of those killed by lynching and evokes the codes of minimalism in its spare lines and metallic aesthetic. As I noted in chapter 1, *New York Times* critic Michael Kimmelman wrote a much cited essay about how minimalism "of all improbable movements of the last 50 years" had become the aesthetic of contemporary commemoration. He notes that minimalist abstraction "in all its allegorical pliancy, turns out to function in a memorial context as the best available mirror for a modern world."[41] Minimal abstract forms have thus become a means through which trauma has been negotiated in terms of design.

The original intentions of the minimalism of modern art, which aimed for pure form with clean lines and a repetition of geometric forms, deliberately devoid of emotion and artistic expression, are transformed when the art itself is deployed in the service of memorialization. The aim of minimalist memorials is not formalism but affect, the creation of forms to mediate loss. The minimalist chairs of the Oklahoma City memorial, for instance, may look, as Kimmelman notes, like Donald Judd boxes, but the moment one sees them as representing one of the dead or a child who was killed, that minimalist aesthetic is placed in the service of mourning. The columns of the lynching memorial are rendered allegorical by their role as keepers of the names of those killed. In other words, modernism's high abstract language becomes something else in memorials, what Kimmelman calls its rhetorical opposite, something "sentimental, narrative, populist." This is precisely because the open language of modernism's forms, as a turn away from the limits of traditional figurative representations, allow for ambiguity, ambivalence, and forms that evoke loss and renewal. In this capacity to mediate trauma, minimalism ironically provides a form of comfort.

Scale is an important feature of the memorial's design, as a way of conveying the enormity of the loss, which borrows from the scale of

National Memorial for Peace and Justice, Corridor 3. Photo: Equal Justice Initiative/Human Pictures.

the Berlin Holocaust memorial, whose enormous scale in the middle of Berlin cannot be ignored. And like the Holocaust memorial, here abstraction and quantification together are used to impress upon viewers the brutal aspects of living beings reduced to quantities. Sanneh states, "Going through these archives, you get overwhelmed by the loss. We wanted a place that was physically large enough and a design that was imposing enough physically so it would help people experience the scale of the loss." The memorial's counting has a deliberate relentlessness in its naming of the thousands who were killed, emphasized by the repetitive form of the markers. The steel markers demand to be noticed; they insert themselves in our vision and space. This monumental scale demands a paying attention, a tallying, a reckoning.

Central corridor of memorial. Photo by author.

As part of that journey, the memorial also actively creates subject positions for viewers that demand an awareness of complicity. As the markers rise over us, they ask us to look up at them, which on one hand makes us feel potentially threatened or vulnerable, and on the other hand places us within the position of the lynching spectator, looking up. Stevenson has often noted that it is important to remember the ways that lynchings were not just killings but spectacles, which attracted large crowds. Victims were hung high in trees even after they were dead, or they were hung on platforms, so that their brutalization could be seen. He states, "The people who carried out this violence could have just shot people and buried them in the ground, but they didn't want it to be a secret, they didn't want it hidden, they didn't want it obscured by dirt and dust. They actually lifted up the bodies because they wanted to terrorize. They wanted the entire community to see it."[42] In this sense, when visitors are encouraged by the design to look up at the hanging markers, they are, depending on their race, asked either to see themselves or their relatives in and as those markers or to see themselves as spectators. The memorial thus is a very different experience, intentionally and inevitably, for Black visitors, white visitors, non-Americans, and so forth, in relation to the question of shame, fear, and complicity.

The memorial's most radical strategy is its aim to have this larger memorial propagate into a whole range of local memorials. To this end, as part of its original design, the memorial has duplicates of each of the markers laid out, almost like a line of coffins, in a field next to it. It has put out a call for the counties that are listed on these markers to come and retrieve them and place them within the county, proximate to where the lynchings took place. As Justin Brown of MASS narrates, "The final monument is all the markers distributed throughout the United States in the places that choose to confront this history and take responsibility for this truth."[43] This strategy is a provocation, demanding a site specificity to memory like the soil that was collected from these sites and an ownership by these counties and towns of these histories of violence. This is narrated by Murphy and others as a healing. It is also intended to be a shaming; as more markers are retrieved, those that remain will mark those counties as refusing to acknowledge their complicity, what Stevenson calls a "report card of which communities have claimed their histories and which haven't."[44] According to Sanneh, more than a hundred are in discussion about doing so, working through EJI's Community Remembrance Project. The process is complex and delicate, and different in each case, with the demand for a lot of local engagement. Teams are asked to create local coalitions and to put up community remembrance markers first. She states, "The memorial is imbued with identity, solemnity, and seriousness, and that is important to the process." This situation of place relates to the question of site specificity and why it was important for this memorial to be in Montgomery, in the Deep South, surrounded by Confederate monuments, rather than in Washington, DC. In many ways, the vision of these individual county markers spread throughout the nation offers a kind of countervision of memorialization to the proliferation of 9/11 memorials throughout the country.

The potential of the duplicate markers to move out into these counties and to disseminate further the message of the memorial that these victims must be recognized, named, and mourned in order for any progress on racial inequality to move forward is a key element in the intended dynamism of the memorial, that it will, in Murphy's words, not be static or stand still. It is a demand, too, that these local counties tell an alternate history to the Confederate histories they currently tell. For Murphy, this is also about community engagement:

> We thought not about just having a statue or a place to visit that would stay the same but one that would change over time. That very DNA of having markers that could be removed from the site and placed in other counties throughout the country where these killings occurred allowed us to create a memorial that was active, one that would engage the communities where these atrocities occurred, would bring people together, like a barn raising, like an active participatory process to really build this movement of truth and reconciliation that we seek.[45]

In this, the memorial can be defined, like the Legacy Museum, as an activist memorial that aims to deploy the memory of those mourned as a means to change the contemporary situation of institutionalized racism, mass incarceration, policy brutality against Black and brown people, and the "presumption of guilt" that Stevenson and others define as haunting Black life.[46]

The abstract understated aesthetic of the memorial's design is contrasted by the figurative sculptures that are placed on the grounds surrounding it, where it also incorporates texts by Toni Morrison and Elizabeth Alexander. The space around the memorial is divided by the designers into four quadrants, the first of which is slavery. As I noted, as visitors enter the memorial space, they first see a figurative group of bronze statues depicting a group or family of seven enslaved figures held together by chains. The presumed patriarch of the group stands in defiance looking out as the others appear tortured and desperate, one woman reaching out toward him while holding a baby. One set of shackles lies empty. The metal leg and wrist irons are rusting, creating streaks

Duplicate markers in field by memorial. Photo by author.

down their partially dressed forms. This work, *Nkyinkyim Installation*, is by Ghanaian artist Kwame Akoto-Bamfo and is part of a larger transAtlantic project by the artist that includes realist sculptures in Ghana. The name refers to an African proverb that discusses resilience and resistance to oppression. According to Stevenson, "For many people it's the first time they have ever seen a sculpture with human beings about slavery."[47] In the video about the sculpture, produced by EJI and filmed by Stevenson in Ghana and Alabama, the work is characterized as evoking "humanity, a determination to survive, and a dignity that can't be stolen by bondage." The narration states, "This time there is respect. And for their children, this time there is love."[48]

Nkyinkyim Installation (2018), by Kwame Akoto-Bamfo. Photo by author.

The second quadrant of the memorial contains the duplicate markers, waiting to be claimed. The theme of the third quadrant is the Great Migration and the civil rights era, with a statue, *Guided by Justice,* by Dana King, that depicts a group of anonymous Black women standing and looking forward as a tribute to the Black women who were central to the Montgomery Bus Boycott. Stevenson often mentions these women, in particular Johnnie Carr, who with Rosa Parks schooled him in activism when he first came to Montgomery. The sculpted women are life size and portrayed as ordinary, wearing bulky coats, holding purses, with one hunched over. They appear to be standing or walking forward, as women who were honoring the boycott would have been. Here, there are footsteps in bronze next to the women where visitors are presumably invited to stand with them. When sculptor Dana King was

Guided by Justice (2018), by Dana King. Photo by author.

asked by Stevenson to create a work honoring these women, she decided to represent a teacher, a grandmother, and a pregnant woman and to depict them in ways that represented the intense labor of the boycott, when Blacks in Montgomery walked miles from home to work and back rather than ride the buses.[49] The statues are realist aesthetically and designed to speak to visitors for whom these women are powerful figures precisely because of their ordinary status.

Finally, the fourth quadrant is focused on mass incarceration, police violence, and racism in the criminal justice system, represented by the sculpture *Raise Up*, by Hank Willis Thomas, in which Black figures stand with their arms raised as their bodies appear to be encased in a rising tide of bronze. Of the three figurative works, this one is the most ambiguous. Are they raising their arms in surrender? In protest? Are they rising out of the metal or are they drowning? Willis Thomas states that the work is based on a photograph by South African photographer Ernest Cole of thirteen South African miners as they undergo a humiliating medical examination in the nude.[50] He intends the work to reflect on police brutality and the racial injustices of the criminal justice system. The statue also evokes the raised arms of protesters against police violence, who enact the words and gestures of those who have been killed: "Hands Up, Don't Shoot!" Of these three artists, Willis Thomas is the most well known, with a recognized body of work that addresses issues of racial justice. He is currently collaborating with MASS on the Gun Violence Memorial Project.[51]

These statues, all made by Black artists, bring figural representation into the aesthetic realm of the abstract and minimalist memorial, and they are intended to evoke actual bodies as opposed to the abstract hanging columns of the memorial. Sanneh states that they did not want the memorial to incorporate lynching photos or gruesome representations, but they were also attuned to the aesthetic context of the South and the diverse audiences of the memorial and felt that the abstract memorial would need to be complemented by figural representations. According to MASS:

> We felt neither the representational nor the conceptual fully invited the deep introspection we were looking to achieve. And so, the memorial seeks to strike the balance between the two, which in turn allows each

Raise Up (2014), by Hank Willis Thomas. Photo by author.

visitor to bring and wrestle with their own interpretations. We wanted to create a platform for people to participate in the act of memorialization, carrying their own perspectives and life experiences into the space of the memorial.[52]

Yet the coexistence of these statues with the memorial is an awkward one. This is largely because in their representation of Black bodies, they present both dignity and humiliation and brutalization. Akoto-Bamfo's depiction of enslaved people, which is described by EJI as a representation of dignity in the context of enslavement, is also about fear, anguish, and exposed bodies in chains. The artist also articulates it as a depiction of shame: "The man with the marks on his face is supposed to be a guardian, yet in this situation, he is not able to protect the mother and the child. We have the mother crying and reaching out for her man, who turns away in shame. He is not able to grant the protection and security that he would have loved to give to the woman."[53] Willis Thomas's work is, by his own description, one about the humiliation of bodies forced to raise their arms before the gaze of the law. These works place viewers in the voyeuristic position of gazing upon pain and humiliation. While this parallels the memorial's aim to create discomfort by placing viewers below the hanging markers, like the spectators of lynchings, here this positioning, precisely because of the role of figuration in exposing bodies to gazes, inevitably means that visitors are gazing upon disempowered and humiliated bodies.

This raises many questions in relation to the visual representation of lynching. The history of lynching is one in which the voyeuristic gaze creates a dehumanizing spectacle of death, with the circulation of numerous photographs and postcards of the crowds watching the brutality of the violence with thrill and fascination. Gazing upon the Black body in pain has thus been coded in the context of this history as a violent act itself. The more recent engagement with lynching photographs, in the book and exhibition *Without Sanctuary*, was criticized for replicating the violence of the original lynching by continuing to circulate these images.[54] Can one gaze upon a lynching image without reiterating that violence? Artist Ken Gonzales-Day engaged with this question in his series *Erased Lynching*, in which he took photographs of lynchings in California and the Southwest, where the majority of those lynched were Latino, Native American, and Asian American. In a strategy that explicitly aims to refuse the gaze, he erased from each image the ropes and the body of the lynching victim. What remains is the crowd. As Eve Tuck and K. Wayne Yang write, "Refusal shifts the gaze from the violating body to the violating instruments—in this case, the lynch mob, which does not disappear when the lynching is over, but continues to live, accumulating land and wealth through the extermination and subordination of the Other."[55]

The question of the visitor's gaze upon the figurative statues at the memorial are particularly raised by the Akoto-Bamfo slave figures, images of which have circulated widely in the media. As Sanneh notes, EJI wanted the first encounter of viewers to be that of human beings, those actual people who were kidnapped and enslaved out of West Africa.[56] Yet how are we supposed to look at the half naked, desperate bodies of these enslaved people without participating in a violent gaze? As one enters the memorial, a sign states that visitors may take pictures *of* the sculptures, but not *with* them. This is a revealing restriction that conjures up potentially offensive picture-taking practices—no selfies with the statues of the enslaved people or of men with their arms up, no posing with these representations of Black bodies, as those crowds once did. Nevertheless, a question still lingers: What does it mean to gaze upon and take a photograph of these enslaved figures?

This conundrum of figuration reveals the power of the modernist representational mode of the memorial itself. The memorial allows for a very different kind of gazing upon the markers and the names, one that is less voyeuristic though one that still potentially implicates viewers in the gaze of the lynching spectator. The memorial achieves this balance precisely because it is not deploying figuration to represent those lynched, but at the same time, we understand that the markers stand in for bodies. In this, the memorial design seems to succeed in representing the dead, avoiding both the minimalist abstraction that has made many memorials somewhat cold modernist forms and the voyeurism of the gaze upon figures being violated. As I have noted, Erika Doss defines trauma as "dissonant, confusing, and chaotic, a kind of dismantling," and in what she terms "terror memorials," minimalism "is often selected to commemorate trauma because it simultaneously evokes this disorientation and resolves it: it conjures trauma's profound dissonance and also speaks to the recovery and reaffirmation—the remaking—of individual and collective harmony."[57] In this sense, the minimalist aesthetic appears to allow for complex, perhaps even inchoate, feelings of resolution, and, as MASS describes it, a final stage of hope, while simultaneously refusing closure. At the same time, the lynching memorial refuses the kind of reaffirmation and resolution described by Doss.

Finally, the memorial is about gravity—an emotional gravity, a gravitational pull—and a temporal suspension. Like the 9/11 memorial, which draws viewers down into the deep black pools, the National Memorial for Peace and Justice creates a pull toward the ground. The steel markers are hanging. When we enter the deep space of the memorial, they are hanging above and over us. There is a tension here, a spatial dynamism, because the markers can feel threatening. One cannot help but imagine them falling. Stevenson states that the terror of lynching can't be understood "without replicating the dynamics" of the lynching spectacle, the looking up at the suspended bodies, the dynamic of the hanging body.[58] And this tension is also a temporal one. Because the columns are suspended, they are never at rest. In this, they seem to convey something out of place. Like the body of the lynching victim, they should not be hanging. One wants to bring them gently to the ground, to put them at ease.

This spatial tension also extends to the replicas of the markers that are lined up in a field next to the memorial, which Murphy describes as in a state of "purgatory." Here too, time is suspended—the markers are, in the parlance of many commentators, "waiting to be claimed." Time waits, the markers hang, gravity pulls downward, gestures wait for answers, objects and time are suspended. One could argue that even after all the markers are claimed by the counties and laid to rest in sites around the country, the memorial will still refuse closure precisely because of the markers that will continue to hang, looming over visitors and reminding us of those bodies hanging. This refusal of closure is the means through which the memorial demands something of the present, and by extension, of the nation. The evocation of bodies still hanging conveys the message that the fight for racial justice is not about a process of healing, even though that is part of the intent of the memorial and the museum. Those markers will continue to hang, as a reminder that the fight for racial justice is never over. These markers, and the bodies they evoke, are not laid to rest. This is memory activated in the present.

The Legacy Museum and the National Memorial for Peace and Justice offer a rescripting of the narratives of the nation, a refusal of narratives of American innocence and exceptionalism. They demand that the legacy of enslavement be traced through racial terrorism to the brutality of Jim Crow, racist policing, and mass incarceration, that this history be told within this landscape and to the nation. The Legacy Museum rejects an uplifting narrative of racial progress in order to demand that visitors see the brutal social impact of mass incarceration and a racist criminal justice system. Similarly, the hanging markers of the memorial offer testimony to the limits of healing and the impossibility of closure.

This points to the limits of memorialization as a reparative form and to the demand that the reparation of such memorialization constitute ongoing forms of reparatory justice work.[59] It is the ongoing nature of the reparation, its never-endedness, that is emphasized by the memorial's form and by Stevenson. We are haunted by the silence about lynching, he states. A haunting, by definition, does not go away.[60] In the museum's emphasis on how the legacy of slavery and lynching exists in the present in terms of mass incarceration and police brutality, and in the memorial's evocative suspension of time and space, this haunting is at work, altering the perceived division between the present and past.

The deployment of human rights discourse at the memorial and museum also constitutes a challenge to US memory culture in general. While the proliferation of memorialization in the US since the 1980s has focused largely on national memory, allowing issues of state terrorism to be erased, memorialization in the memory boom in other parts of the world, in particular in Latin America, has often been deployed within the framework of human rights in ways that have produced active engagements with social justice movements of the present. In understanding terrorism, even state terrorism, as part of the story of the United States, this memorial and museum engage with human rights discourse, and the question of who must be held accountable and how, what truths need to be told, and what reparations must be made are central. Those accountable for racist terror and its effects, both perpetrators and beneficiaries—the US state itself—must recognize how this legacy is enacted, legally, economically, culturally, socially, in the present. In Argentina, the mothers of disappeared children, Madres of the Plaza de Mayo, have demanded that the state "*Aparicíon con vida,*" "Bring them back alive." As Adam Rosenblatt has written, this "counterfactual" demand, which cannot be fulfilled, operates to delegitimize the state, to make explicit that the state cannot repair what it has done.[61] To understand slavery, lynching, and racial violence as state terrorism is to see how what the state has done and sanctioned *cannot be repaired* through memorialization alone. As the hanging markers of the memorial will never, by design, come to rest on the ground, the memorial points to this future of ongoing struggle.

Yet Stevenson's words and the work of EJI to confront these violent histories, despite their refusal to tell a story of uplift, is ultimately one of hope, which is why it can offer a bridge to a new era, beyond the post-9/11 era, in which memory can potentially be transformed into social justice activism in the present, against mass incarceration. As Stevenson states, "I want to talk about this history of enslavement and of native genocide and of lynching and segregation, not because I am interested in punishing America. I want to liberate us. I really do believe there is something better waiting for us."[62] Such a new era would demand a national reckoning not only of the United States' violent pasts but also of its violence as an imperial entity. Such a reckoning would break through the narratives that have allowed those violent histories to be obscured within narratives of innocence, exceptionalism, and patriotism, and it would embrace a politics of aspiration and renewal, opening new ways of engaging with memory in the present.

Conclusion

On January 6, 2021, an armed mob of Trump supporters stormed and breached the US Capitol in what would come to be understood as an insurrection incited by president Donald Trump himself. In the days that followed, as the security failures were dissected and analyzed, the public was reminded, again and again, that the Capitol building had been for the last almost twenty years a fortress of post-9/11 security. That is because intelligence analysis of the 9/11 attacks had established that Flight 93, which crashed in Pennsylvania, was targeting the US Capitol building, a mere eighteen minutes flying time farther. The Capitol had thus become in 2001 a site of extreme and increasingly normalized security protocols, all in relation to potential foreign security threats.

That the threat to the US Capitol in 2021 was from domestic terrorism, as opposed to foreign terrorist organizations, was made abundantly clear on January 6. On that day, not only was the threat from right-wing and white-supremacist organizations realized, but the participation and complicity of some police officers and former military personnel in the attempted takeover of the building and the government was also brought to light. The violence was rendered visible on social media and in the countless videos and photos that were shared and then analyzed for weeks. This incident, the most serious attempted coup in the nation's history, starkly revealed the divisions of the nation, with two polarized views of the election, of corruption, and of government. Each side believed their moral position and legal position about the election to be the more truthful. Those who invaded the Capitol believed, through an enormous disinformation campaign led by Trump, that their mission was to save the country from massive election fraud and the fraudulent agenda of the Democrats. The fervor of this belief helped unleash the insurrection with the idea that it was the only truly patriotic option. Those who affirmed the evidence that the election had been fair and had been won decidedly by President Biden saw the insurrection as an act of domestic terrorism and sedition fueled by conspiracy theories. The polarization of the country seemed in that moment to have reached its most extreme.

The transformation of the threat on the Capitol building from attack by foreign terrorists to attack by domestic terrorists and angry citizens demonstrates the shift from the post-9/11 era to a new era for the nation. Whereas the fear of foreign attack and the wars that followed 9/11 were defining features of the two decades after 9/11, the era of the Trump administration, the global pandemic, and the election of 2020 demonstrated that the defining structures of feeling had shifted into new terrain, from fear of the Other to a polarizing rage at politicians and fellow citizens, from defending the nation to civil war, with a threat from within rather than outside. That this explosive division had been a long time coming has been noted by many, precisely because of its roots in economic disparities and polarized views on the role of government. On December 30, 2020, historian Heather Cox Richardson wrote an expansive overview of the last twenty years of US society in her "Letters from An American" column that was widely read in 2020–21 as a chronicle of a traumatic time and transition in US politics. Richardson sees the years leading up to 2020 as the "end game of the Reagan Revolution" that began in 1980 and that pursued years of deregulation, increased anti-government sentiment, and a dismantling of the New Deal state. In 2020, the global pandemic, according to Richardson, exposed the devastating consequences of rejecting the "activist government that has protected us since 1933."[1]

Thus, the post-9/11 era began as a time of defense, securitization, and fear of foreign terrorism and ended as a time of deep internal political division and terrorism within the nation. The crises of 2020–21 also had the effect of cracking open and exposing the racial, economic, and ideological divides of the nation in ways that potentially produced the means to name and confront them. Police killings of unarmed Black people were exposed, videotaped, protested, and widely discussed. White supremacy was rendered highly visible not as the fringe movement it had been perceived to be but as a central aspect of dominant white culture in America and of US political culture. These aspects of American culture were *seen* in the time of crisis as never before. That has the potential to shift public discourse and fuel change. Whether it can eventually produce social change is not yet clear, but that cracking open cannot be undone; these aspects of US culture cannot be unseen. Activism thus arises on both sides, with right-wing activism defending Confederate monuments and Black Lives Matter demanding that the police be fundamentally restructured.

The arc of this book is from the proliferation and fervor of 9/11 memorialization as a form of patriotism and national unity in the early 2000s to the challenge of memory activism of the lynching memorial and museum in the late 2010s, an activism that demands a rethinking of the narrative script of the nation. Memorialization became a key social arena through which national identity was affirmed in the post-9/11 era and through which national narratives were effectively questioned in the late 2010s, demanding a reassessment of the founding myths of the nation, a reckoning with its past and present of racial strife and violence, and a confrontation with how monuments and memorials had been deployed to affirm white supremacy through US history, in particular of the Civil War.

The complex role played by cultural memory in these changing and contested concepts of the nation reveals the way that memorialization—who is remembered, who is grieved, who is designated as worthy of public and collective memorialization—tells us a great deal about the values of a nation. And for these reasons, that memory can be a powerful site for activist interventions that demand social justice. Black Lives Matter, in demanding "Say their names," intervenes into the public domain via memory, demanding that those killed unlawfully by police deserve to be remembered, to be mourned, to be grieved, to be named. The memorial markers of the National Memorial for Peace and Justice pull the forgotten and anonymous victims of lynching from history into the present, demanding that they be grieved. The memorial demands that they be made whole in death and, even more importantly, that what happened to them will not be erased from the national story. And the Legacy Museum demands that this history be seen in the present, that the legacies of slavery and lynching be recognized as the foundations of contemporary mass incarceration and the inequities of the criminal justice system and its treatment of non-white citizens. That these movements have produced a backlash, with an increasing fervor around openly defending white supremacy and the symbols of Confederacy is no surprise, as they do constitute a threat to society as it stands.

The Legacy Museum and the National Memorial for Peace and Justice are emblematic of this turn, in the early 2020s, in the national conversation about race, terrorism, and the legacies and ongoing dynamics of white supremacy in US culture. The museum and lynching memorial convey the hope that the national conversation on race and justice can be changed. They stand in comparison to the memory projects of 9/11. 9/11 memory projects ask us to mourn those arbitrarily caught up in the violence of that day, but in mourning them, we are not asked to reflect on what followed in the wake of the day or to consider how those deaths were deployed politically. The lynching memorial, by contrast, explicitly asks us to mourn and then to see the larger historical picture in a way that demands that we think about the current lives that are impacted by the same system of racial injustice in the system of mass incarceration. This is a memory project that makes demands in the present. It is also a repudiation of the narrative of American innocence.

On the eve of the inauguration of President Biden in January 2021, the president and vice president elect held a memorial service at the Lincoln Memorial for which rows of lights were illuminated along both sides of the memorial's reflecting pool. In the year of the pandemic, this was the first national recognition of those who were lost to COVID-19, which at that point numbered over four hundred thousand—more, it was noted at the time, than all the Americans who died in World War II. The number of dead had become so large as to be unimaginable and difficult to grasp. It is rare for pandemics to be memorialized, but as the AIDS epidemic and the AIDS Quilt demonstrated, sometimes memorials are needed as forms of activism, to demand that those who died are remembered and mourned as part of the nation. Disproportionately representing older people, people of color, and the working poor, the COVID-19 US dead need to be mourned collectively as Americans, as a testimony that never again should a government turn its back on vulnerable citizens and a threat to their lives.[2] In the era that follows the post-9/11 era, wherever it takes the nation, a reckoning with the devastation, loss, and travesty of the COVID-19 pandemic in the United States, a pandemic augmented and exacerbated by government indifference and incompetence, will need to take place.

ACKNOWLEDGMENTS

The question of how memory has shaped American culture over the last two decades has been one that has continuously pulled me back into its orbit. After I published *Tourists of History* in 2007, which touched on memory projects in Oklahoma City and New York in the early 2000s, I moved on to other topics and projects, but the question of memory was never far from my thinking, and I kept working on 9/11 and post-9/11 memory. In 2008, I wondered if the financial crisis had shifted away from the national discussion of 9/11 memory to newer narratives of inequality and sacrifice, yet then that seemed to fade. After Donald Trump was elected to the presidency in 2016, the nascent aspects of this project seemed to me to have been rendered meaningless. I could not see why any of it mattered in what I perceived to be the extraordinary threat to democracy posed by Trump. In the years that followed, I continued to try to define this book and what it should include, moving forward in fits and starts. Then, in March 2020, the world shut down, and the dramatic shift in national discourse opened new paradigms and modes, and there was a moment in late spring when I thought, now I understand what this book is about, the post-9/11 era that is now over. So in many strange ways, this project that I have worked on for over ten years is my pandemic book.

I have been wrestling with this material for such a long time that I am deeply indebted to the insights and challenges of many readers, audiences, and reviewers. To Marianne Hirsch, Katherine Hite, Susan Mosakowski, Brett Gary, Lisa Gitelman, Giovanna Di Chiro, and John Bodnar, who all read chapters and provided incisive and valuable input, I am deeply grateful. You challenged me to clarify and hone my argument and to situate this book in relation to the extraordinary present moment in which it will be released. Katie and I went on several research trips together, to Shanksville, Pennsylvania, and Montgomery, Alabama, and discussing those sites together was enormously helpful. Two readers for

NYU Press were equally challenging and insightful, and I thank them, as I thank readers for *Memory Studies* and the editors of *American Quarterly* that published essays now incorporated into chapter 2. I was fortunate to be in conversation with Jonathan Bach and Brigitte Sion about the opening of the 9/11 museum and to meet with the architects of Davis Brody Bond with them. I am indebted to the input over the years of Sarah Banet-Weiser, Lauren Berlant, Alison Landsberg, James Young, Nicholas Mirzoeff, Natasha Zaretsky, Nitin Sawhney, Diana Taylor, Jo Labanyi, Lori Novak, Erika Doss, Joseph DeLappe, Susan Murray, Erica Robles-Anderson, and Radha Hegde.

Over the last twelve years, I have given numerous presentations on this material, where I have been posed challenging and insightful questions. Many thanks to those who invited me and engaged with this material: the Institute for the Arts and Humanities, University of North Carolina, Chapel Hill; the King Juan Carlos Center, New York University; the Department of Communication at the University of Stockholm; the Department of Cultural Studies, George Mason University; the Mémorial de Caen, France; the University of Southern California Gould School of Law; the Illinois Program for Research in the Humanities, University of Illinois, Champaign-Urbana; the Humanities Center, SUNY Stony Brook; Northeastern University; Carnegie Mellon University; el Museo de la Memoria y los Derechos Humanos, Santiago, Chile; Carpe Diem, Lisbon, Portugal; Center for Material Culture, University of Delaware; the Lisbon Consortium Summer Institute; the University of Richmond; the University of Hartford; the American University of Beirut; the Rethinking Peace Studies Conference, Japan ICU Foundation, Tokyo; the Sweden American Studies Association Biennial Conference, University of Gothenburg; the Mellon-Sawyer Seminar Series, University of Oxford/Oxford Brookes University; Cultures and Commemorations of War, Oxford University; Rochester Institute of Technology; the Strassler Center for Holocaust and Genocide Studies, Clark University; the Global Urban Humanities Institute, University of California, Berkeley; the University of California, Davis; Georgia State University; the Columbia University Cultural Memory Seminar; and the American Studies Association. Throughout this time, ongoing conversations through the Columbia Cultural Memory Seminar have been inspiring, thanks to Marianne

Hirsch, Andreas Huyssen, Leo Spitzer, and all the scholars involved. I was honored as well during this time to be a part of the extraordinary group of scholars in the Women Mobilizing Memory project, from New York, Santiago, and Istanbul.

In 2016–17, I was honored to be a faculty fellow of the NYU Center for the Humanities, where I workshopped early versions of this work. Thanks to Gwynneth Malin, Jane Tylus, Uli Baer, Nicole Starosielski, and the full group for their input and for working through those early months of the Trump election shock. I am grateful to the Center for the Humanities for a publication grant for the costs of photo permissions, with thanks to Molly Rogers and Uli Baer. I recently workshopped material with my colleagues in the Department of Media, Culture, and Communication, an extraordinary group of graduate students and faculty whose intellectual acumen puts me in awe. The staff at MCC have also been enormously helpful, efficient, and skilled, in particular Annette Morales, Melissa Lucas-Ludwig, Dove Pedlosky, Tracy Figueroa, Rebecca Brown, Danielle Resto, and Darrell Carter. Research assistance over the years from Angela Arias-Zapata, Michelle Pfeifer, and Kari Hensley helped provide me with a rich archive of materials to work with.

During the time I worked on this book I was honored to supervise many wonderful dissertations by students whose ideas informed my own, including Hatim el-Hibri, Scott Selberg, Liz Patton, Kari Hensley, the late Naomi Angel, Nadja Millner-Larsen, Lana Lin, Jennifer Heuson, Beza Merid, Inês Beleza Barreiros, and Diana Kamin.

At NYU Press, I am grateful to Ellen Chodosh for long-term support and friendship and to Eric Zinner for talking with me about the project over the years and patiently awaiting its completion. Thanks to Furqan Sayeed for being resourceful and expertly shepherding it through, to Martin Coleman for supervising its production, and to Richard Feit for skilled editing.

To friends and family, thank you: Joanna Hefferen, Joanne Ross, JoAnn Hanley, Sherry Millner, Ernie Larsen, John Epstein, Lynn Spigel, Susan Murray, Bob Riley, Kara Kirk, Barbara Osborn, Ella Taylor, Noel Phillips, Bill Bridgers, Anna McLellan, Andrew and Kathy Shepard, and all the Rhinecliff crowd. And to those I miss dearly, Jytte Jensen, Nathalie Magnan, Eric Schumann, John Giancola, and Lesley Stern. My sister Barbara Peterson has been a source of steady support as has Moira

Peterson, Bill Peterson, and Leigh Peterson, and my thanks to Carl and Cheryl-Anne Sturken and Kelly and Kyra Sturken.

Dana Polan has lived with this project for many years, during which time he managed to publish several books. I thank him for his tireless support and his insightful input. His presence makes my life possible. Leo Polan has traveled the globe to many sites of memory with me, and as he moves toward defining his own future, I am eager to see how the world opens up for him.

Lauren Berlant, who died as this book went to press, helped shape my thinking for decades and was an extraordinary friend. I will miss her voice always.

My mother, Marie Sturken, who was an artist of great talent and an extraordinarily vibrant person, died in 2018 at age ninety-six. Marie traveled with me to many sites of memory over the years, and one of the last museum tours we took together was to the 9/11 museum and memorial in New York. She was a model of how to live life to the fullest. It is to her memory that I dedicate this book.

NOTES

INTRODUCTION
1. Lepore, *These Truths*, chapter 16.
2. Butler, *Precarious Life*, 20.
3. Gordon, *Ghostly Matters*, xvi.
4. Doss, *Memorial Mania*, 59.
5. See Bayoumi, *This Muslim American Life*.
6. "New Costs of War Study: 37 Million Displaced by U.S. Post-9/11 Wars," Watson Institute, Brown University, https://watson.brown.edu. See also Ismay, "At Least 37 Million People Have Been Displaced."
7. Sturken, *Tourists of History*, introduction.
8. Crawford and Lutz, "Human Costs of the Post-9/11 Wars."
9. Rhodes, "The 9/11 Era Is Over."
10. Huyssen, *Present Pasts*; and Essen, "State of the Art in Memory Studies."
11. Rothberg, *Multidirectional Memory*, 3.
12. For an overview of the context of the National Mall monuments and memorials, see Savage, *Monument Wars*.
13. Montgomery, "A Wave of War Memorials."
14. Gopnik, "Stones and Bones," 39.
15. Aronson and Knowles, "What Would the Covid-19 Memorial Look Like?"; on the AIDS Quilt, see Sturken, *Tangled Memories*, chapter 5.
16. See the "Terrorism" section in "What We Investigate," FBI website, www.fbi.gov.
17. Singh, *Race and America's Long War*, 14.
18. Immerwahr, *How to Hide an Empire*, 343–44.
19. Ibid., 400.
20. Ibid., 382.
21. Singh, *Race and America's Long War*, 30.

1. MONUMENTS AND VOIDS
1. Anastas, "Atrocity Exhibition."
2. Rybczynski, "Black Holes."
3. Cagüeñas, "Reversed Rapture," 475.
4. See Sturken, *Tourists of History*, chapter 4.
5. Aronson, *Who Owns the Dead?*, 1.
6. Ibid., chapter 2.

7   Langewiesche, *American Ground*, 205.
8   For the book *Memory Remains*, artist Francesc Torres was given access to photograph these objects when they were all in the hangar.
9   For the story of the team that identified artifacts to be preserved at Ground Zero, see Adler, "Recovering History"; and Opotow and Pryiomka, "Memory, Site, and Object."
10 Regan, "What Happened to the Remnants of the World Trade Center?"
11 "Port Authority Concludes Successful Program to Distribute 9/11 World Trade Center Artifacts," Port Authority of New York and New Jersey press release no. 139, August 11, 2016, www.panynj.gov.
12 Ibid.
13 de Montebello, "The Iconic Power of an Artifact."
14 Young, "Sites of Reckoning."
15 Quoted in Adler, "Recovering History," 26.
16 Schifman, "The Entire History of Steel."
17 "First Steel Produced for Historic Freedom Tower," World Trade Center, www.wtc.com.
18 Fedorinova, "One World Trade Center Reveals Yet Another Problem for Steel."
19 https://www.defense.gov/Experience/USS-New-York-A-City-on-the-Sea/.
20 The 9/11 museum's memorial registry is https://registries.911memorial.org/#/memorials. See also Sanchez, "22 of the Most Powerful 9/11 Monuments."
21 See Sturken, *Tourists of History*, introduction.
22 Doss, *Memorial Mania*, 2.
23 Crawford, *Human Costs of the Post-9/11 Wars*.
24 Doss, *Memorial Mania*, 167.
25 Pederson, "The Other Memorials," 66–73.
26 Finnegan, "Monument."
27 Fischl, "A Memorial That's True to 9/11." See also Doss, *Memorial Mania*, 164–65.
28 Keyser, "Controversy Delays 9–11 Memorial."
29 Cutkomp, "Saratoga Arts' Tempered by Memory Sculpture."
30 https://registries.911memorial.org/#/memorials/2433408d-79e9-429e-9c75-23d635db4b8d, and https://libeskind.com/work/memoria-e-luce-911-memorial/.
31 Lubell, "9/11 Memorials Aren't Limited to NY and DC."
32 "Pentagon Memorial Designers' Statement, Background Information, Project Description, & Bios," Pentagon Memorial website, https://pentagonmemorial.org.
33 "The 9/11 Pentagon Memorial," *CBS News*, September 6, 2008, www.youtube.com/watch?time_continue=81&v=icJsGPGnsqo.
34 McKee, "Memory Block."
35 Ibid.
36 I discuss many of the proposed designs in *Tourists of History*, chapter 5.
37 Levine, *9/11 Memorial Visions*.
38 Young, *The Stages of Memory*, chapter 1; and Dowd, "The Unbearable Lightness of Memory."
39 Shapira, "Reflecting Absence"; see also Young, "The Memorial Process," 150.

40 Management of the project was done by the architecture firm David Brody Bond, which would also design the museum. Sagalyn, *Power at Ground Zero*, 365–66.
41 Young, *The Stages of Memory*, 68.
42 Arad, "Building the 9/11 Memorial," 86–87.
43 Meeting with Davis Brody Bond architects Steven Davis, Carl Krebs, and Mark Wagner, April 22, 2014, with Jonathan Bach and Brigitte Sion.
44 Nobel, *Sixteen Acres*, 255.
45 The report by construction executive Frank J. Sciame in 2011 was the final decision in eliminating the underground memorial galleries. See Young, *The Stages of Memory*, 69–70. See also Sagalyn, *Power at Ground Zero*, 360–72.
46 The official catalogue of the memorial is Blais and Rasic, *A Place of Remembrance*.
47 Kimmelman, "Art/Architecture: Out of Minimalism."
48 Doss, *Memorial Mania*, 133.
49 I discuss the Vietnam Veterans Memorial at length in *Tangled Memories*, chapter 2.
50 Gopnik, "Stones and Bones."
51 Young, *The Stages of Memory*, 75.
52 Shapira, "Reflecting Absence."
53 Filler, "At the Edge of the Abyss."
54 Kimmelman, "Finding Space for the Living at a Memorial."
55 Ibid.
56 Shapira, "Reflecting Absence"; Arad, "Building the 9/11 Memorial," 88.
57 Cascone, "Jon Stewart, Michael Arad, and Others Talk."
58 Cuozzo, "From Zero to 100," 34.
59 Young, *The Stages of Memory*, 77.
60 Beamer with Abraham, *Let's Roll*.
61 This story was told to me and Katherine Hite on our visit to the memorial in May 2017 by memorial ambassador Clay Mankamyer, who is a retired state trooper from Shanksville and whose grandchildren were at the school.
62 Riley, *Angel Patriots*.
63 Ibid., chapters 6 and 7.
64 Ibid., 72; Hamill, "Picture Made on 9/11," and "When Serenity Ended."
65 Jordan, "Transcending Hollywood," 201.
66 The story of the Flight 93 Memorial Chapel is told in Riley, *Angel Patriots*, chapter 4, and Thompson, *From Memory to Memorial*, 59–73.
67 Thompson, *From Memory to Memorial*, 128–33.
68 Hawthorne, "Reading Symbolism in the Sept. 11 Era," 175–79.
69 Saffron, "Review: Gripping Site," 138.
70 Ibid., 139.
71 Photographs of the reinternment service and the boulder are in the coffee-table book sold at the visitor center gift shop, featuring photographs by Chuck Wagner and quotes from family members and others, *Reflections from the Memorial*.
72 Paul Murdoch, at memorial dedication in 2015, *PBS Newshour*, September 10, 2015, www.pbs.org.

73 Noel, "The Countryside of 9/11."
74 See for example Last, "The Memorials We Deserve," 23–29.
75 Paul Murdoch, speaking at the opening of the Flight 93 National Memorial Visitor Center, quoted in Sullivan, "A New 9/11 Memorial to Flight 93."
76 Not far from the Flight 93 memorial is a small monument to coal miners and rescue workers for the Quecreek Mine Rescue Site, where, in July 2002, nine miners who were trapped in a flooded mine were rescued after several days by the drilling of a rescue shaft on a local farm.
77 Riley, *Angel Patriots*, 102–4.
78 Ibid., 216–18.
79 The story of Flight 93 has also been leveraged for political agendas, most strangely as a metaphor for the 2016 election. Michael Anton, who would go on to serve for a year in the Trump administration, wrote a pseudonymous March 2016 essay, "The Flight 93 Election," in which he compared letting Hillary Clinton win the election with passengers refusing to storm the cockpit of the Flight 93 flight. He would publish it as a book: Anton, *After the Flight 93 Election* (Encounter Books, 2019).

2. THE OBJECTS THAT LIVED, THE VOICES THAT REMAIN

1 Emily Edwards, "The Stories Behind the Markings," *Interpreting the Last Column* (blog), accessed July 20, 2021, https://911memorial.org/.
2 *Fox News Insider*, "FNC Reporter Donates Brick."
3 Londoño, "Returning Home."
4 Axelrod, "Beyond Ground Zero."
5 Journalist Seymour Hersh has contested the official story of bin Laden's killing in his book *The Killing of Osama bin Laden*.
6 See Balfour, "Unlikely Cryptfellows," 4. In his essay on training docents in the museum, Noah Rauch tells the story of a docent who asked if he could spit on the brick. "A Balancing Act," 16–21.
7 The 9/11 Tribute Museum, which was originally a temporary museum created by the families in 2006 just south of the site, has continued to operate. The museum specializes in tours of the overall site by survivors and is a separate entity from the 9/11 museum.
8 Sagalyn, *Power at Ground Zero*, 671.
9 On Thinc Design, see Tom Hennes, "Reflections on the Opening of the 9/11 Memorial Museum."
10 Greenwald, "Through the Lens of Memory," 29–30.
11 Gopnik, "Stones and Bones."
12 The range of this consultation is described in the museum's publication; see Greenwald, "Through the Lens of Memory," 11–30. The designers were also key participants in these conversations.
13 Weisser, "Archaeology, Architecture, and Creating a Space for Memory," 59.
14 See Gopnik, "Stones and Bones"; and Anastas, "Atrocity Exhibition."
15 Cuozzo, "9/11 Museum Café Drops Booze, Gourmet Food."

16 Dupré, *One World Trade Center*, 172.
17 Sagalyn, *Power at Ground Zero*, 311, 321, and 327.
18 Greenwald, "Through the Lens of Memory," 32.
19 I was given a tour of the newly opened museum, with Jonathan Bach and Brigitte Sion, by architect Mark Wagner of DBB on July 24, 2014. See also Opotow and Pryiomka, "Memory, Site, and Object," which incorporates an interview with Wagner.
20 Jacobs, "Letter from Ground Zero."
21 Sagalyn, *Power at Ground Zero*, 674.
22 See Greenwald, "Through the Lens of Memory," 17.
23 Meeting with Davis Brody Bond architects Steven Davis, Carl Krebs, and Mark Wagner, April 22, 2014, with Jonathan Bach and Brigitte Sion.
24 I wrote at length about the fetishizing of the footprints in *Tourists of History*.
25 The appropriateness of this quotation from Virgil has been much discussed, since it refers to two Trojan soldiers who have just murdered enemy soldiers in their sleep, and some have stated that it is more appropriate for the attackers than for the victims of 9/11. See Poole, "Performing Trauma," 1–18; and Dunlap, "A Memorial Inscription's Grim Origins."
26 Frost, "No Safe Spaces," 225.
27 Ramirez, "The Complexities of Displaying World Trade Center Dust," 183–87.
28 I borrow the idea of a "survivor object" from the Survivor Objects conference, organized by the Center for Material Culture Studies at the University of Delaware in November 2014. My thanks to those at the conference for their valuable feedback.
29 For more, see *The Last Column, a Symbol of Resilience*, https://www.youtube.com/watch?v=4-heOLpMq3M.
30 Paliewicz, "Bent but Not Broken," 5, 11.
31 Shulman, "Impact Steel," 30–35.
32 Huyssen, *Twilight Memories*, 33.
33 Bennett, *Vibrant Matter*, xvi.
34 Cotter, "The 9/11 Story Told at Bedrock."
35 The museum publication, *The Stories They Tell: Artifacts from the National September 11 Memorial Museum, A Journey of Remembrance*, recounts the complex trajectories of several of these objects.
36 Trebay, "A Moment in Time Captured in Pieces," E1.
37 See his widow Lisa Beamer's memoir, *Let's Roll*.
38 Ibid.
39 Aronson, *Who Owns the Dead?*, 1.
40 "World Trade Center Operational Statistics," Office of the Chief Medical Examiner, www.nyc.gov. The OCME has continued to occasionally identify remains (identifying Scott Michael Johnson from a bone fragment in July 2018, for example). Pager, "Keeping Its Promise to Families," A21.
41 The primary organization to contest the status of the refuse at Fresh Kills was the World Trade Center Families for Proper Burial (WTCFPB), whose 2005 lawsuit

demanding that the fine dust from the World Trade Center site be placed in special containers and returned to Ground Zero was dismissed in July 2008. Led by a family whose son's wallet and remains were found at Fresh Kills, WTCFPB contended, with supporting testimony from workers and experts, that a significant amount of the debris at Fresh Kills had not been properly sifted. The plan to turn Fresh Kills into a park, with an area designated as a memorial site, has not allayed the sense of injustice over the possible existence of remains at the landfill. Aronson, *Who Owns the Dead?*, chapter 2.

42 Ibid., 2.
43 Lipton and Glanz, "DNA Science Pushed to the Limit," A1; Aronson, *Who Owns the Dead?*, 98–105.
44 Aronson, *Who Owns the Dead?*, 109.
45 Farrell, "In 'Ceremonial Transfer,'" A20. See also Aronson, *Who Owns the Dead?*, 227–28.
46 Steve Kandell narrates his experience of visiting this room, with its window onto wooden cabinets of remains, in his essay, "The Worst Day of My Life."
47 Ng and Friedman, "9/11 Museum."
48 At the Oklahoma City memorial, the designers successfully argued, and families agreed, that the unidentified remains should not be placed within the memorial (they are interred at the state Capitol). See Sturken, *Tourists of History*, 113.
49 Kandell, "The Worst Day of My Life."
50 Dunlap and Beachy, "Seeking the Final Faces," A1.
51 Ibid.
52 Butler, *Frames of War*, 38–39.
53 The museum conducted a focus group specifically on the composite and other artifacts in 2010. See Greenspan, *Battle for Ground Zero*, 218.
54 Here it reads, "Visitors are advised that the exhibition presents images and content reflecting the violence of the attacks and their consequences. The exhibition may not be appropriate for visitors 10 years old and younger. Adults accompanying younger visitors should exercise discretion before entering."
55 Kuang, "The Near-Impossible Challenge of Designing the 9/11 Museum."
56 Ross Poole argues, in contrast, that the "chronological, and also spatial, incoherence is designed to provide a representation of the shock as well as the pathos, courage, and death of that morning. . . . The lack of a meaningful trajectory *is* the meaningful trajectory." Poole, "Performing Trauma," 6.
57 Frost, "No Safe Spaces," 228.
58 Greenwald, "Through the Lens of Memory," 23–25.
59 Davidson, "Getting to 9/11."
60 Jake Barton, interview with the author, June 24, 2019.
61 Greenwald explains how the museum staff consulted with families, in this case with Todd Beamer's parents, about whether to include the audio of the hijackers speaking, which they felt was important to do. This last phrase is in text but not audio because the recordings are still under seal. Greenwald, "Through the Lens of Memory," 27.

62 Cohen, "At Museum on 9/11," A1.
63 The debates within the museum about how to present this history are discussed in Chanin, "The Challenges of Documenting History."
64 Otterman, "Film at 9/11 Museum."
65 Cohen, "At Museum on 9/11."
66 Sodaro, "Prosthetic Trauma," 117–29.
67 Molotch, "How the 9/11 Museum Gets Us."
68 Dunlap, "Freedom Center in Doubt"; and Dunlap, "Governor Bars Freedom Center," A1.
69 Frost, "No Safe Spaces," 235.
70 Sagalyn, *Power at Ground Zero*, 676.
71 Lynne Sagalyn describes the battle over the International Freedom Center in great detail in *Power at Ground Zero*, 306–32.
72 Ibid., 332–34. See also Shemtob and Opotow, "Conflict and Change," 24–30.
73 This was on the Local Projects website, which has now been updated to read "We are on a mission to push the boundaries of emotional storytelling." http://local-projects.com/work.
74 Hill, "Museum as Megamachine."
75 Senk, "The Memory Exchange," 4; and Sodaro, *Exhibiting Atrocity*, 156.
76 Senk, "The Memory Exchange," 5.
77 Hennes, "Reflections on the Opening of the 9/11 Memorial Museum."
78 *Fast Company*, "A Tour of the 9/11 Museum."
79 Senk, "The Memory Exchange," 5.
80 Sodaro, *Exhibiting Atrocity*, 143.
81 Jake Barton interviewed in video by *Wall Street Journal*, 2014, www.wsj.com.
82 It also was restricted to those news organizations that were willing to provide licenses—and that had the lawyers to negotiate those licensing agreements—for the material. See Klein, "Timescape and Memory," 440.
83 Alderson, "Interactive."
84 Sodaro, *Exhibiting Atrocity*, 159.
85 Kennicott, "The 9/11 Memorial Museum."
86 Jeanne Allen, "New Yorkers Avoid 9/11 Museum in Droves," *Nonprofit Quarterly*, https://nonprofitquarterly.org.
87 https://www.youtube.com/user/911memorial.
88 Smith, "9/11 Museum a Tough Sell at Home," A15, A17.
89 Edelman, "9/11 Memorial Still Operating at a Loss."
90 Edelman, "9/11 Memorial Paying Security."
91 Edelman, "The 9/11 Museum's Absurd Gift Shop."
92 Philip, "Families Infuriated by 'Crass Commercialism.'"
93 I discuss the proliferation of 9/11 kitsch in *Tourists of History*.
94 Kandell, "The Worst Day of My Life."
95 Ibid.
96 O'Neill, "Of Course There Is a Gift Shop." See also Zurcher, "9/11 Museum Gift Shop."

97 Edelman, "The 9/11 Museum's Absurd Gift Shop."
98 Appadurai, "Introduction," 3–63.
99 Huyssen, *Twilight Memories*, 33.

3. GLOBAL ARCHITECTURE, PATRIOTIC SKYSCRAPERS, AND A CATHEDRAL SHOPPING MALL

1 The observatory is operated by Legends Hospitality. Its spokesperson told the *New York Times* that there was debate in the company and at the Port Authority about whether to depict the brief life of the tower in the video. The video was designed and produced by the Hettema Group and Blur Studio. See Dunlap, "On Time Lapse Rocket Ride."
2 de Certeau, "Walking in the City," 92.
3 Kaplan, *Aerial Aftermaths*, 8. The introduction to the book has a long, evocative engagement with the destruction of the World Trade Center, de Certeau, and the aerial views of the twin towers.
4 The observatory was paid for by Legends Hospitality with a fifteen-year lease. The complexity of the partnership is outlined by Lynne Sagalyn in *Power at Ground Zero*, 703–6.
5 Barron, "That Smell at the Top of One World Trade?"
6 Sorkin, "Lower Manhattan and the Tragedy of Business as Usual."
7 Sagalyn, *Power at Ground Zero*, 667–78.
8 Kimmelman, "Santiago Calatrava's Transit Hub."
9 Sagalyn has a chart of all of the costs in *Power at Ground Zero*, 668.
10 Sorkin, "Lower Manhattan and the Tragedy of Business as Usual."
11 Darton, "The Janus Face of Architectural Terrorism."
12 Graham, *Vertical*, 169.
13 Darton, "The Janus Face of Architectural Terrorism."
14 Ibid.
15 Huxtable, "The New York Process," A20.
16 Sagalyn, *Power at Ground Zero*. See also Greenspan, *Battle for Ground Zero*.
17 In Judith Dupré's *One World Trade Center: Biography of the Building*, there are profiles of all the major players in the reconstruction of the site, including real estate developers, architects, engineers, security professionals, politicians, and bureaucrats, and there is not one woman among them.
18 Sagalyn, *Power at Ground Zero*, 91.
19 Campanile, "Inside Lower Manhattan's Amazing Post-9/11 Rebound."
20 Stein, *Capital City*, 38–39.
21 Goldberger, *Up from Zero*, 57.
22 Graham, *Vertical*, 157.
23 Ong, "Hyperbuilding."
24 Graham, *Vertical*, 163.
25 Plitt, "NYC's Supertall Skyscraper."
26 Stefanos Chen, "New York City's Evolving Skyline."

27 Goldberger, *Up from Zero*, 57. See also Ali and Al-Kodmany, "Tall Buildings and Urban Habitat."
28 Bullough, *Moneyland*, 23. See also Fernandez, Hofman, and Aalbers, "London and New York as a Safe Deposit Box."
29 Story and Saul, "Towers of Secrecy." This was the first of a five-part series.
30 Saul, "Mayor Bloomberg Wants Every Billionaire on Earth."
31 Brennan, "Chapter 2."
32 Goldberger, "Too Rich, Too Tall, Too Thin?," 170.
33 432 Park is now the subject of conflicts over structural problems of water damage and elevator malfunctions that may be due to wind sway. Bekiempis, "High Anxiety."
34 Foer, "Russian Style Kleptocracy."
35 Capps, "Why Architects Are Outraged." Sadly, Michael Sorkin would lose his life to COVID-19 in April 2020.
36 In a subsequent special issue of the *Avery Review* on the debate, Ananya Roy wrote that the profession of architecture had long had a deeply embedded relationship of complicity with colonialism and imperialism, as well as with systems of racialized power. She critiques this as the "infrastructure of assent." Roy, "The Infrastructures of Assent."
37 Martin, "The Demagogue Takes the Stage."
38 Dupré, *One World Trade Center*, 10.
39 Ibid., 6.
40 Goldhagen, "One World Trade Center."
41 Sagalyn, *Power at Ground Zero*, 264–65.
42 Ibid., 271.
43 Filler, "New York's Vast Flop."
44 Steinhaer, "Trump Proposes Putting Up 2 Towers."
45 Dupré, *One World Trade Center*, 70.
46 Anastas, "Atrocity Exhibition."
47 Dupré, *One World Trade Center*, 48.
48 Cuozzo, "Forget 'Freedom,'" 23.
49 Dupré, *One World Trade Center*, 50.
50 Kimmelman, "A Soaring Emblem of New York," A1.
51 Ali and Al-Kodmany, "Tall Buildings and Urban Habitat."
52 Quoted in Sagalyn, *Power at Ground Zero*, 218.
53 Dupré, *One World Trade Center*, 87.
54 Lamster, "Hope Rises from Ground Zero," 31.
55 Kimmelman, "A Soaring Emblem," A1.
56 Dunlap and Heisler, "1 World Trade Center Gains Popularity."
57 Goldhagen, "One World Trade Center."
58 Ouroussoff, "An Appraisal."
59 Quoted in Sagalyn, *Power at Ground Zero*, 688.
60 Nocera, "9/11's White Elephant."

61 Koblin, "A Mad Dash to Points South."
62 See the "Buildings" page in the "About" section of the WTC website, www.wtc.com.
63 Filler, "New York's Vast Flop."
64 Samuel Stein has an concise summary of Trump's real estate career in *Capital City*, chapter 4.
65 Martin, "The Demagogue Takes the Stage."
66 Muschamp, "An Appraisal"; and Kimmelman, "Architecture: Ground Zero."
67 Huxtable, "A Landmark Destination."
68 Dunlap, "No Grand Opening Planned."
69 Kimmelman, "Santiago Calatrava's Transit Hub."
70 Kimmelman, "Moynihan Train Hall," C1.
71 Calatrava and Kausel, *Santiago Calatrava Conversations with Students*, 43.
72 Goldhagen, "Santiago Calatrava's Overrated Architecture."
73 DenHoed, "The Transformation of Calatrava's Oculus"; Cuozzo, "Bad to the Bone"; Kimmelman, "Santiago Calatrava's Transit Hub"; Filler, "New York's Vast Flop."
74 Kimmelman, "Santiago Calatrava's Transit Hub," C1.
75 Schilling, "World Trade Center Mall Offers Change."
76 Fazzare, "Santiago Calatrava Explains How He Designed the Oculus."
77 Goldberger, "Beyond the Hype."
78 Tangel and Morris. "Station Embodies Resolve," A15; and Gonchar, "World Trade Center Transportation Hub."
79 Video on *Architectural Digest* website, www.architecturaldigest.com.
80 Filler, "The Bird Man."
81 Sagalyn, *Power at Ground Zero*, 566. When Christopher Ward came in as executive director of the Port Authority in 2008, he demanded that there be structural columns, and thereafter, the columns were referred to by workers as the Chris Ward columns.
82 Sagalyn, *Power at Ground Zero*, 261–62; Jacobs, "Calatrava's Transportation Hub."
83 *Santiago Calatrava*, video, directed by Alexandra Livieris, 2016. www.youtube.com/watch?v=h9qSRbUDWEI.
84 Fazzare, "Santiago Calatrava Explains."
85 Filler, "The Bird Man"; see also Sagalyn, *Power at Ground Zero*, 507.
86 Kim, "Oculus Skylight, Which Stayed Closed for 9/11 Tribute."
87 Rosengaard, "Calatrava's Oculus," 8–9.
88 Jacobs, "Calatrava's Transportation Hub."
89 Kimmelman, "Moynihan Train Hall," C1.
90 Brake, "Calatrava's Transit Hub."
91 Efimenko, *On Doves*, 46. I am indebted to many of the insights in this thesis.
92 Ibid.
93 DenHoed, "The Transformation of Calatrava's Oculus."
94 Martin, "The Demagogue Takes the Stage."

95 Filler, "The Bird Man."
96 Goldhagen, "Santiago Calatrava's Overrated Architecture."
97 Wainwright, "Snapping Point." See also Lange, "Is Instagram Ruining Architecture?" Some also make the argument that social media has created a previously nonexistent feedback loop from the public to architects, so that the people's responses to buildings (and plans for buildings) have a greater influence. See Kushner, "Why the Buildings of the Future Will Be Shaped by . . . You."
98 DenHoed, "The Transformation of Calatrava's Oculus."
99 Sorkin, "Lower Manhattan and the Tragedy of Business as Usual."

4. VISIBILITY AND ERASURE

1 See the Fallen Heroes Project website, www.fallenheroesproject.org/.
2 See "Letters from Families" at the Fallen Heroes Project website, www.fallenheroesproject.org.
3 Gilbertson, *Bedrooms of the Fallen*.
4 Filkins, *The Forever War*, chapter 11.
5 Gilbertson, "Absences," in *Bedrooms of the Fallen*, 83.
6 Horton and Gregg, "Use of Military Contractors"; and Peltier, "The Growth of the 'Camo Economy.'"
7 There are many sources for these statistics, including "Casualty Statistics," www.defense.gov; Costs of War Project, Watson Institute, Brown University, https://watson.brown.edu; Crawford and Lutz, "Human Cost of Post-9/11 Wars"; and "US Military Fatalities in Iraq and Afghanistan as of February 21 2021, by State," *Stastista*, www.statista.com.
8 "New Costs of War Study: 37 Million Displaced by U.S. Post-9/11 Wars, Watson Institute, Brown University, https://watson.brown.edu. See also Ismay, "At Least 37 Million People Have Been Displaced."
9 Singh, *Race and America's Long War*, 2.
10 Grandin, *The End of the Myth*, 5.
11 Sturken, *Tourists of History*, chapter 1.
12 She emphasizes the term *commercialization* because most of these for-profit firms are not subject to the rules of the private market when they receive no-bid contracts from the government, for which they charge exorbitant rates. Peltier, "The Growth of the 'Camo Economy.'"
13 "Remarks by the President at the National Defense University," White House Office of the Press Secretary, May 23, 2013, https://obamawhitehouse.archives.gov. See also Baker, "Pivoting from a War Footing."
14 Savage, "What Will Our Iraq Memorial Look Like?"
15 Representative Tom McClintock, "Global War on Terrorism Memorial Act," Congressional Record, daily edition, 163 (July 28, 2017), H6544. See also "Monuments and Memorials Authorized under the Commemorative Works Act in the District of Columbia: Current Development of In-Progres and Lapsed Works," Congressional Research Service, April 24, 2018, www.everycrsreport.com.

16 See Gourevitch's foreword in Gilbertson, *Bedrooms of the Fallen*, x.
17 Bacevich, *Breach of Trust*, 104–7.
18 Friedman, *A Soldier's Portfolio*.
19 Two Freedom of Information suits were filed, in April 2004 by Russ Kick, the webmaster of www.memoryhole.com, and in April 2005 by professor Ralph Begleiter of the University of Delaware. See the National Security Archive (at George Washington University) website, www.gwu.edu/~nsarchiv/.
20 Rebecca Adelman writes at length about the complexities of the ban in *Beyond the Checkpoint*, 37–43.
21 Bodnar, *Divided by Terror*, 4–6.
22 Mirzoeff, *The Right to Look*, 2–3.
23 Shabout, "Dafatir," 185, 199.
24 Doss, *Memorial Mania*, 245.
25 Bodnar, *Divided by Terror*, 145–47.
26 Doss, *Memorial Mania*, 250–51.
27 American Friends Service Committee, "Costs of War," www.afsc.org/.
28 Godfrey, "Questionnaire," 69–70.
29 Hirsch, "In Memoriam," 132–33, 178; and Potter, "Collecting Leaves, Assembling Memory."
30 Hirsch, "In Memoriam," 178.
31 Purchased with funds from Sarah Ann and Werner Kramarsky, Mr. and Mrs. David Schiff, Melissa and Robert Soros, Marion C. and Charles Burson, Toby Devan Lewis Foundation, the Judith Rothschild Foundation, Nora and Guy Barron, Pam Joseph and Rob Brinker, Greg Kucera and Larry Yocom, Ted and Maryanne Ellison Simmons, and the Stanley Family Fund of the Community Foundation of New Jersey.
32 Peraica, "An Interview with Joseph DeLappe."
33 DeLappe and Simpson, "Virtual Commemoration," 616.
34 Hackett, "This Memorial Destined for Oblivion."
35 DeLappe and Simpson, "Virtual Commemoration," 619.
36 Goodman, "105,000 Tattoos."
37 Kamat, "Interview with Iraqi Artist Wafaa Bilal," 317.
38 See Joseph Delappe's website, www.delappe.net.
39 "Costs of War: US Veterans & Military Families," Watson Institute, Brown University, https://watson.brown.edu.
40 Nessen, Lounsbury, and Hetz, *War Surgery in Afghanistan and Iraq*.
41 Savage, "What Will Our Iraq Memorial Look Like?"
42 *2019 National Veteran Suicide Prevention Annual Report*, Office of Mental Health and Suicide Prevention, US Department of Veterans Affairs, www.mentalhealth.va.gov.
43 "Costs of War: US Veterans & Military Families."
44 Duckworth, "Tucker Carlson Doesn't Know What Patriotism Is."
45 Leitz, *Fighting for Peace*, 17.

46 The pipeline, which was approved by President Trump and went into operation in May 2017, has been halted and restarted and the subject of legal battles ever since.
47 Leitz, *Fighting for Peace*, 179, 175.
48 See the website of About Face: Veterans Taking Action against Militarism and Endless Wars, https://aboutfaceveterans.org/.
49 *The Ground Truth*, directed by Patricia Foulkrod (2006). See Holden, "The Broken Souls."
50 Igielnik and Parker, "Majorities of U.S. Veterans."
51 *Soldiers Stories from Iraq and Afghanistan*, www.youtube.com/watch?v=AHe1Ln-JcWE.
52 Adelman, *Figuring Violence*, chapter 4.
53 Finkel, *Thank You for Your Service* (the book and the film).
54 Adelman, *Figuring Violence*, 225–26.
55 Gell, "George W. Bush."
56 Wagner-Pacifici, "Portraits of Courage," 114.
57 Nina Berman's website is at www.ninaberman.
58 Biernoff, *Portraits of Violence*, 40–41. Biernoff writes extensively on this image in the Introduction and chapter 1 of this book.
59 Ibid., 4.
60 Beyerstein, "The Face of War."
61 See the Global War on Terrorism Memorial Foundation website and Facebook page: www.gwotmemorialfoundation.org/ and www.facebook.com.
62 See the National Infantry Museum website at https://nationalinfantrymuseum.org.
63 Kim, "Veterans Say It's Not Too Soon to Build a National Memorial."
64 Montgomery, "A Wave of War Memorials Is Coming to D.C."
65 Yeazel, "A Global War on Terror Memorial Is Unnecessary."
66 Ismay, "A Navy Veteran"; and Kalmbacker, "'Wall of Veterans.'"
67 Page, "Upset by Veterans."
68 Savage, "What Will Our Iraq War Memorial Look Like?"
69 Singh, *Race and America's Long War*, 17; and Sontag, "Regarding the Torture of Others."
70 Singh, *Race and America's Long War*, 30.

5. THE MEMORY OF RACIAL TERROR

1 Stevenson, "A Presumption of Guilt."
2 Hasian and Paliewicz, *Racial Terror*, chapter 2.
3 Doss, *Memorial Mania*, 122. I discuss the Oklahoma City bombing and the characterizations of Timothy McVeigh as an evil loner in *Tourists of History*, chapter 3.
4 EJI's interactive lynching website shows the shifts in populations from the South to the West, Midwest, and North from 1910 to 1970, https://lynchinginamerica.eji.org/explore/migration.
5 Mock, "Why We Should Stop Calling It the 'Great Migration.'"
6 Toobin, "The Legacy of Lynching."

7   Lori Pierce and Kaily Heitz give an excellent summary of the history of counting lynchings in "Say Their Names," 972–75.
8   Equal Justice Initiative, *Lynching in America*. The reference to the courthouse lawn is from Ifill, *On the Courthouse Lawn*.
9   Stevenson, "A Presumption of Guilt."
10 *The Legacy Museum*, "You Are Here," n.p.
11 A video about this marker is on the Community Remembrance Project website: https://eji.org/projects/community-remembrance-project/.
12 From a video in the exhibition of the Legacy Museum.
13 From the HBO documentary *True Justice: Bryan Stephenson's Fight for Equality*, directed by George Kunhardt and Peter W. Kunhardt (2019).
14 Newkirk, "The Great Land Robbery"; see also Presser, "Kicked off the Land."
15 For an interesting analysis of the soil of the plantation as memory, see Martens and Robertson, "How the Soil Remembers Plantation Slavery."
16 Pierce and Heitz, "Say Their Names," 963.
17 Toobin, "The Legacy of Lynching."
18 Hobbs and Freudenberger, "A Visit to Montgomery's Legacy Museum."
19 Stevenson, introduction to *The Legacy Museum*, n.p.
20 Stevenson, *Just Mercy*, and *Just Mercy*, directed by Destin Daniel Cretton (2019; Warner Bros).
21 Kennicott, "A Powerful Memorial."
22 Phone interview by author with Sia Sanneh, July 14, 2020. All quotes from Sanneh are from this interview.
23 On mass incarceration, see Alexander, *The New Jim Crow*.
24 Landsberg, "Post-Postracial America".
25 Interview by author with Jake Barton, New York, June 24, 2019. Unless otherwise noted, all quotes from Barton are from this interview.
26 Landsberg, "Post-Postracial America."
27 Fleetwood, *Marking Time*, introduction.
28 Jackson, *Through All the Pain I Still Evolved*.
29 Hasian and Paliewicz critique the idea that the museum can have its intended transformative effect on US race relations. Hasian and Paliewicz, *Racial Terrorism*, 217.
30 Pierce and Heitz, "Say Their Names," 970.
31 Levin, "Lynching Memorial"; and Hobbs and Freudenberger, "A Visit to Montgomery's Legacy Museum."
32 From the video *Why Build a Lynching Memorial*, on the EJI website, https://museumandmemorial.eji.org/memorial.
33 Murphy outlines this philosophy in his widely viewed TED talk, "Architecture That's Built to Heal."
34 Pasnik, Mansfield, and Yang, *Justice Is Beauty*.
35 Murphy, "Architecture That's Built to Heal."
36 Chakrabarti, "Lynching Memorial's Designer."
37 Cheng, "Figuration, Abstraction and Empathy."

38 Email correspondence with Regina Yang of MASS Design Group, July 24, 2020.
39 Murphy, "Architecture That's Built to Heal."
40 Email correspondence with Regina Yang.
41 Kimmelman, "Art/Architecture; Out of Minimalism."
42 Kennicott, "A Powerful Memorial."
43 Brown, in "Conversation: Memory and Monument," 321.
44 Brooke Gladstone, "The Worst Thing We've Ever Done."
45 Chakrabarti, "Lynching Memorial's Designer."
46 Stevenson, "A Presumption of Guilt"; and https://eji.org/issues/presumption-of-guilt/.
47 Gladstone, "The Worst Thing We've Ever Done."
48 "EJI Releases Video on Sculpture about Enslavement," https://museumandmemorial.eji.org.
49 Jones, "KPIX Anchor-Turned-Sculptor."
50 Picard, "'Public Art Is Propaganda, Frankly.'"
51 "The Gun Memorial Project," MASS Design Group, https://massdesigngroup.org.
52 Email correspondence with Regina Yang.
53 Helm, "The New Lynching Memorial and Legacy Museum."
54 See Allen, *Without Sanctuary*; Hasian and Paliewicz, *Racial Terror*, 103–11; and Markovitz, *Legacies of Lynching*, conclusion.
55 Tuck and Yang, "R-Words: Refusing Research," 241.
56 Helm, "The New Lynching Memorial and Legacy Museum."
57 Doss, *Memorial Mania*, 133.
58 Gladstone, "The Worst Thing We've Ever Done."
59 Hasian and Paliewicz, "Taking the Reparatory Turn"; and "The National Memorial for Peace and Justice."
60 Gordon, *Ghostly Matters*, xvi.
61 Rosenblatt, "Aparicíon con Vida."
62 Klein, "Bryan Stevenson on How America Can Heal."

CONCLUSION

1 Heather Cox Richardson, "Letters From an American," January 30, 2020, https://heathercoxrichardson.substack.com/.
2 For proposals and ideas circulating about COVID-19 memorials, see Bogost, "How Will the Future Remember Covid-19?"; and Vergara, "Picturing the Loss."

BIBLIOGRAPHY

Adelman, Rebecca. *Beyond the Checkpoint: Visual Practices in America's Global War on Terror*. Amherst: University of Massachusetts Press, 2014.

———. *Figuring Violence: Affective Investments in Perpetual War*. New York: Fordham University Press, 2019.

Adler, Jerry. "Recovering History: The Story of Hangar 17." In *Memory Remains: 9/11 Artifacts at Hangar 17*, edited by Clifford Chanin, photographs by Francesc Torres, 15–26. Washington, DC: National Geographic Press, 2011.

Alderson, Rob. "Interactive: Jake Barton on Designing Media Exhibits for the 9/11 Museum." *It's Nice That*, May 19, 2014. www.itsnicethat.com.

Alexander, Michelle. *The New Jim Crow: Mass Incarceration in the Age of Colorblindness*. Tenth Anniversary Edition. New York: New Press, 2020. First published 2010.

Ali, Mir M., and Kheir Al-Kodmany. "Tall Buildings and Urban Habitat of the 21st Century: A Global Perspective." *Buildings* 2 (2012): 384–423.

Allen, James, ed. *Without Sanctuary: Lynching Photography in America*. Santa Fe, NM: Twin Palms, 1999.

Anastas, Benjamin. "Atrocity Exhibition." *Los Angeles Review of Books*, July 24, 2014. https://lareviewofbooks.org.

Appadurai, Arjun. "Introduction: Commodities and the Politics of Value." In *The Social Life of Things: Commodities in Cultural Perspective*, edited by Arjun Appadurai, 3–63. Cambridge, UK: Cambridge University Press, 1988.

Arad, Michael. "Building the 9/11 Memorial." In *New York after 9/11*, edited by Susan Opotow and Zachary Baron Shemtob: 86–105. New York: Fordham University Press, 2018.

Aronson, Jay D. *Who Owns the Dead? The Science and Politics of Death at Ground Zero*. Cambridge, MA: Harvard University Press, 2016.

Aronson, Jay D., and Scott Gabriel Knowles. "What Would the Covid-19 Memorial Look Like?" *Washington Post*, April 28, 2020. www.washingtonpost.com.

Axelrod, Jim. "Beyond Ground Zero: 9/11 Museum Exhibit Focuses on Bin Laden Death." *CBS This Morning*, September 11, 2014. www.youtube.com/watch?v=xg7jIPmchOc.

Bacevich, Andrew J. *Breach of Trust: How Americans Failed Their Soldiers and Their Country*. New York: Metropolitan Books, 2013.

Baker, Peter. "Pivoting from a War Footing, Obama Acts to Curtail Drones." *New York Times*, May 23, 2013. www.nytimes.com.

Balfour, Lindsay Anne. "Unlikely Cryptfellows: Hospitality, Difference, and Spectrality at the 9/11 Museum." *Journal of Aesthetics & Culture* 7 (2015), 1–9. https://doi.org/10.3402/jac.v7.28217.

Barron, James. "That Smell at the Top of One World Trade? It's on Purpose." *New York Times*, August 7, 2019. www.nytimes.com.

Bayoumi, Moustafa. *This Muslim American Life: Dispatches from the War on Terror.* New York: New York University Press, 2015.

Beamer, Lisa, with Ken Abraham. *Let's Roll: Ordinary People, Extraordinary Courage.* Wheaton, IL: Tyndale, 2002.

Bekiempis, Victoria. "High Anxiety: Super-Rich Find Supertall Skyscraper an Uncomfortable Perch." *Guardian*, February 7, 2021. www.guardian.com.

Bennett, Jane. *Vibrant Matter: A Political Ecology of Things.* Durham, NC: Duke University Press, 2010.

Berman, Nina. *Purple Hearts: Back from Iraq.* London: Trolley Books, 2004.

Beyerstein, Lindsay. "Face of War." *Salon*, March 10, 2007. http://salon.com.

Biernoff, Suzannah. *Portraits of Violence: War and the Aesthetics of Disfigurement.* Ann Arbor: University of Michigan Press, 2017.

Blais, Allison, and Lynn Rasic, eds. *A Place of Remembrance: Official Book of the National September 11 Memorial.* Washington, DC: National Geographic, 2011.

Blight, David W. "How Trumpism May Endure." *New York Times*, January 9, 2021. www.nytimes.com.

Bodnar, John. *Divided by Terror: Patriotism in Post-9/11 America.* Chapel Hill: University of North Carolina Press, 2021.

Bogost, Ian. "How Will the Future Remember Covid-19?" *Atlantic*, November 24, 2020. www.theatlantic.com.

Brake, Alan G. "Calatrava's Transit Hub." *Dezeen*, May 7, 2016.

Brennan, Shane. "From Sunshine to Solar Resources: Elemental Dynamics of Light, Heat, Height and Visual in New York City." From *Practices of Sunlight: Visual and Cultural Politics of Solar Energy in the United States.* PhD diss., New York University, 2017.

Bullough, Oliver. *Moneyland: The Inside Story of the Crooks and Kleptocrats Who Rule the World.* New York: St. Martin's, 2019.

Butler, Judith. *Frames of War: When Is Life Grievable?* London: Verso, 2009.

———. *Precarious Life: The Powers of Mourning and Violence.* London: Verso, 2004.

Cagüeñas, Diego. "Reversed Rapture: On Salvation, Suicide, and the Spirit of Terrorism." *Public Culture* 30, no. 3 (2018): 465–82. https://doi.org/10.1215/08992363-6912139.

Calatrava, Santiago, and Cecelia Lewis Kausel. *Santiago Calatrava Conversations with Students—The MIT Lectures.* Princeton, NJ: Princeton Architectural Press, 2002.

Campanile, Carl. "Inside Lower Manhattan's Amazing Post-9/11 Rebound." *New York Post*, September 6, 2016. https://nypost.com.

Capps, Kriston. "Why Architects Are Outraged over a Letter to Trump." *Citylab*, November 15, 2016. www.citylab.com.

Cascone, Sarah. "Jon Stewart, Michael Arad, and Others Talk about the Meaning of the Newly Unveiled Design of the 9/11 Memorial Glade." *Artnet*, May 31, 2018. https://news.artnet.com.
Chakrabarti, Meghna. "Lynching Memorial's Designer Seeks Healing through Architecture." *Here & Now*, September 23, 2016. www.wbur.org.
Chanin, Clifford, ed. *Memory Remains: 9/11 Artifacts at Hangar 17*. Photographs by Francesc Torres. Washington, DC: National Geographic Press, 2011.
———. "The Challenges of Documenting History in a Memorial Museum: Presenting the Perpetrators." In *No Day Shall Erase You: The Story of 9/11 As Told at the National September 11 Memorial Museum*, edited by Alice M. Greenwald, 154–57. New York: Skira Rozzoli, 2016.
Chanin, Clifford, and Alice M. Greenwald, eds. *The Stories They Tell: Artifacts from the National September 11 Memorial Museum, A Journey of Remembrance*. New York: Skira Rizzoli, 2013.
Chen, Stefanos. "New York City's Evolving Skyline." *New York Times*, June 5, 2019. www.nytimes.com.
Cheng, Irene. "Figuration, Abstraction and Empathy: The National Memorial for Peace and Justice." Paper presented at the Techniques of Memory Symposium, Global Urban Humanities Institute, UC Berkeley, April 2019.
Cohen, Patricia. "At Museum on 9/11, Talking through an Identity Crisis." *New York Times*, June 2, 2012. www.nytimes.com.
Cotter, Holland. "The 9/11 Story Told at Bedrock, Powerful as a Punch to the Gut." *New York Times*, May 14. 2014, www.nytimes.com.
Crawford, Neta C. *Human Costs of the Post-9/11 Wars: Lethality and the Need for Transparency*. Watson Institute for International and Public Affairs, Brown University, November 2018, https://watson.brown.edu.
Crawford, Neta C., and Catherine Lutz. "Human Costs of the Post-9/11 Wars: Direct War Deaths in Major War Zones." Watson Institute for International and Public Affairs, Brown University, November 2019, https://watson.brown.edu.
Cuozzo, Steve. "9/11 Museum Café Drops Booze, Gourmet Food." *New York Post*, July 10, 2014. https://nypost.com.
———. "Bad to the Bone." *New York Post*, August 3, 2014. https://nypost.com.
———. "Forget 'Freedom': Good Riddance to WTC Moniker." *New York Post*, March 30, 2009, 23. https://nypost.com.
———. "From Zero to 100: Is It Right That New York's Most Hallowed Ground Has Become Party Central?" *New York Post*, September 11, 2016, 34. https://nypost.com.
Cutkomp, Aubree. "Saratoga Arts Tempered by Memory Sculpture: An Apparent End to the Controversy." *Thefreegeorge*, August 16, 2011. http://thefreegeorge.com.
Darton, Eric. "The Janus Face of Architectural Terrorism: Minoru Yamasaki, Mohammad Atta and the World Trade Center." *Opendemocracy.net*, November 8, 2001. www.opendemocracy.net.
Davidson, Justin. "Getting to 9/11: How a Museum's Creators Memorialized Our Collective Agony." *New York Magazine*, May 14, 2014.

de Certeau, Michel. "Walking in the City." In *The Practice of Everyday Life*, translated by Steven Rendell, 91–110. Berkeley: University of California Press, 1984.

de Montebello, Philippe. "The Iconic Power of an Artifact." *New York Times*, September 25, 2001. www.nytimes.com.

DeLappe, Joseph, and David Simpson. "Virtual Commemoration: The Iraqi Memorial Project." *Critical Inquiry* 37, no. 4 (Summer 2011): 615–26.

DenHoed, Andrea. "The Transformation of Calatrava's Oculus on the Anniversary of 9/11." *New Yorker*, September 11, 2017. www.newyorker.com.

Doss, Erika. *Memorial Mania: Public Feeling in America*. Chicago: University of Chicago Press, 2010.

Dowd, Maureen. "The Unbearable Lightness of Memory." *New York Times*, November 30, 2003. www.nytimes.com.

Duckworth, Tammy. "Tucker Carlson Doesn't Know What Patriotism Is." *New York Times*, July 9, 2020. www.nytimes.com.

Dunlap, David W. "A Memorial Inscription's Grim Origins." *New York Times*, April 3, 2014. www.nytimes.com.

———. "Freedom Center in Doubt." *New York Times*, September 25, 2005. www.nytimes.com.

———. "Governor Bars Freedom Center at Ground Zero." *New York Times*, September 29, 2005. www.nytimes.com.

———. "No Grand Opening Planned for $4 Billion Transit Hub." *New York Times*, February 24, 2016. www.nytimes.com.

———. "On Time Lapse Rocket Ride to Trade Center's Top, Glimpse of Doomed Tower." *New York Times*, April 19, 2005. www.nytimes.com.

Dunlap, David W., and Susan C. Beachy. "Seeking the Final Faces for a 9/11 Tapestry of Grief, Loss, Life and Joy." *New York Times*, September 10, 2016. www.nytimes.com.

Dunlap, David W., and Todd Heisler. "1 World Trade Center Gains Popularity in the Pantheon of New York Kitsch." *New York Times*, September 7, 2016. www.nytimes.com.

Dupré, Judith. *One World Trade Center: Biography of the Building*. New York: Little, Brown, 2016.

Edelman, Susan. "9/11 Memorial Paying Security Firm $1 million to Patrol Site." *New York Post*, November 17, 2018. https://nypost.com.

———. "9/11 Memorial Still Operating at a Loss." *New York Post*, December 9, 2017. https://nypost.com.

———. "The 9/11 Museum's Absurd Gift Shop." *New York Post*, May 18, 2014. https://nypost.com.

Efimenko, Alexandra. *On Doves, Dinosaurs, and Shopping Cathedrals: The World Trade Center Hub and the Tale of Redevelopment*. Master's thesis, Gallatin School of Individualized Study, New York University, 2018.

Equal Justice Initiative. *Lynching in America: Confronting the Legacy of Racial Terror*. 3rd ed. Montgomery, AL: EJI, 2017. https://eji.org.

———. *The Legacy Museum: From Enslavement to Mass Incarceration*. Montgomery, AL: EJI, 2018.

Essen, Patrick. "State of the Art in Memory Studies: An Interview with Andreas Huyssen." *Politika*, June 2018. www.politika.io.

Farrell, Stephen. "In 'Ceremonial Transfer,' Remains of 9/11 Victims Are Moved to Memorial." *New York Times*, May 10, 2014, A20. www.nytimes.com.

Fast Company. "A Tour of the 9/11 Museum with the Man Who Designed It." September 11, 2017. www.youtube.com/watch?v=JSP5xbZCN8A.

Fazzare, Elizabeth. "Santiago Calatrava Explains How He Designed the Oculus for Future Generations." *Architectural Digest*, October 24, 2017. www.architecturaldigest.com.

Fedorinova, Yuliya. "One World Trade Center Reveals Yet Another Problem for Steel." *Bloomberg*, August 29, 2017. www.bloomberg.com.

Fernandez, Rodrigo, Annelore Hofman, and Manuel B. Aalbers. "London and New York as a Safe Deposit Box for the Transnational Wealth Elite." *Environment and Planning A* 48, no. 12 (2016): 2443–61.

Filkins, Dexter. *The Forever War*. New York: Vintage, 2009.

Filler, Martin. "At the Edge of the Abyss." *New York Review of Books*, September 21, 2011. www.nybooks.com.

———. "New York's Vast Flop." *New York Review of Books*, March 9, 2017. www.nybooks.com.

———. "The Bird Man." *New York Review of Books*, December 15, 2005. www.nybooks.com.

Finkel, David. *Thank You for Your Service*. New York: Picador, 2013.

———. *Thank You for Your Service*, film, directed by Jason Hall, 2017.

Finnegan, William. "Monument." *New Yorker*, June 25, 2007. www.newyorker.com.

Fischl, Eric. "A Memorial That's True to 9/11." *New York Times*, December 19, 2003. www.nytimes.com.

Fleetwood, Nicole R. *Marking Time: Art in the Age of Mass Incarceration*. Cambridge, MA: Harvard University Press, 2020.

Foer, Franklin. "Russian Style Kleptocracy Is Infiltrating America." *Atlantic*, March 2019. www.theatlantic.com.

Fox News Insider. "FNC Reporter Donates Brick from Bin Laden Compound to 9/11 Museum." July 6, 2014. http://insider.foxnews.com.

Friedman, Devin, and the Editors of GQ. *A Soldier's Portfolio: This Is Our War: Servicemen's Photographs of Life in Iraq*. New York: Artisan, 2006.

Frost, Laura. "No Safe Spaces: Notes on the National September 11 Museum." *Journal of Urban Cultural Studies* 4, nos. 1&2 (2017): 221–39. https://doi.org/10.1386/jucs.4.1-2.221_1.

Gell, Aaron. "George W. Bush Opens Up about Veterans, Iraq, and the Healing Power of Art." *Task & Purpose*, March 3, 2017. https://taskandpurpose.com.

Gilbertson, Ashley. *Bedrooms of the Fallen*. Chicago: University of Chicago Press, 2014.

Gladstone, Brooke. "The Worst Thing We've Ever Done." *On the Media*, June 1, 2018. www.wnycstudios.org.

Godfrey, Mark. "Questionnaire: In What Ways Have Artists, Academics, and Cultural Institutions Responded to the U.S.-Led Invasion and Occupation of Iraq?" *October* 123 (Winter 2008): 69–70.

Goldberger, Paul. "Beyond the Hype, Santiago Calatrava's $4 Billion Transportation Hub Is a Genuine People's Cathedral." *Vanity Fair*, March 2, 2016. www.vanityfair.com.

———. "Too Rich, Too Tall, Too Thin?" *Vanity Fair* 56, no. 5 (May 2014). www.vanityfair.com.

———. *Up from Zero: Politics, Architecture, and the Rebuilding of New York*. New York: Random House, 2004.

Goldhagen, Sarah Williams. "One World Trade Center." *Architectural Record*, January 16, 2015. www.architecturalrecord.com.

———. "Santiago Calatrava's Overrated Architecture." *New Republic*, January 22, 2006. https://newrepublic.com.

Gonchar, Joann. "World Trade Center Transportation Hub," *Architectural Review*, April 1, 2016.

Goodman, Amy. "105,000 Tattoos: Iraqi Artists Wafaa Bilal Turns His Own Body into a Canvas to Commemorate Dead Iraqis and Americans." *Democracy Now*, March 9, 2010. www.democracynow.org.

Gopnik, Adam. "Stones and Bones: Visiting the 9/11 Memorial and Museum." *New Yorker*, July 7 & 14, 2014. www.newyorker.com.

Gordon, Avery. *Ghostly Matters: Haunting and the Sociological Imagination*. Minneapolis: University of Minnesota Press, 2008. First published 1997.

Graham, Stephen. *Vertical: The City from Satellites to Bunkers*. London: Verso, 2016.

Grandin, Greg. *The End of the Myth: From the Frontier to the Border Wall in the Mind of America*. New York: Metropolitan Books, 2019.

Greenspan, Elizabeth. *Battle for Ground Zero: Inside the Political Struggle to Rebuild the World Trade Center*. New York: Palgrave Macmillan, 2013.

Greenwald, Alice M. "Through the Lens of Memory: Creating the 9/11 Memorial Museum." In *No Day Shall Erase You: The Story of 9/11 As Told at the National September 11 Memorial Museum*, 11–30. New York: Skira Rozzoli, 2016.

Hackett, Regina. "This Memorial Destined for Oblivion." *Seattle PI*, September 10, 2006, http://www.seattlepi.com.

Hamill, Sean D. "Picture Made on 9/11 Takes a Toll on Photographer." *New York Times*, September 10, 2007. www.nytimes.com.

———. "When Serenity Ended in Shanksville on 9/11." *Coalspeaker*, https://coalspeaker.com.

Hasian, Marouf, Jr., and Nicholas Paliewicz. *Racial Terrorism: A Rhetorical Investigation of Lynching*. Jackson: University of Mississippi Press, 2021.

———. "Taking the Reparatory Turn at the National Memorial for Peace and Justice." *International Journal for Communication*, 14 (2020): 2227–45. http://ijoc.com.

———. "The National Memorial for Peace and Justice, Dark Tourist Argumentation, and Civil Rights Memoryscapes." *Atlantic Journal of Communication*, April 2020: 1–17. https://doi.org/10.1080/15456870.2020.1741590.

Hawthorne, Christopher. "Reading Symbolism in the Sept. 11 Era." *Los Angeles Times*, October 5, 2005. www.latimes.com.

Helm, Angela. "The New Lynching Memorial and Legacy Museum Force Us to Bear Witness to Our Whole American Truth." *Root*, April 25, 2018. www.theroot.com.

Hennes, Ted. "Reflections on the Opening of the 9/11 Memorial Museum, from the Lead Exhibition Designer." TED Blog, May 22, 2014. https://blog.ted.com.

Hersh, Seymour M. *The Killing of Osama bin Laden*. London: Verso, 2016.

Hill, Mike. "Museum as Megamachine: On the 9/11 Memorial Museum, with a Nod to Lewis Mumford." Open Humanities Press, October 17, 2014. http://openhumanitiespress.org.

Hirsch, Faye. "In Memoriam." *Art in America* (April 2008): 132–33, 178.

Hobbs, Allyson, and Nell Freudenberger. "A Visit to Montgomery's Legacy Museum." *New Yorker*, July 17, 2018. www.newyorker.com.

Holden, Stephen. "The Broken Souls of Men Turned into War Machines." *New York Times*, September 15, 2006. www.nytimes.com.

Horton Alex, and Aaron Gregg. "Use of Military Contractors Shrouds True Costs of War. Washington Wants It That Way, Study Says." *Washington Post*, June 30, 2020, www.washingtonpost.com.

Huxtable, Ada Louise. "A Landmark Destination: The Bus Station." *Wall Street Journal*, June 15, 2004, D7. www.wsj.com.

———. "The New York Process: Don't Expect Anything Uplifting from the Pols and Realtors Now Pondering the WTC Site," *Wall Street Journal*, September 17, 2001, A20. www.wsj.com.

———. "Too Much of a Good Thing?" *Wall Street Journal*, December 8, 2005, D8. www.wsj.com.

Huyssen, Andreas. "International Human Rights and the Politics of Memory: Limits and Challenges." *Criticism* 53, no. 4 (2011): 607–24.

———. *Present Pasts: Urban Palimpsests and the Politics of Memory*. Stanford, CA: Stanford University Press, 2003.

———. *Twilight Memories: Marking Time in a Culture of Amnesia*. New York: Routledge, 1995.

Ifill, Sherrilyn. *On the Courthouse Lawn: Confronting the Legacy of Lynching in the Twenty-First Century*. New York: Beacon, 2007.

Igielnik, Ruth, and Kim Parker. "Majorities of U.S. Veterans, Public Say the Wars in Iraq and Afghanistan Were Not Worth Fighting." Pew Research Center. www.pewresearch.org.

Immerwahr, Daniel. *How to Hide an Empire: A History of the Greater United States*. New York: Farrar, Straus and Giroux, 2019.

Ismay, John. "A Navy Veteran Had a Question for the Feds in Portland. They Beat Him in Response." *New York Times*, July 20, 2020. www.nytimes.com.

———. "At Least 37 Million People Have Been Displaced by America's War on Terror." *New York Times Magazine*, September 8, 2020. www.nytimes.com.
Jackson, Kuntrell. *Through All the Pain I Still Evolved*. Self-published, 2020, www.kuntrelljackson.com.
Jacobs, Karrie. "Letter from Ground Zero: Delirious World Trade." *Architect*, July 30, 2014. www.architectmagazine.com.
———. "Calatrava's Transportation Hub Finally Takes Flight." *Architect*, March 3, 2016. www.architectmagazine.com.
Jones, Kevin L. "KPIX Anchor-Turned-Sculptor Contributes Piece to Lynching Memorial." KQED, April 29, 2018. www.kqed.org.
Jordan, John W. "Transcending Hollywood: The Referendum on *United 93* as Cinematic Memorial." *Critical Studies in Media Communication* 25, no. 2 (June 2008): 196–223.
Kalmbacker, Colin. "'Wall of Veterans' Arriving in Portland to Protect Black Lives Matter Protestor from Trump's DHS Troops." *MSN News*, July 25, 2020. www.msn.com.
Kamat, Anjali. "Interview with Iraqi Artist Wafaa Bilal." *Arab Studies Journal* 18, no. 1 (Spring 2010): 316–29.
Kandell, Steve. "The Worst Day of My Life Is Now New York's Hottest Tourist Attraction." *BuzzFeed News*, May 19, 2014. www.buzzfeednews.com.
Kaplan, Amy. "Violent Belongings and the Question of Empire Today: Presidential Address to the American Studies Association, Hartford, Connecticut, October 17, 2003." *American Quarterly* 56, no. 1 (March 2004): 1–18.
Kaplan, Caren. *Aerial Aftermaths: Wartime from Above*. Durham, NC: Duke University Press, 2018.
Kennicott, Phillip. "A Powerful Memorial in Montgomery Remembers the Victims of Lynching." *Washington Post*, April 24, 2018. www.washingtonpost.com.
———. "The 9/11 Memorial Museum Doesn't Just Display Artifacts, It Ritualizes Grief on a Loop." *Washington Post*, June 7, 2014. www.washingtonpost.com.
Keyser, Tom. "Controversy Delays 9-11 Memorial 'Tempered by Memory.'" *Times Union*, September 11, 2011. www.timesunion.com.
Kim, Caitlin. "Veterans Say It's Not Too Soon to Build a National Memorial for the Afghanistan and Iraq Wars." American Homefront Project, March 3, 2020, https://americanhomefront.wunc.org.
Kim, Elizabeth. "Oculus Skylight, Which Stayed Closed for 9/11 Tribute, Will Need $200,000 Seal." *Gothamist*, September 23, 2019.
Kimmelman, Michael. "A Soaring Emblem of New York, and Its Upside-Down Priorities." *New York Times*, November 30, 2014, A1. www.nytimes.com.
———. "Architecture: Ground Zero Finally Grows Up." *New York Times*, February 1, 2004. www.nytimes.com.
———. "Art/Architecture; Out of Minimalism, Monuments to Memory." *New York Times*, January 13, 2002. www.nytimes.com.
———. "Finding Space for the Living at a Memorial." *New York Times*, May 28, 2014. www.nytimes.com.

———. "Moynihan Train Hall. It's Stunning and a First Step." *New York Times*, January 14, 2021, C1. www.nytimes.com.

———. "Santiago Calatrava's Transit Hub Is a Soaring Symbol of a Boondoggle," *New York Times*, March 3, 2016, C1. www.nytimes.com.

Klein, Ezra. "Bryan Stevenson on How America can Heal." *Ezra Klein Show*, podcast, July 20, 2020. www.vox.com.

Klein, Lauren F. "Timescape and Memory: Visualizing Big Data at the 9/11 Memorial Museum." In *The Routledge Companion to Media Studies and Digital Humanities*, edited by Jentery Sayers, 433–42. New York: Routledge, 2018.

Koblin, John. "A Mad Dash to Points South." *New York Times*, July 23, 2014. www.nytimes.com.

Kuang, Cliff. "The Near-Impossible Challenge of Designing the 9/11 Museum." *Wired*, May 14, 2014. www.wired.com.

Kushner, Marc. "Why the Buildings of the Future Will Be Shaped by . . . You." TED Talk, March 2014. www.ted.com.

Lamster, Mark. "Hope Rises from Ground Zero." *Architectural Review*, October 2011, 31.

Landsberg, Alison. "Memory vs. History: The Politics of Temporality at the Legacy Museum in Montgomery, Alabama." In *The Routledge Memory Activism Handbook*, edited by Jenny Wustenberg and Yifat Gutman. New York: Routledge, forthcoming.

———. "Post-Postracial America: The Politics of Memory at Legacy Museum in Montgomery." Paper presented at E Pluribus Unum conference, Clark University, Worcester, MA, April 2019.

Lange, Alexandra. "Is Instagram Ruining Architecture?" *New York Times*, September 7, 2019. www.nytimes.com.

Langewiesche, William. *American Ground: Unbuilding the World Trade Center*. New York: North Point, 2002.

Last, Jonathan V. "The Memorials We Deserve." *Weekly Standard*, May 28, 2007, 23–29.

Leitz, Lisa. *Fighting for Peace: Veterans and Military Families in the Anti-Iraq War Movement*. Minneapolis: University of Minnesota Press, 2014.

Lepore, Jill. *These Truths: A History of the United States*. New York: Norton, 2018.

Levin, Sam. "Lynching Memorial Leaves Some Quietly Seething: 'Let Sleeping Dogs Lie.'" *Guardian*, April 28, 2018. www.theguardian.com.

Levine, Lester J. *9/11 Memorial Visions: Innovative Concepts from the 2003 World Trade Center Site Memorial Competition*. Jefferson, NC: McFarland, 2016.

Lipton, Eric, and James Glanz, "DNA Science Pushed to the Limit in Identifying the Dead of Sept. 11." *New York Times*, April 22, 2002, A1. www.nytimes.com.

Londoño, Ernesto. "Returning Home, a Veteran War Reporter Wrestled with Old Wounds." *New York Times*, December 15, 2004. www.nytimes.com.

Lubell, Sam. "9/11 Memorials Aren't Limited to NY and DC—They're Everywhere." *Wired*, September 10, 2016. www.wired.com.

Markovitz, Jonathan. *Legacies of Lynching: Racial Violence and Memory*. Minneapolis: University of Minnesota Press, 2004.

Martens, Raina, and Bill Robertson. "How the Soil Remembers Plantation Slavery." *Edgeeffects*, March 28, 2019. https://edgeeffects.net.

Martin, Reinhold. "The Demagogue Takes the Stage." *Placesjournal*, March 2017. https://placesjournal.org.

McKee, Bradford. "Memory Block: The Pentagon's Inaccessible Memorial." *Slate*, March 27, 2003. https://slate.com.

Mirzoeff, Nicholas. *The Right to Look: A Counterhistory of Visuality*. Durham, NC: Duke University Press, 2011.

Mock, Brentin. "Why We Should Stop Calling It the 'Great Migration.'" *Citylab*, July 4, 2018. www.citylab.com.

Molotch, Harvey. "How the 9/11 Museum Gets Us." *Public Books*, September 1, 2014. www.publicbooks.org.

Montgomery, David. "A Wave of War Memorials Is Coming to D.C. Are We All at Peace with That?" *Washington Post*, July 31, 2018. www.washingtonpost.com.

Murphy, Michael. "Architecture That's Built to Heal." TED talk, February 2016, https://massdesigngroup.org.

Muschamp, Herbert. "An Appraisal; PATH Station Becomes a Procession of Flight." *New York Times*, January 23, 2004. www.nytimes.com.

Nessen, Shawn Christian, David Edmond Lounsbury, and Stephen P. Hetz. *War Surgery in Afghanistan and Iraq: A Series of Cases, 2003–2007*. Falls Church, VA: Office of the Surgeon General/Borden Institute, 2008.

Newkirk, Vann R., II. "The Great Land Robbery." *Atlantic*, September 2019. theatlantic.com.

Ng, Alfred, and Dan Friedman, "9/11 Museum, Which Sits on Unidentified Remains of Attack Victims, Hosts Alcohol-Fueled Party Night before Opening." *New York Daily News*, May 21, 2014. www.nydailynews.com.

Nobel, Philip. *Sixteen Acres: Architecture and the Outrageous Struggle for the Future of Ground Zero*. New York: Metropolitan Books, 2005.

Nocera, Joe. "9/11's White Elephant." *New York Times*, August 19, 2011. www.nytimes.com.

Noel, Josh. "The Countryside of 9/11." *Chicago Tribune*, August 15, 2013. www.chicagotribune.com.

O'Neill, Luke. "Of Course There Is a Gift Shop at the 9/11 Museum." *Mediaite*, May 18, 2014. www.mediaite.com.

Ong, Aihwa. "Hyperbuilding: Spectacle, Speculation and the Hyperspace of Sovereignty." In *Worlding Cities: Asian Experiments and the Art of Being Global*, edited by Ananya Roy and Aihwa Ong, 205–26. Hoboken, NJ: Blackwell, 2011.

Opotow, Susan, and Karyna Pryiomka. "Memory, Site, and Object: The September 11 Memorial Museum." In *New York After 9/11*, edited by Susan Opotow and Zachary Baron Shemtob, 230–51. New York: Fordham University Press, 2018.

Opotow, Susan, and Zachary Baron Shemtob, eds. *New York After 9/11*. New York: Fordham University Press, 2018.

Otterman, Sharon. "Film at 9/11 Museum Sets Off Clash over Reference to Islam." *New York Times*, April 24, 2014. www.nytimes.com.
Ouroussoff, Nicolai. "An Appraisal; Tower of Impregnability, The Sort Politicians Love." *New York Times*, June 30, 2005. www.nytimes.com.
Page, Sydney. "Upset by Veterans Who Stormed the Capitol, These Vets Decided to Clean Up Trash the Mob Left on the Streets of D.C." *Washington Post*, January 14, 2021. www.washingtonpost.com.
Pager, Tyler. "Keeping Its Promise to Families, New York Identifies Another 9/11 Victim." *New York Times*, July 25, 2018, A21. www.nytimes.com.
Paliewicz, Nicholas S. "Bent but Not Broken: Remembering Vulnerability and Resiliency at the National September 11 Memorial Museum." *Southern Communication Journal* 82, no. 1 (2017): 1–14. https://doi.org/10.1080/1041794X.2016.1252422.
Pasnik, Mark, Jeffrey Mansfield, and Regina Yiho Yang, eds. *Justice Is Beauty*. New York: Monacelli Press, 2019.
Pederson, Martin C. "The Other Memorials." *Metropolis* (September 2011): 66–73.
Peltier, Heidi. "The Growth of the 'Camo Economy' and the Commercialization of the Post-9/11 Wars." Watson Institute for International and Public Affairs, Brown University, June 30, 2020. https://watson.brown.edu.
Peraica, Ana. "An Interview with Joseph DeLappe." In *Victims Symptom (PTSD and Culture)*, edited by Ana Peraica, 70–72. Theory on Demand No. 3. Amsterdam: Institute of Networked Cultures, 2008. https://www.networkcultures.org.
Philip, Abby. "Families Infuriated by 'Crass Commercialism' of 9/11 Museum Gift Shop." *Washington Post*, May 19, 2014. www.washingtonpost.com.
Picard, Charmaine. "'Public Art Is Propaganda, Frankly': Hank Willis Thomas Discusses Gun Violence and the Urgent Need for Alternative Memorials." *Art Newspaper*, October 31, 2019. www.theartnewspaper.com.
Pierce, Lori, and Kaily Heitz. "Say Their Names." *American Quarterly* 72, no. 4 (December 2020): 961–77.
Plitt, Amy. "NYC's Supertall Skyscraper Boom, Mapped." *NYcurbed*, March 6, 2020. http://nycurbed.com.
Poole, Ross. "Performing Trauma: Commemorating 9/11 in Downtown Manhattan." *Memory Studies* 13, no. 4 (2018): 452–69. https://doi.org/10.1177/1750698017749979.
Potter, Amanda. "Collecting Leaves, Assembling Memory: Jane Hammond's *Fallen* and the Function of War Memorials." *Archives of American Art Journal* 47, nos. 3–4 (Fall 2008): 67–77.
Presser, Lizzie. "Kicked off the Land." *New Yorker*, July 15, 2019. www.newyorker.com.
Ramirez, Jan Seidler. "The Complexities of Displaying World Trade Center Dust." In *No Day Shall Erase You: The Story of 9/11 As Told at the National September 11 Memorial Museum*, edited by Alice M. Greenwald, 183–87. New York: Skira Rozzoli, 2016.
Rauch, Noah. "A Balancing Act: Interpreting Tragedy at the 9/11 Memorial Museum." *Journal of Museum Education* 43, no. 1 (2018): 16–21.

Regan, Michael D. "What Happened to the Remnants of the World Trade Center?" *PBS Newshour*, September 10, 2016. www.pbs.org/newshour.

Rhodes, Ben. "The 9/11 Era Is Over: The Coronavirus Pandemic and a Chapter of History That Should Have Expired Long Ago." *Atlantic*, April 6, 2020. www.theatlantic.com.

Riley, Alexander T. *Angel Patriots: The Crash of United Flight 93 and the Myth of America*. New York: New York University Press, 2015.

Rosenblatt, Adam. "Aparcíon con Vida: Disappearance and the Politics of the Counterfactual from Argentina to Ayotzinapa." Paper presented at the Latin American Studies Association Annual Meeting, Lima, Peru, 2017.

Rosengaard, Mikkel. "Calatrava's Oculus," *Architectural Review* 238, no. 1422 (August 2015): 8–9.

Rothberg, Michael. *Multidirectional Memory: Remembering the Holocaust in the Age of Decolonization*. Stanford, CA: Stanford University Press, 2009.

Roy, Ananya. "The Infrastructures of Assent: Professions in the Age of Trumpism." *Avery Review* 21 (January 20, 2017): 5–15.

Rybczynski, Witold. "Black Holes: There Is Nothing Comforting about the 9/11 Memorial." *Slate*, September 10, 2011. https://slate.com.

Saffron, Inga. "Review: Gripping Site." *Metropolis* (September 2016): 138–39.

Sagalyn, Lynne B. *Power at Ground Zero: Politics, Money, and the Remaking of Lower Manhattan*. New York: Oxford University Press, 2016.

Sanchez, Gabriel H. "22 of the Most Powerful 9/11 Monuments around the World." *Buzzfeed*, September 11, 2016. www.buzzfeed.com.

Saul, Michael Howard. "Mayor Bloomberg Wants Every Billionaire on Earth to Live in New York City." *Wall Street Journal*, September 20, 2013. www.wsj.com.

Savage, Kirk. *Monument Wars: Washington, D.C., the National Mall, and the Transformation of the Memorial Landscape*. Berkeley: University of California Press, 2009.

———. "What Will Our Iraq Memorial Look Like?" *Washington Post*, May 27, 2011. www.washingtonpost.com.

Schifman, Jonathan. "The Entire History of Steel." *Popular Mechanics*, July 9, 2018. www.popularmechanics.com.

Schilling, Dave. "World Trade Center Mall Offers Change to Reflect on 9/11—with Retail Therapy." *Guardian*, September 11, 2016. http://theguardian.com.

Senk, Sarah. "The Memory Exchange: Public Mourning at the National 9/11 Memorial Museum." *Canadian Review of American Studies* 48, no. 2 (2018): 254–76. https://doi.org/10.3138/cras.2017.029.

Shabout, Nada. "Dafatir: Testimonies of Forgotten Times." In *Theater of Operations: The Gulf Wars 1991–2011*, edited by Peter Eleey and Ruba Katrib: 181–203. New York: MoMA PS1, 2019.

Shapira, Harel. "Reflecting Absence: An Interview with Michael Arad." *Public Books*, August 20, 2013. www.publicbooks.org.

Shemtob, Zachary Baron, Patrick Sweeney, and Susan Opotow. "Conflict and Change: New York's Birth after 9/11." In *New York after 9/11*, edited by Susan Opotow and Zachary Baron Shemtob, 14–40. New York: Fordham University Press, 2018.

Shulman, Michael. "Impact Steel: The Force of Violence." In *The Stories They Tell: Artifacts from the National September 11 Memorial Museum, A Journey of Remembrance*, edited by Clifford Chanin and Alice M. Greenwald, 30–34. New York: Skira Rizzoli, 2013.

Silliman, Stephen W. "The 'Old West' in the Middle East: U.S. Military Metaphors in Real and Imagined Indian Country." *American Anthropologist* 110, no. 2 (June 2008): 237–47.

Singh, Nikhil Pal. *Race and America's Long War*. Berkeley: University of California Press, 2017.

Sion, Brigitte, ed. *Death Tourism: Disaster Sites as Recreational Landscape*. New York: Seagull Books, 2014.

Smith, Jennifer. "9/11 Museum a Tough Sell at Home." *Wall Street Journal*, May 23, 2016. www.wsj.com.

Sodaro, Amy. *Exhibiting Atrocity: Memorial Museums and the Politics of Past Violence*. New Brunswick, NJ: Rutgers University Press, 2018.

——— . "Prosthetic Trauma and Politics in the National September 11 Memorial Museum." *Memory Studies* 12, no. 2 (2019): 117–29.

Sontag, Susan. "Regarding the Torture of Others." *New York Times*, May 23, 2004. www.nytimes.com.

Sorkin, Michael. "Lower Manhattan and the Tragedy of Business as Usual." *Metropolis*, September 8, 2014. www.metropolismag.com.

Stein, Samuel. *Capital City: Gentrification and the Real Estate State*. New York: Verso, 2019.

Steinhauer, Jennifer. "Trump Proposes Putting Up 2 Towers at Trade Center Site." *New York Times*, May 19, 2005. www.nytimes.com.

Stevenson, Bryan. "A Presumption of Guilt." *New York Review of Books*, July 13, 2017. www.nybooks.com.

——— . *Just Mercy: A Story of Justice and Redemption*. New York: Spiegel & Grau, 2014.

Story, Louise, and Stephanie Saul. "Towers of Secrecy: Stream of Foreign Wealth Flows to Elite New York Real Estate." *New York Times*, February 8, 2015, A1. www.nytimes.com.

Sturken, Marita. "Containing Absence, Shaping Presence at Ground Zero." *Ghosts, Exhumations, and Uncomfortable Truths* in *Memory Studies* 13, no. 3 (2020): 313–21.

——— . *Tangled Memories: The Vietnam War, the AIDS Epidemic, and the Politics of Remembering*. Berkeley: University of California Press, 1997.

——— . "The 9/11 Memorial Museum and the Remaking of Ground Zero," *American Quarterly* 67, no. 2 (June 2015): 471–90.

——— . "The Objects that Lived: The 9/11 Museum and Material Transformation," *Memory Studies* 9, no. 1 (2016): 13–26.

——— . *Tourists of History: Memory, Kitsch, and Consumerism from Oklahoma City to Ground Zero*. Durham, NC: Duke University Press, 2007.

Sullivan, Kevin. "A New 9/11 Memorial to Flight 93: 'Our Loved Ones Left a Legacy for All of Us.'" *Washington Post*, September 10, 2015. www.washingtonpost.com.

Tangel, Andrew, and Keiko Morris. "Station Embodies Resolve." *Wall Street Journal*, February 13–14, 2016, A15. www.wsj.com.

Tharoor, Ishaan. "Is the 9/11 Era Over?" *Washington Post*, September 11, 2020. www.washingtonpost.com.

Thompson, J. William. *From Memory to Memorial: Shanksville, America, and Flight 93*, University Park: Pennsylvania State University Press, 2017.

Toobin, Jeffrey. "The Legacy of Lynching, on Death Row." *New Yorker*, August 22, 2016. www.newyorker.com.

Trebay, Guy. "A Moment in Time Captured in Pieces." *New York Times*, August 13, 2014. www.nytimes.com.

Tuck, Eve, and K. Wayne Yang. "R-Words: Refusing Research." In *Humanizing Research: Decolonizing Qualitative Inquiry with Youth and Communities*, edited by Django Paris and Maisha T. Winn, 223–47. Thousand Oaks, CA: Sage, 2014.

Vartanian, Hrag. "It's Time to End the 9/11 Tribute in Light." *Hyperallergic*, September 10, 2020. www.hyperallergic.com.

Vergara, Camilo José. "Picturing the Lost." *Public Books*, November 26, 2020. www.publicbooks.com.

Wagner-Pacifici, Robin. "Portraits of Courage: Caught in the Sovereign's Gaze." *European Journal of Cultural Studies* 24, no.1 (2021): 107–22. https://doi.org/10.1177/1367549420985844.

Wainwright, Oliver. "Snapping Point: How the World's Leading Architects Fell under the Instagram Spell." *Guardian*, November 23, 2018. www.theguardian.com.

Weisser, Amy. "Archaeology, Architecture, and Creating a Space for Memory." In *No Day Shall Erase You: The Story of 9/11 as Told at the National September 11 Memorial Museum*, edited by Alice M. Greenwald, 58–61. New York: Skira Rozzoli, 2016.

Williams, Paul. *Memorial Museums: The Global Rush to Commemorate Atrocities*. New York: Berge, 2007.

Yeazel, Chris. "A Global War on Terror Memorial Is Unnecessary." *War on the Rocks*, June 28, 2019. https://warontherocks.com.

Young, James, E. "Sites of Reckoning Symposium: Memorial, Museums & Fractured Truth(s) in the Aftermaths of Mass Violence." Keynote address, George State University, March 2020.

———. "The Memorial Process: A Juror's Report from Ground Zero." In *The Contentious City: The Politics of Recovery in New York City*, edited by John Mollenkopf, 140–62. New York: Russell Sage Foundation, 2005.

———. *The Stages of Memory: Reflections on Memorial Art, Loss, and the Spaces Between*. Amherst: University of Massachusetts Press, 2016.

Zurcher, Anthony. "9/11 Museum Gift Shop: Hoodies and Anger." *BBC News*, May 21, 2014.

INDEX

About Face: Veterans Against the War, 208
abstraction: as architect/terrorist concept, 137–138; as memorialization aesthetic, 15, 61, 199, 250, 251, 254, 258, 261; in 9/11 memorials, 15, 42, 55; in skyscraper designs, 138. *See also* Arad, Michael; Legacy Museum; minimalism; National Memorial for Peace and Justice; steel; Vietnam Veterans Memorial
Abu Ghraib prison (Iraq), 17, 114, 183, 207, 219, 227
Adelman, Rebecca, 211
Age of Terror: Art Since 9/11, exhibit (Imperial War Museum, London), 186
AIDS Memorial Quilt, 268
Akoto-Bamfo, Kwame, 255–256, 259–266, 260
Alexander, Elizabeth, 254
al-Qaeda, 11, 35, 106, 112, 113, 137, 152
American Civil War and Reconstruction. *See* Legacy Museum; monument removals
American empire, 18–21, 112, 208, 217, 219–220
American exceptionalism: in American innocence narrative, 8, 10, 19, 234, 262, 264; in defining post-9/11 era, 8, 127; in national identity, 8, 18, 19, 234, 262, 264; in production of 9/11 memory, 12, 27–29, 51, 56, 74, 127–128; role of memory in, 12, 16. *See also* 9/11
American Friends Service Committee, 191
American Institute for Architects (AIA), 145

American Servicemen and Women Who Have Died in Iraq and Afghanistan (But Not Including . . . , project (Prince), 196–198
A Million Thanks, book and film (Finkel), 211
and Counting, performative (Bilal), 202–203
Arad, Michael: design of National 9/11 Memorial Glade, 61–62; minimalism of, 55; name designs in 9/11 memorial, 57; pool designs for 9/11 Memorial, 26, 53–55
architecture: absence, loss and evocations by, 25, 53; absence and void as Ground Zero, 51–63, 106; aesthetic strategies of, 15, 53, 60, 67, 69, 138, 156, 159–160, 164–165, 169, 171, 233, 244, 250; of airport memorials, 37–38; as anti-humanist, 138; authenticity of site in, 27–28, 45–46, 51, 83, 87, 89, 106, 134; celebrity architects in, 22, 46, 135, 145, 245; centrality of, 5, 15–16, 22, 52–53, 127, 134–141, 135, 146, 159, 161, 170, 171; gift shop themes of, 124–125; at high-end, 22, 51, 134, 136, 141–145, 169; justice strategies in, 145–146, 244–245; as kitsch, 151, 162, 169; memory experience and, 2, 5, 15–16, 16, 22, 25, 87, 124, 134, 160; negative space in, 25; profession of, 145–146, 148, 170; real estate interests and, 22, 133–136, 141–146, 148, 156, 158; rebuilding Lower Manhattan and, 129–171; scale and, 28, 56, 85–87, 134–135, 137, 163;

303

architecture (cont.)
  security design and, 153–154; storytelling in, 106, 136, 151, 169, 233; symbolism in, 5, 15, 25, 58, 59, 135, 138, 139, 141, 142–144, 149, 151, 152, 159–162, 164–166, 169; terrorism experience and, 5, 136–138, 140; trauma responses and, 5, 15, 93, 169; visitors experience and, 22, 87, 124, 233, 246. *See also* Calatrava, Santiago; Libeskind, Daniel; Oculus (World Trade Center Transportation Hub, NYC); One World Trade Center; Silverstein, Larry (and Properties)
Arlington National Cemetery, 51, 217
Arlington West, memorial (Veterans for Peace, Santa Barbara, CA), 187–189, 187–190, 191, 207
Aronson, Jay, 100–101, 277–78n41
art: about counting, 186, 197; dafatir bookforms as, 187; drone warfare responses of, 204–206; justice strategies and, 240; loss evocation and, 173; museumization and, 95, 96–97, 216; post-9/11 wars and, 23, 172–178, 186, 186–206, 186–216, 204–216; steel in, 42; visibility politics and, 186–206
Associated Press, 65, 199
Atlantic, 144
Atta, Mohamed, 11, 137
audio: affect of, 22, 108, 111, 116, 127; in exhibitions, 22, 48, 64–65, 106, 108–111, 115–116, 127; recordings from 9/11, 22, 65, 105, 109, 110, 111, 278n61; storytelling and witnessing with, 108, 110–111, 115, 116, 176, 278n78
Auschwitz-Birkenau Memorial and Museum, 98
Awad, Nadia, 201

Bacevich, Andrew, 182–183
Bach, Josh, 124
Barton, Jake, 110, 115–117, 119, 233, 236, 240
Beamer, Lisa, 64

Beamer, Todd, 64, 65, 98, 100
Beckman, Julie, 46, 47, 48
Bedrooms of the Fallen, photography (Gilbertson), 173, 176–177, 182
benches, 46–49, 61, 66
Bennett, Joan, 98, 105
Berger, Joshua, 202
Berman, Nina, 214–216
Bern, Marc, 126
Bernstein, Tom A., 114
Beyer Binder Bell, 139
Biden, Joseph R.: COVID-19 memorialization by, 268; election of, 4; inauguration of, 268; January 6th Insurrection and, 265–266; in National September 11 Museum exhibit, 74
Biernoff, Suzannah, 214
Biggs, Sanford, 240
Bilal, Wafaa, 202–204
Bingham, Mark, 65
bin Laden, Osama, 11, 19; assassination of, 18, 79, 81; brick from compound (Pakistan) of, 79–82, 113
Bjarke Ingels (BIG), 156
Black Lives Matter, 1, 3, 15, 24, 207, 240, 267
Blackwell, Marlon, 145
Bloomberg, Michael, 84, 144
Bodnar, John, 184, 189–190, 206–207
Body Count, project/installation (Thomas), 202
Boston Marathon Memorial, 98
Breaux, Joel, 39
Bridle, James, 204
Brown, Bernard C., II, 47
Brown, Justin, 253
Brown, Michael, 240
Bullough, Oliver, 143
Burj Khalifa (Dubai), 142
Bush, George W.: administration of, 7, 11, 17, 113; art by, 212–214; Global War on Terror of, 7, 17, 18; Iraq war of, 113–114; in National September 11 Museum

exhibit, 74; *Portraits of Courage* book by, 212–214; reputation of, 20, 212–214; veteran events with, 212
Butler, Judith, 5, 103–4, 199

Cagüeñas, Diego, 25
Calatrava, Santiago, 14, 51, 135, 159–170
Cantor Fitzgerald, 98, 102
Carey, Michael and Mia, 172, 174
Carlson, Tucker, 207
Carr, Johnnie, 256
Chelsea Piers, 114
Cheney, Dick, 7, 20, 119, 214
Cheng, Irene, 245–246
Chicago Tribune, 72
Chief Medical Examiner, Office of (OCME, NYC), 100, 101, 277n40
Childs, David, 149–151, 152, 154, 156
Christine's Tree memorial (Eaton, CT), 37
Chrysler Building (NYC), 34, 133, 144
CIA (Central Intelligence Agency), 10, 79, 81
Circle, The, proposal (Janssen), 199
Citicorp Building (NYC), 133
Civil Rights Memorial (Montgomery, AL), 231
Clark, Louise, 189
Clinton, Hillary, 114, 117, 276n79; in National September 11 Museum exhibit, 74
Collateral Damage, installation (Engler), 202
Collateral Damage, performative (Berger), 202
Commemorative Works Act, 181–182
Condé Nast, 151, 154, 156, 167
Confederate monuments. *See* monument removals
Contini, Anita, 139
Cost of War, exhibit (Eyes Wide Open), 193
Cost of War Project, Brown University, 178

Cottom, Asia S., 47
Council on Tall Buildings and Urban Habitat, 152
COVID-19 Memorial Ceremony (Lincoln Memorial, WDC), 268
COVID-19 pandemic, 1, 2, 4, 6, 10, 11, 15, 18, 136, 145, 146, 148, 158, 266, 268–269
Crabapple, Molly, 236
Crawford, Anthony, 227–228
crises of 2020–21, 4, 11, 148, 225, 266; as end of post-9/11 era, 10
Cuozzo, Steve, 63, 151

Darton, Eric, 137–138
Davidson, Justin, 109
Davis, Jefferson, 226
Davis Brody Bond (DBB), 31, 85, 86, 87
death counts: of AIDS epidemic, 268; of Blacks by police, 1, 15; in comparisons, 1–3; of COVID-19 pandemic, 1, 3, 10, 268; Global War on Terror, 216; of Iraq war, 23; of lynchings, 23, 221, 226, 242–243, 251, 286n7; of 9/11, 1, 3, 8, 30, 31–32, 37, 57, 94, 98, 100; of post-9/11 wars, 8, 10, 16, 23, 179, 186, 198, 202, 202–204; as unidentified or undocumented, 30, 100; of World War II, 2, 3, 268. *See also* Chief Medical Examiner, Office of (OCME, NYC)
de Certeau, Michel, 131, 154
DeLappe, Joseph, 198–199, 201, 204, 206
de Portzamparc, Christian, 144
design: of audio retellings, 108; authenticity of site in, 48–49, 90; centrality of, 5, 21; by committee, 83–84; contests and competitions in, 48–49, 51–53, 67, 216; global memory in, 12; justice strategies in, 228, 233, 244–245; mediated experience in, 108, 115–116, 170; memory boom and, 15; memory experience and, 2, 5, 84–93; of merchandise, 124; name elements in memorialization and, 48–49, 57, 102; of narrative, 111–112;

design (*cont.*)
responses to terrorism and, 5; restraint in, 69, 72; scale and, 56, 61, 250–251; security and, 59, 135, 153–154; storytelling in, 69, 73, 108, 115; symbolism in, 5, 85, 139, 146, 149, 165, 263; of viewpoints, 69, 246, 253; visibility politics and, 198; visitor experience and, 86–87, 106, 120. *See also* figuration; minimalism; skyscrapers; steel
Dexter Avenue King Memorial Church (Montgomery, Al.), 231
Dickens, Rodney, 47
digital media: affect and, 114; collective memory and, 22, 114–120, 170; design of, 57, 83, 115, 116, 116–119, 233; difficult content and, 233; mapping with, 35; Oculus and, 167, 170; One World Observatory and, 130–132; post-9/11 wars and, 183, 185–186, 195, 202
DiNapoli, Thomas, 141
Di-Natale, Dominic, 79, 81
DNA identification, 100, 101, 228, 230, 254; and Community Soil Collection Project (EJI), 228, 230
Dog Tag Memorial Garden (North Church, Boston), 191
Doss, Erika, 5, 14, 36, 39, 76, 189–190, 190, 224, 261
Dover Air Force Base, 184
Drawing Center, 85
drone warfare, 114, 131; artistic responses to, 204–206; during Obama Administration, 7, 17, 180, 182. *See also* Global War on Terror
Dubin, Jorge, 45
Du Bois, W. E. B., 223
Duckworth, Tammy, 207
Dunlap, David, 153, 160
Dupré, Judith, 150, 151, 152
Durant, Sam, 186

Efimenko, Alexandra, 167–168
El-Gamal, Sharif, 115
Empire State Building (NYC), 34, 133, 144
Empty Sky, memorial (Jamroz and Schwartz, Jersey City, NJ), 37–38
End of Serenity, The, photograph (McClatchey), 66
Engler, Elise, 202
Equal Justice Initiative (EJI): Community Remembrance Project of, 226–228, 253; Community Soil Collection Project of, 228–231; goals of, 14, 224, 233, 238, 242; location of, 231, 232; *Lynching in America* report of, 226; lynching research and archive of, 18, 221–222, 226; racial terrorism definitions by, 18, 23, 223–224, 226. *See also* Legacy Museum; mass incarceration; National Memorial for Peace and Justice; Stevenson, Bryan
Erased Lynching Series, photography (Gonzales-Day), 260
Exposition Universelle of 1889 (Paris), 129
Eyes Wide Open, the Human Costs of the Iraq War, exhibit (American Friends Service Committee), 191–193, 193

Falkenberg, Dana and Zoe, 47
Fallen, installation (Hammond), 193, 195–196
Fallen Heroes Project (Reagan), 172–176, 198
Farmer, Paul, 244
FBI (Federal Bureau of Investigation), 112
Ferguson, Missouri, 240
figuration, 199–200; Black bodies in, 259–261; in lynchings visualization, 236, 258–262; as memorialization aesthetic, 12, 16, 193, 250; in 9/11 memorials, 41–42, 96–97; of post-9/11 wars, 178, 183, 193, 199–201, 210–211, 214, 218; in racist historical monuments, 2, 15. *See also* iraqimemorial.org; National Memorial for Peace and Justice; photographs; steel

Filkins, Dexter, 176–177
Filler, Martin, 58, 150, 158, 165, 169
Finch, Spencer, 92, 92–93, 93
Finkel, David, 211
Finnegan, William, 39
Fire Department of New York (FDNY), 31–32, 36–37, 101, 121, 122; emergency communications of, 109; Engine Ladder Company 10 memorial of, 37; Ladder Company 3 of, 94; merchandise of, 122
firefighters: in memorial sculptures, 41; stories of, 108, 109, 121. *See also* Fire Department of New York; 9/11
First White House of the Confederacy (Montgomery, AL), 231
Fischl, Eric, 41–42
Fleetwood, Nicole, 238
Flight 11, American Airlines, 37, 57, 94, 111
Flight 77, American Airlines, 46
Flight 93, United Airlines: absence of images from, 63; courage aboard, 74–75, 76; films about, 65, 75; 9/11 flight of, 63, 64, 65, 265; religious narratives of, 63–64, 76; victims of, 66, 69, 71, 82
Flight 93 Memorial Chapel (Friedens, PA), 66, 68
Flight 93 National Memorial (Shanksville, PA), 63–76; absence at, 65; among official sites, 13, 14, 21, 45–46, 73, 74, 76, 102; architecture, 67–71; controversies about, 67, 69; date opened of, 67; design contest for, 67, 69; design of, 56, 67, 69–73; *End of Serenity* photograph at, 65–66; gift shop of, 74, 275n71; human remains at, 46, 71; land purchased for, 67; landscape of, 21, 61, 63–65, 67, 71, 73; map of, 72; minimalism at, 72; monumentalism at, 72; National Park Service (NPS) role in, 46, 67, 70–72, 74, 111; objects in, 98–99; rural aspect of, 21, 73; as tourist attraction, 14; Tower of Voices, 69; Visitor Center of, 69, 70
Flight 175, United Airlines, 37

Floyd, George, 1, 15
Foer, Franklin, 144
Foner, Eric, 114
Former Sergeant Mike Moriarty . . . , photograph (Karady), 209–210
Foster, Norman, 148, 156
Foster + Partners, 156
Foulkrod, Patricia, 208–209, 285n49
432 Park (NYC), 144, 281n33
Four World Trade Center, 51, 154; date opened, 156; design of, 156
Fox News, 79
Foye, Patrick J, 160
Freedom Rides Museum (Montgomery, AL), 231
Freeman, John Craig, 202
Fresh Kills Landfill (Staten Island), 30, 31, 100, 277–278n41
Frost, Laura, 107–108, 114
Fuller, Mark, 45

Gallagher, Mike, 217
Gambale, Giovanna, 98, 99
Gartenburg, James, 109
Gaudi, Antoni, 162
Ghaib, Ghassan, 187
gift shops, *See* Flight 93 National Memorial; Legacy Museum; National September 11 Museum
Gilbertson, Ashley, 173, 176–177, 182
Glick, Jeremy, 65
Global War on Terror: artistic responses to, 173–177, 204–206; branding as, 17, 180; cost of, 217; drone warfare in, 7, 17, 180, 181; memorialization issues, 177–178, 180–181; memory projects of, 23, 217; as national defense, 6; during Obama Administration, 7; Pakistan, Yemen, Syria and Afghanistan in, 7, 8, 17, 180, 206; timeline challenge of, 16, 177–180, 180, 181–182. *See also* Abu Ghraib prison; Iraq War; long war; Obama, Barack; post-9/11 wars; War in Afghanistan

Global War on Terrorism Memorial (National Mall): Commemorative Works Act exemption of, 181–182; 216; planning for, 13, 23, 181; timeline challenge of, 217
Global War on Terror Memorial (Columbus/Fort Benning, GA), 216
Godfrey, Mark, 193
Goldberger, Paul, 142, 144, 162, 163
Goldhagen, Sarah Williams, 148, 152–154, 162, 169–170
Gonzales-Day, Ken, 260
Google Earth, 131
Gopnik, Adam, 14, 56, 84
Gordon, Avery, 5
Gourevitch, Philip, 182
Graham, Kevin and Jeffrey, 172, 174
Graham, Stephen, 142
Grand Central Station (NYC), 162
Grandcolas, Laura, 109
Grandin, Greg, 179
Gravity Media, 120
Greenfield, Alice, 139
Greengrass, Paul, 65, 75
Greenwald, Alice M., 83, 111, 114
Ground Truth, The, film (Foulkrod), 208–209
Ground Zero (2001+ NYC): absence at, 51–63; among official sites, 15, 21–22, 31, 63; architecture, 5, 15, 22, 25, 31, 53, 134–145; death counts at, 30, 51; debris from, 30, 100; design competitions for, 51–53; dust at, 29–31; footprints of twin towers at, 21, 26, 42, 53–54, 56, 83, 84, 89, 91, 92, 106, 124–125; human remains recovered at, 100; Last Column removal from, 5; master plan for, 51–53, 55, 91–92, 133, 149–151, 169; material remains and presence at, 100–105; post-9/11 wars at, 8; proximity to, 37, 45, 114, 115; as publicly funded private venture, 15, 158; rebuilding at, 5, 8, 15, 22, 29, 51, 82–83, 134–136, 140, 143, 150, 160, 162–163, 167, 170, 171; rebuilding cost of, 22; recovery mission at, 77; as sacred, 28, 33, 42, 45, 56, 59, 69, 76, 82, 114, 114–115, 120, 159, 169; security at, 60; unbuilt proposals for, 199; urban landscape of, 136, 139, 149, 156, 158, 159; as visitor destination, 83; World Trade Center Memorial Competition, 198–199. *See also* Arad, Michael; Chief Medical Examiner, Office of; DNA identification; Fresh Kills Landfill; Oculus; One World Trade Center; Port Authority of New York and New Jersey; Silverstein, Larry; skyscrapers; steel
Guantánamo Bay prison (Cuba), 7, 8, 17, 113, 180, 219
Guardian, 162
Guided by Justice, sculpture (King), 256–257
Gulf War, 183
Gulf War Memorial (Cumberland, Md.), 216
Gun Violence Memorial Project (Willis Thomas / MASS Design), 258

Hammond, Jane, 193, 195–196
Hank Williams Museum, 231
Hanlon, Brian, 41
Hart, Bob, 37
Heaton, Jeff, 189
Heisler, Todd, 153
Heitz, Kaily, 231, 241
Hennes, Tom, 116
heroes and heroism, 4, 31–32, 36, 55, 57, 64–65, 73, 74–76, 82, 93, 100, 120, 134, 191, 214, 245–246. *See also* Fallen Heroes Project
Heyer, Heather, 15
hijackers, 11, 64, 65, 71, 75, 98, 111, 112, 278n61
Hill, Mike, 115
Hinton, Anthony Ray, 228, 230, 239
Hite, Katherine, 239

Holder, Eric, 117
Holocaust, 12, 113, 224
Holocaust Memorial (Berlin), 12, 63, 251
Homage to al-Mutanabbi Street, dafatir (Ghaib), 187–188
Hudson Yards (NYC), 146, 148, 158
Hugs for Our Soldiers, 211
human rights discourse, 18, 113–114, 145, 208, 219, 224, 238, 263; in Latin America, 12, 17–18, 263
Hussein, Saddam, 179, 183
Huxtable, Ada Louise, 139, 160
Huyssen, Andreas, 126

Immerwahr, Daniel, 19
Imperial War Museum (London), 186, 193
Institute of Contemporary Art (London), 186
International Freedom Center (IFC), 83, 85, 114
iraqimemorial.org, 198–204
Iraq Veterans Against the War, 208
Iraq War: artistic responses to, 16, 113, 172–177, 183–217, 186–206; beginning of, 7, 179–180; costs of, 20, 178; end of US involvement in, 180; erasure and visibility of, 16, 23, 177–178, 182–206; Falluja in, 176, 179; 9/11 in justifying narrative for, 7, 8, 17, 35–36, 111, 113, 179–180; as quagmire, 11; wounded veterans of, 23, 178, 186, 196–198, 206–216. *See also* Bush, George W.; Global War on Terror; long war; post-9/11 wars; War in Afghanistan
Isay, Dave, 115
ISIS (Islamic State of Iraq and Syria), 35, 114, 179, 180
Islamophobia, 115
Ivey, Robert, 145

Jackson, Kuntrell, 239
Jamroz, Jessica, 37
Janssen, Peter and Ward, 199

January 6th Insurrection, 2, 4, 16, 207, 218, 220, 225, 265–266
Jim Crow, 237, 262
John F. Kennedy International Airport (NYC), Hangar 17 at, 31, 32
Jordan, John W., 65
Judd, Donald, 250
Just Mercy (Stevenson), 232; film, 232

Kamardinova, Gavkharoy, 102
Kandell, Steve and Shari, 102, 125, 278n46
Kane, Howard Lee, 102
Kaplan, Caren, 131
Karady, Jennifer, 209–210
Karaloannoglou, Athanasia, 199
Kasman, Keith, 46
Kathy Mazza Memorial Park (Oyster Bay, NY), 37
Kennicott, Philip, 120, 232, 232–233
Kimmelman, Michael, 55, 59, 61, 152, 153, 160, 161, 250
King, Dana, 256–257
King, Martin Luther, Jr., 231
Kitgali Genocide Memorial, 244
Klein, Lauren, 119
Korean War Memorial, 243

Lafayette Crosses, memorial (Heaton, Clark and MacMichael, Hillside, CA), 189–190, 191
Landsberg, Alison, 233–234, 236
Lawrence, Vanessa, 109
Layman Design, 83, 106
Lee, Robert E., 226
Legacy Museum (Montgomery, AL): as activist museum, 4, 24, 128, 223, 233–234, 238–239, 240, 254, 267; architecture of, 5, 233; authenticity in, 232; Community Soil Collection Project in, 204, 228–231; complicity engagement in, 234–235, 240–241; cost of, 232; date opened of, 4, 14, 23, 231, 242; difficult content in, 236, 237; digital media in, 236;

Legacy Museum (*cont.*)
exhibition design of, 254; family contexts in, 224–225, 235, 236, 238; gift shop of, 242; goals of, 232, 233–234, 240; as history museum, 233–234, 240; interactive technologies in, 238–239; mass incarceration at, 223–224, 232–233, 236, 238–240, 242; in memorialization context of 9/11, 223–224, 225, 228, 232, 233, 234–235, 236–237; as memory museum, 223, 233–234, 240; memory witnessing in, 235–236; Montgomery bus boycott in, 237; narrative eras in, 233–234, 236–238, 262–263; past and present in, 233–234, 235–236; photographs in, 236, 237, 237–238; prison visiting booth at, 238–240; segregation in, 224, 232, 233, 236–238, 242, 264; slavery in, 223, 223–227, 229, 232–236, 238, 240, 242, 243; storytelling in, 233, 238–239; subjective position of visitors in, 235–236; tourism and, 14, 231–232; trauma engagement in, 240–242. *See also* lynchings; mass incarceration; Montgomery (Alabama)
Legends Hospitality, 280n1, 280n4
Leitz, Lisa, 207–208
Lepore, Jill, 2–3
Libeskind, Daniel: master plan (Memory Foundations) for Ground Zero of, 52–53, 55, 91–92, 133, 149–151, 169; studio of, 42
Lin, Maya, 48, 52, 55, 139
Lincoln Memorial (National Mall), 13, 268
Local Projects, 57, 83, 87, 108, 110, 115, 233
Logan Airport 9/11 Memorial, Boston (Moskow Linn), 37
long war: costs of, 182–183; definitions of, 177, 179, 216; global war on terror as, 177, 180; memorialization issues of, 180; peace movement veterans in, 208; post-9/11 wars as, 17, 177, 178–180;

prolongation of, 179, 182; undeclared wars as, 208. *See also* Global War on Terror; Iraq War; post-9/11 wars; War in Afghanistan
Lopez, Linda, 98
Lot's Tribe, installation (Magrath), 199–200
Lower Manhattan Development Corporation (LMDC), 52, 55, 85, 139, 149
lynchings: activist memorialization of, 4, 6, 15; collective grieving and, 5; and Community Remembrance Project (EJI), 227–228; and Community Soil Collection Project (EJI), 228; counting of, 23, 204, 223–225, 226, 242–243, 244, 246; definitional distinctions of, 226; in memory boom, 243–244; multidirectional memory and, 4, 18, 23, 219, 220; photographs of, 236, 258, 260; as racial terrorism, 17, 18, 223, 226, 236, 244, 263; in reckoning of national identity, 24, 220, 223, 232, 234–235, 244, 263; as spectacles, 225, 229–230, 252, 262; victims of, 4, 18, 220, 223, 228–229, 236–237, 242–243, 246–250, 260, 262; visualization of, 204, 260–261. *See also* Equal Justice Initiative (EJI); Legacy Museum; National Memorial for Peace and Justice; Stevenson, Bryan; visitor experience
Lyon train station (Calatrava), 162

MacMichael, Lynn, 189
Madres of the Plaza de Mayo, 263
Magrath, Michael, 199–200
Maki, Fumihiko, 156
Marine Wedding, photograph (Berman), 214–216
Marked for Life, proposal (Karaloannoglou), 199
Marriott (Vista International) Hotel, 98
Martin, Reinhold, 146, 159, 169
Mascherino, Alphonse, Rev., 65

MASS Design Group, 145, 228, 244–249, 253, 258–261, 261
mass incarceration, 14, 18, 23, 219, 223, 224, 231–232, 236, 238, 240, 254, 258, 262–264, 268
McClatchy, Val, 65
McClintock, Tom, 181–182
McKee, Bradford, 48
McPherson, Vanzetta, 230
McQueen, Steve, 193
Memoria e Luce, memorial (Daniel Libeskind Studio, Padua, Italy), 42
memorialization: as activist, 4, 14–16; aesthetic strategies in, 12, 15, 37, 55, 56, 250, 261; at authentic sites, 27–28, 45–46, 51, 76, 102; of Confederacy, 14–15, 27; excess of, 21, 26–27, 36, 45, 76, 217, 219, 225; Global War on Terror and, 172–178, 180–182; memory boom and, 12–16; naming in, 15, 48, 57; as narration, 4, 14–16, 18, 21, 27; as nationalism, 4–5, 21; of 9/11 memory, 2, 7, 21, 23, 26–31, 35–36, 44–45, 51–52, 61, 67, 76, 102, 134, 136, 219, 223, 224, 225; in post-9/11 era, 1–7, 16, 21, 27; of post-9/11 wars, 23, 173–182, 193–202; of terrorism victims, 36, 223–225, 250, 263–264; as tourism, 14. *See also* steel
Memorial to the Iraq War, exhibit (Institute of Contemporary Art, London), 186
memory: as activist, 14–16, 18, 128, 220, 234, 254, 262, 264; architecture and design of, 5, 12, 15–16, 21, 84–85, 87, 110, 170, 244, 244–254; as collective, 2, 5, 12, 115–120; commodification of, 126–127; competitive issues of, 12–16, 177–178; as consumerism, 14, 123, 126–128, 168; countervisual strategies of, 178, 186, 193; as cultural force in US identity, 2, 12, 15–16, 220, 243–244, 263; in defining terrorism, 16–18, 17; digital media in collective memory, 22, 115–120; erasure and visibility of, 177–178, 182–188, 193, 196–198, 211–213, 216, 223, 231; global

cultural force of, 11–12, 16, 224, 263; Global War on Terror and, 172–178, 180–182, 217; materiality in service of, 126–127; as memory boom, 11–18, 181, 243, 263; as multidirectional, 12–13, 13; of 9/11 and its effects, 1–6, 8, 12, 13–16, 18, 20–24, 26–29, 31–32, 35–36, 42–43, 45–46, 51, 52, 67, 73, 76, 84–85, 93, 103, 117, 134, 165, 219; politics of, 1–11, 14, 179, 180, 186; projects at end of post-9/11 era, 267–268; projects of post-9/11 wars, 178, 179, 186–216; proliferation of, 11–14, 21; of racial terror, 221–264; as redefining terrorism, 16–17, 16–18; responses to terrorism and, 5; soil as, 231, 253; as tourism, 14; visibility politics and, 186–216. *See also* memorialization; minimalism
Meyer, Danny, 85
Miller, Billy, 176–177
Milwaukee Art Museum (Calatrava), 162, 165
minimalism: Corten steel in, 248; as memorialization aesthetic, 12, 15, 55, 56, 250, 261; in 9/11 memorials, 37, 55, 56; in skyscraper designs, 156. *See also* Arad, Michael; Flight 93 National Memorial (Shanksville, PA); Four World Trade Center. Legacy Museum; National September 11 Memorial (NYC); Vietnam Veterans Memorial
Minneapolis Police Department, 1
Mirzoeff, Nicholas, 186
Molotch, Harvey, 113
Moneyland, book (Bullough), 143
Montebello, Philippe de, 33
Montgomery (Alabama): Anthony Crawford plaque in, 228; Black women's activism in, 258; bus boycott in, 231, 237, 256, 258; civil rights tourism in, 231; Confederate memorial landscape of, 226–227; enslaved population (1860) of, 227; in Legacy Museum, 237, 256, 258;

Montgomery (*cont.*)
  Legacy Museum in, 4, 14, 23, 220, 231, 232, 237; lynching of John Temple in, 230; mayors of, 231–232; National Memorial for Peace and Justice in, 4, 12, 14, 23, 220, 221, 231, 245, 253; slave market markers in, 227; warehouses for enslaved people in, 232. *See also* Equal Justice Initiative (EJI); Legacy Museum; National Memorial for Peace and Justice
monument removals: Christopher Columbus, 1; Confederate and racist landscape of, 1, 2, 6, 13, 15–16, 27, 35, 224, 226–227, 244, 253–254, 267; in reckoning of national identity, 1–2, 15–16, 16, 21
Moriarity, Mike and Randi, 209–210
Morrison, Toni, 254
Moskow Linn, 37
Moynihan Train Hall, 166–167
Murdoch, Paul, 72, 73
Murdoch, Paul and Milena, 67, 71
Murphy, Michael, 244–246, 248, 253, 254, 262, 286n33
Muschamp, Herbert, 160
Museum of Modern Art / PS1 (New York), 186
museums: as activist museums, 23, 24, 220, 223, 233, 240–242, 267–268; algorithms in, 57, 118–119; authenticity of place in, 27, 45–46, 83, 95, 127, 232; of civil rights movement, 14, 231; complicity engagement in, 223, 234–235, 240–241; goals of, 22, 82, 232; as history museums, 22, 82, 98, 116–118, 120, 232–235; memorial-historical conflict in, 82–83, 114, 233–234, 262–263; as memorial museums, 22, 112, 117, 121, 122, 127, 223; as memory museums, 11, 14, 82, 103, 117, 120, 126, 234, 240–242; post-9/11 wars in, 186, 193–196, 205, 216; storytelling in, 83, 93, 102, 115–118, 135, 233, 236–238; trauma engagement at, 93, 112–113, 125, 240–242. *See also* Legacy Museum; National September 11 Museum (NYC)

NAACP, 223, 226
Nadar (Gaspard-Félix Tournachon), 129
Napoli, Paul, 126
National Defense University, 180
National Desert Storm and Desert Shield Memorial, 13
National Guard, 7, 173, 182, 183, 208, 210, 218
national identity: as comfort culture, 19–20; defining factors of, 8; at end of post-9/11 era, 8, 18; impact of terrorism on, 219, 220; as innocence, 19, 26, 35, 50, 64, 76, 97, 125, 127, 223, 234, 238, 262, 264; as isolationist, 12; post-9/11 memory conflicts of, 2, 24, 26, 27, 50, 64, 208, 267; role of memory in, 12, 223. *See also* American exceptionalism; lynchings
National Infantry Museum, 216
National Liberty Memorial (National Mall Liberty Fund), 13, 217
National Mall, 13, 16, 23, 61, 181, 216–217, 243
National Memorial for Peace and Justice (Montgomery, AL), 242–268; as activism, 15, 223, 244, 245, 246, 254–255, 261, 267, 268; among civil rights tourist sites, 231; among EJI projects, 231, 242–243; among memory boom sites, 243; architectural design of, 244–259; architectural principles in, 245; Community Soil Collection Project (EJI) in, 3, 228, 242, 267; complicity engagement in, 243–244, 252–254, 254; Confederate racist landscape and, 6, 15, 244, 253, 254; cost of, 232; counting dead strategies of, 204, 246, 252; date opened of, 4, 14, 23, 221, 242; design of,

12, 42, 145, 221–222, 242–251; figurative art in, 12, 255–256; global influences in, 244–244; gravity in, 260, 261–262; in human rights discourse, 263; lynching as racial terror at, 15, 223, 225, 262; as lynching memorial, 15, 222; markers (duplicate) in, 254–256, 262; markers (steel) in, 251, 261–262, 263, 267; in memorialization context of 9/11, 223–224, 224, 225–226, 243, 253–254, 261–262; memorialization spectrum and, 223; in memory boom, 243; minimalism in, 245, 250; naming in, 15, 241–243, 246–248, 250, 254; *Nkyinkyim Installation* at, 255–256, 262, 267, 268; in post-9/11 era, 225; scale of, 250–251, 251; as tourist destination, 14

National Museum of African American History and Culture (WDC): 242; date opened of, 14, 243

National Native American Veterans Memorial (National Mall), 213, 217

National 9/11 Pentagon Memorial (Arlington, VA), 45–51; among official sites, 13, 21, 28, 45–46, 82, 102, 106, 121; architects of, 46; as authentic site, 45–46; date opened of, 46; design of, 21, 46, 49–50; inaccessibility of, 50; naming in, 46–48; site of, 50–51

National Park Service (NPS), 67, 84. *See also* Flight 93 National Memorial

National Register of Historic Places, 84

National Security Archive, 184

National September 11 Memorial (NYC), 25–26, 51–63; absence at, 25, 51, 53, 100; architectural memory of, 61; architecture, 52–55, 58, 61; as authentic site, 26; design contest of, 52–53; gravity at, 25; Ground Zero site of, 51–53; human remains in, 46; meaningful adjacencies in, 57; Memorial Glade at, 61–62; minimalism at, 55; naming at, 57–58; national innocence at, 26; picture tak-

ing at, 62–63; pools of, 21, 25–26, 53–56, 58, 59, 63, 85, 163; as primary 9/11 memorial, 26; scale of, 56–57; security at, 51, 53–55, 60; tourism at, 59, 61; use restrictions at, 59–60

National September 11 Museum (NYC), 77–128; absence in, 22, 85, 89, 94, 100, 103, 124, 127; algorithms in, 57, 118–119; among official sites, 13, 14, 21, 82, 102; archeological aspects of, 22, 91, 93, 105; architectural designs for, 84–85, 87, 89, 92, 106; architectural principles in, 87; artists exhibitions in, 41; audio in, 86, 278–279n41; authenticity at, 91–92; bin Laden brick in, 79–82, 107, 113; collective memory in, 115–120; as commercial enterprise, 46, 84, 121, 126; complicity engagement in, 234–235; composite debris in, 105; content warnings in, 106; cost of, 83; date opened of, 77, 83; design of, 31, 84; digital media in, 22, 35, 57, 77, 83, 86, 104–105, 108, 115–120; entrance fee, 84; exhibition designers of, 83; exhibition principles of, 83–84; footprints of twin towers in, 89, 90, 91–92, 125; Foundation Hall in, 77, 78, 82, 87, 90, 93, 106, 118; gift shop of, 14, 22, 34, 84, 86, 120–127, 170, 242; goals of, 22, 82, 102, 103, 115; hijackers in, 112; historical exhibition in, 22, 106, 112, 117; human remains in, 102; impact steel in, 87, 92, 94–97; Islamophobia in, 111, 113, 120; Last Column in, 77–79, 90, 106–107, 116; logo of, 123; materiality memory and, 122, 124–125, 127; materiality transformation and, 79; material remains and presence at, 100–105; meaningful adjacencies in, 118–119; memorial gallery in, 83, 89, 92, 102–104; as memorial museum, 22; memorial quilts in, 92; as memory and historical museum, 103, 120; naming at, 102, 118–119;

National September 11 Museum (*cont.*) narrating the day of, 106, 111–114; nationalist story of, 22; personal objects at, 97–100; photographs in, 22, 102–105, 106, 107–108, 112; pools in, 83, 85, 89; proposal and development of, 82–83; *Rendering the Unthinkable: Artists Respond to 9/11*, exhibition, 41; ribbon walkway in, 87, 90–92; *The Rise of al-Qaeda* in, 112; scale at, 77–78, 91; security at, 60, 84–85, 121; shoes in, 97, 97–98, 98, 176, 191; slurry wall in, 84, 87, 92, 93, 118; storytelling at, 29, 79, 81, 94, 97, 102–105, 115, 119; survivor objects in, 93–100; survivors' stairs in, 87; Timescape in, 118–119; Tribute Walkway in, 92, 94; tridents in, 34, 85–86, 88; twin towers merchandise in, 124–125; visitor statistics at, 83; voids in, 83, 85, 89; witness experience at, 116–119; World Trade Center 1993 bombing at, 102

Nelson Byrd Woltz Landscape Architects, 71

New York Daily News, 102

New Yorker, 39, 84, 170, 232

New York Police Department (NYPD), 32, 60, 75, 77, 84, 101, 121, 153–154; merchandise of, 101, 122. *See also* One World Trade Center

New York Post, 63, 121, 126, 151

New York State Museum (Albany), 31

New York Times, 33, 55, 103, 111, 133, 143, 152, 153, 160, 180n1, 207, 245, 250

9/11: authenticity in sites of, 27–28, 45–46, 48, 49, 50, 51, 53, 83, 87, 95, 127; debris relocation from, 30, 91, 100, 105, 277–278n41; dust of, 29–30, 93, 100, 108, 278–279n41; exceptionalist narrative of, 4, 8, 10, 27–29, 51, 56, 74, 134; rescue and recovery workers of, 20, 41, 61, 77, 84, 106, 126; as shaping event, 5–8, 12–13, 20, 36, 51. *See also* Flight 93 National Memorial; Ground Zero (2001+ NYC); National 9/11 Pentagon Memorial (Arlington, VA); National September 11 Memorial (NYC); National September 11 Museum (NYC); 9/11 memorials; steel

9/11 Memorial (Fuller, Palm Beach Gardens, FL), 27, 45

9/11 memorials, 35–51; at airports, 37–38; around New York harbor, 37, 39; controversies over, 39, 41; excess of, 21, 26–27, 45, 76, 219, 225; figurative statues in, 41; of first responders, 61–62; kitsch merchandise of, 121; in New Jersey, 37, 39, 41; official sites of, 21, 22, 45; proliferation of, 6, 13–14, 21, 26–29, 35–36, 45, 76, 178, 223, 254, 267; registry of, 35; tristate concentration of, 36. *See also* steel

9/11 Tiles for America, memorial (NYC), 37

Nkyinkyim Installation, sculpture (Akoto-Bamfo), 255–256

Nobel, Philip, 54

Nocera, Joe, 154, 156

Noel, Joshua, 72

Nouvel, Jean, 145

Obama, Barack: drone warfare use by, 7, 17, 180, 181; election of, 7, 180, 224, 233; Global War on Terror of, 7, 180; Iraq War policies of, 180; in National September 11 Museum (NYC), 74; post-9/11 wars of, 3, 11, 17; troop surge under, 182. *See also* Guantánamo Bay prison

Occupy Wall Street, 3, 7, 60

Oculus (World Trade Center Transportation Hub, NYC), 159–170; cathedral-like features of, 22, 159, 160–161, 164, 168–169; commission of, 159–160; cost of, 135, 159, 161, 165, 166; criticism of, 159–163, 165–169; date opened of, 160; design of, 14, 52, 135, 159–164; kitsch elements of, 169; 9/11 memory at, 14, 52,

165, 167, 168, 170; picture taking at, 164, 170; as shopping mall, 14, 60, 160, 167, 169, 170; social media influence at, 170; as tourist site, 14, 161, 164, 167, 170; as transportation hub, 60, 135, 162–164, 165
Oklahoma City bombing, 16, 285n3
Oklahoma City National Memorial and Museum, 48, 49, 56, 112, 243, 250, 269, 278n48
One57 (NYC), 144
1,000 Drones—A Participatory Memorial, The, installation (DeLappe), 204–206
O'Neill, Luke, 126
One World Observatory (NYC), 129–133, 280n1, 280n4
One World Trade Center, 146–159; anchor tenant in, 151, 154, 156, 157; architectural design of, 146, 149–154; cost of, 135; criticism of, 16, 148, 150, 152–154; date opened of, 153; digital media in, 131–132; elevator (Sky Pod), 129, 130; as Freedom Tower, 33, 135, 149–151, 154; height, 129, 151; kitsch merchandise of, 153; naming as, 132, 151; NYPD security redesign of, 153–154; public sector tenants in, 154; signature address of, 151. *See also* One World Observatory (NYC)
Ong, Aihwa, 142
Ong, Betty, 111
Operation Iraqi Freedom, 210
Ouroussoff, Nicolai, 154

Paliewicz, Nicholas, 94
Palmer, Orjo, 109
Park 51 Project (NYC), 115
Parks, Rosa, 231, 256
Partners in Health, 244
Passiak, Amy, 32
Pataki, George, 53, 114, 117, 149
Patriot Act, 3, 8, 113, 114, 144–145
Peltier, Heidi, 179
Penn Station (NYC), 160, 166

Pentagon: bin Laden burial by, 81; as crash site and target, 106, 137; 9/11 steel reuse project of, 34; policy on coffin images of, 184, 188; war dead archive of, 184. *See also* National 9/11 Pentagon Memorial
Permasteelisa, 42
Petronas Towers (Kuala Lumpur), 142
Pfeifer, Joseph W., 31
photographs: censorship of, 107–108, 183–185, 186; by embedded photojournalist, 173; of enslaved people, 236; of lynchings, 236, 258, 260; from 9/11 events, 65–66; at 9/11 memorial, 63; of post-9/11 wars, 183, 209; of racial terror, 236; of torture, 219; and tourists, 21, 62–63, 164, 170, 172, 261; of traumatic memory, 209; of war dead, 172, 173, 176, 184–185, 198, 202; of wounded veterans, 209–210, 212, 214–216
Pierce, Lori, 231, 241
police: brutality and racial reckonings of, 1, 2, 4, 10, 15, 20, 24, 60, 207, 221, 222, 240, 258, 263, 266–267; departments as 9/11 repositories, 31; and George Floyd, 1, 15; in memorial sculptures, 41; and 9/11 sites, 14, 84, 121; "Say Their Names" and, 15, 267. *See also* heroes and heroism; January 6th Insurrection; National September 11 Memorial; National September 11 Museum; New York Police Department; 9/11; One World Trade Center; Port Authority of New York and New Jersey
Poole, Ross, 278n56
Port Authority of New York and New Jersey, 22, 31, 137, 152, 158, 180n1; death counts of, 32; Freedom Tower project of, 140; Ground Zero ownership of, 140; mandate of, 148; naming of One World Trade Center and, 151; Oculus (World Trade Center Transportation Hub) project of, 159–160, 165, 166;

Port Authority (*cont.*)
  office locations of, 135, 154; PATH trains of, 84, 89, 159, 160, 164, 166; police department of, 60, 101, 121; steel distribution program of, 31, 34, 44, 52; toll increase of, 156. *See also* Kathy Mazza Memorial Park
Portraits of Courage, book (Bush), 212–214
post-9/11 era: antiwar art projects of, 186; beginning of, 2; definition of, 2, 4, 5, 6–10, 28–29; as disruption, 29, 76; end of, 5, 10, 14, 15, 16–20, 208, 223, 225, 263–264, 266–267; memorials as meaning in, 14, 27, 120, 127, 223; politics of memory in, 1–6. *See also* American exceptionalism
post-9/11 wars: artistic responses to, 23, 172–178, 186, 186–206, 206–216, 212; costs of, 7, 8; counting the wounded of, 178, 186, 196–198; death cataloguing of, 187; defined as, 17–18, 177; erasure issues of, 11, 23, 178, 182–186, 212; images in networked culture of, 185; images of death honors from, 183–184; inclusive theaters of, 8, 18, 180; memorialization issues of, 18, 35, 177–178, 180–181, 216–219; trauma and, 23, 176–178, 206, 208–209, 212, 218; US veterans of, 20, 23, 79, 178, 182, 183–184, 186, 187, 190, 190–191, 206–220, 218–219; visibility as political mode of, 185–186; volunteer armies of, 7, 173, 182, 218; wounded veterans issues of, 23, 178, 206, 206–216. *See also* Bush, George W.; drone warfare; Global War on Terror; Iraq war; long war; Obama, Barack; War in Afghanistan
Power at Ground Zero, book (Sagalyn), 139
Prince, Emily, 196–198
Proposal; for Iraq War Memorial (Durant), 186
Purple Hearts, book (Berman), 214
Putin, Vladimir, 39

Queen and Country, artwork (McQueen, Imperial War Museum), 193
Quinn, Christine, 117

Racism, 1, 14, 20, 223, 254, 258
Raise Up, sculpture (H. W. Thomas), 258–259
Rambusch, Viggo Bech, 37
Ramirez, Jan Seidler, 99, 103
Reagan, Michael, 172–175, 211
Recovering Equilibrium, memorial (Krivanek and Breaux, Los Angeles International Airport), 38–39
Reed, Steven, 232
Reflect, sculpture (Satow, Rosemead, CA), 42, 44
Reflecting Absence, (Arad and Walker, 9/11 Memorial, NYC), 53
Rhodes, Ben, 10–11
Richardson, Heather Clark, 266
Riches, Jim and Jimmy, 121
Ricks, Alan, 244
Riley, Alexander T., 64
Rise of al-Qaeda, The, exhibit (National September 11 Museum), 112
Rising, The, memorial (Schwartz, Valhalla, NY), 37
Rockefeller Center, 41
Rodriguez, Michael "Rod," 217
Rogers, Richard, 156
Rogers, Rob, 2, 3
Rogers Stirk Harbour + Partners (RSHP), 156
Rosa Parks Museum (Montgomery, AL), 231
Rosenblatt, Adam, 263
Rothberg, Michael, 12–13
Roy, Ananya, 281n36
Rumsfeld, Donald, 20, 179
Rybczynski, Witold, 25

Saffron, Inga, 69
Sagalyn, Lynne, 139

Sanneh, Sia, 224, 245, 246, 250, 251, 253, 258, 260
Saul, Stephanie, 143
Savage, Kirk, 181, 206, 211, 218–219
Savett, Noah, 42
Scherer, Christopher G., 173, 177, 211
Schilling, Dave, 162
Schwartz, Frederic, 37–38
Semper Memento (Dubin, Laguna Beach, CA), 27, 45
Senk, Sarah, 116
September 11 Memorial Garden and Trail (Athens, GA), 37
Serra, Richard, 248
Seven World Trade Center, 149, 156
Shabout, Nada, 187
Sherrill, Stephen, 187
Shoot an Iraqi, installation (Bilal), 202
Silverstein, Larry (and Properties), 33, 135, 146, 148, 149–150, 151, 152–153, 156, 158–159
Simpson, David, 199, 201
Singh, Nikhil Pal, 19, 20, 179, 219, 219–220
Skidmore Owings Merrill (SOM), 149–150, 156
Skwerek, Mark, 202
skyscrapers: construction of, 34; height as symbolism of, 152; history of, 34, 133, 142, 142–143; as oversized, 79, 138; as residential properties, 143–145; supertall, 108, 142; as targets, 137; urban landscape of, 9–10, 129–133, 143–145
Slate, 48
Snøhetta, 85, 86
social media: architecture and, 170, 283n97; image sharing on, 1, 59, 62–63, 170, 183, 222, 265; museum platforms and, 116–117
Sodaro, Amy, 112–113, 117, 119
Soldiers' Stories of Iraq and Afghanistan project/exhibit (Karady), 209–210
Sonoma Valley Museum of Art, 205
Sorkin, Michael, 134, 135, 145, 171

Souls, Joe, 228
Southern Poverty Law Center, 231
Spanish American War, 180
Speer, Albert, 154
Spielberg, Steven, 232
Springsteen, Bruce, 37
Standing Rock Indian Reservation protests, 207
Statue of Liberty, 39, 133, 152
steel: Corten, 228, 248, 251; as day of 9/11 narrative, 28–33, 79; distribution of, 21, 31, 31–32, 42; in Eiffel Tower, 129; impact steel from 9/11, 87, 92, 94–97; as modernist abstraction, 42; in modern skyscrapers, 33–34, 143; in National Memorial for Peace and Justice, 246, 251, 261; in New York City buildings, 34; in 9/11 memorialization and memorials, 21, 27–29, 28, 30, 30–35, 36, 37, 42–45, 52, 61, 77, 94–97, 106, 107, 124, 216; in Oculus ribs, 163; as symbolism, 34–35, 94; in Trump era, 33; in US economy, 33–34; in US Navy ships, 34. *See also* architecture; National September 11 Museum
Stein, Samuel, 141
Stern, Robert A. M., 145
Stevenson, Bryan: on Black women's activism, 256, 258; on complicity engagement at memorial, 253; at dedication of Anthony Crawford plaque, 228; on Deep South as memory site, 231; on enslaved majority in Montgomery (1860), 227; founding of Equal Justice Initiative (EJI) by, 224; Jackson case won before Supreme Court, 239; and *Just Mercy* film and book, 232; lynching as racial terror narrative of, 18, 224, 261–262, 264; on lynching as spectacle, 252–253; marketing by, 242; MASS Design Group and, 244–245; on memorial experience, 248, 250; on museum experience, 238;

Stevenson, Bryan (*cont.*)
in *Nkyinkyim Installation* video, 255; on post-9/11 continuities of terrorism, 225; on racial oppression eras, 23, 232, 248; on reparatory justice, 263; on sculptural figuration of slavery, 255; on Soil Collection Project of EJI, 229; on southern iconography of Confederacy, 226–227
Stewart, Jon, 61
Story, Louise, 143
StoryCorps project, 115
Strange, Todd, 231–232
Svonavec family, 67

Tea Party, 3
Tempered by Memory, sculpture (Alstine and Savett, Saratoga Springs, NY), 42–43
Temple, John, 230
terrorism: in defining post-9/11 era, 2, 4, 5, 6, 6–12, 219, 266; definition of, 4–6, 16–17, 219–220, 224–225, 262–263; as domestic-based, 5, 16, 18, 20, 225, 265–266; as foreign-based, 5, 6, 16, 18, 219, 225, 265, 266; as globalized, 6, 12, 16, 180, 181, 218–219; as Islamic-fundamentalist based, 19, 111–114, 223; in Latin American memory, 12, 17–18, 263; material transformation of, 28; in memorialist aesthetic, 33, 35, 36, 39–40, 55, 76, 82, 261–262; memory activism and, 4, 217, 220; in narrativized culture, 76, 136, 140, 219; Patriot Act and, 144; as racial terrorism, 4, 5, 6, 14, 17, 18, 23, 222–225, 229, 233, 236–237, 244, 248, 252–253, 262, 263, 268; rebuilding response to, 140–141, 165; as state-sanctioned terrorism, 12, 17, 18, 180, 263; traumatic memory and, 208; as US-based, 18, 219–220, 223, 225, 263; victims of, 31–32, 36, 181–182, 223, 225, 243. *See also* architecture; Global War on Terror; January 6th Insurrection; long war; One World Trade Center; post-9/11 wars
Theater of Operations: The Gulf Wars, 1991–2011, exhibit (Museum of Modern Art / PS1, NYC), 186
Thinc Design, 83, 87, 116, 124
This War, proposal (Awad), 201
Thomas, Hank Willis, 240, 258–259, 260
Thomas, Prince Varguese, 202
Three World Trade Center, 51, 156
Time-Warner Center (NYC), 143
To The Struggle Against World Terrorism (Tear Drop), memorial (Tsereteli, Bayonne, NJ), 39–40
trauma, 2, 12, 28, 76, 111, 208, 236, 266; architecture and, 5, 15, 93, 169; comfort objects and, 127; definition of, 55, 261; inclusive memory and, 14, 18, 20; indifference to, 184; minimalist aesthetics and, 55, 250; museum/memorial experience of, 93, 241; photojournalism and, 94, 106, 111, 112–113, 173, 176–177. *See also* post-9/11 wars
Tribeca Film Festival, 65
Trump, Donald J.: administration of, 10, 11, 17, 19, 20, 220; drone warfare of, 17; election of, 3, 7, 145; Freedom Tower opinion of, 150; impeachments of, 4; isolationism of, 10; January 6th Insurrection and, 220, 225, 265–266; Muslim ban of, 111; real estate career of, 158–159; slogans of, 33, 159; tariff war of, 33. *See also* steel
Trying to Remember the Color of the Sky on That September Morning, installation (Finch, NYC), 92, 93
Tsereteli, Zurab, 39
Tuck, Eve, 260
Tumbling Woman, sculpture (Fischl), 41
Two World Trade Center, 156

Unibail-Rodamco-Westfield, 197
United 93, film (Greengrass), 65, 75

United States Holocaust Memorial Museum (WDC), 114
US Capitol: in antiwar art, 186, 201; as target, 64, 75, 137, 266. *See also* January 6th Insurrection
US Congress, 13, 180–181
U.S./Iraq War Memorial (Freeman and Skwerek), 202
US Navy: reuse of steel by, 34; SEALs (Navy Sea, Air, and Land Teams) of, 79; veterans of, 47, 218

Van Alstine, John, 42
Veterans, US. *See* Iraq War; long war; photographs; post-9/11 wars; US Navy; Veterans for Peace; Vietnam Veterans Memorial (National Mall); War in Afghanistan
Veterans for Peace, 182, 187, 207
Vietnam Veterans Memorial (National Mall): date opened of, 13, 217; design of, 48, 55–56, 191; in memory boom, 13, 217, 243
Vietnam War, 190, 206, 207
Viñoly, Rafael, 144, 145
visitor experience: of activism, 232, 233, 234, 235, 238, 262; of aerial views, 129; of audio recordings, 64–65, 108–111; of authenticity, 50, 58, 63, 69–70, 92, 232, 239–240; design factors in, 14, 48–50, 58, 69, 72, 86–87, 92–93, 106, 113, 129, 168–169, 232–241, 245–248, 254, 256–258, 260; destination popularity in, 14, 83, 231, 242; difficult material in, 106, 236; of empathy, 93, 103, 241; of grief and horror, 25, 39, 50, 77, 93, 104, 107, 128; of historical narratives, 87, 103–104, 106–117, 128, 168, 231–234, 236–238, 242–243, 248, 256–258, 262; of human remains, 69, 101–102, 105; of incarceration, 238–240; with interactive video, 238–240; of pools, 25, 55, 57; prior knowledge of, 73, 81, 237–238; as stages of transformation, 248, 253; as subject positioning, 120, 235, 240, 244, 245, 261; of trauma, 106, 108; of victims with names, 48, 58, 73, 93, 104, 242–243, 245–248, 253, 262; as witnesses in collective memory, 22, 77, 117–118, 119–120, 235–236, 238–240, 261, 262

Wagner, Mark, 23, 31, 277n19
Walker, Peter, 53, 61, 62
Ward, Christopher, 33, 140, 282n81
War in Afghanistan, 3, 8, 11, 16, 17, 18, 20, 113; among post-9/11 wars, 17; artistic responses to, 172–177, 187, 189, 191, 193, 196–198; beginning of, 7, 179–180; costs of, 20, 178; erasure and visibility of, 16, 23, 177–178, 182–186, 189; landscape images of, 183; memory projects about, 172–178; in National September 11 Museum (NYC), 13; 9/11 justifying narrative for, 36, 179; as quagmire, 11; in US era of disruption, 2–3; volunteer armies in, 7; wounded veterans of, 23, 178, 186, 196–198, 206–216. *See also* Iraq War; long war; post-9/11 wars
Washington Monument (National Mall), 13, 150
Washington Post, 120, 232
Wells, Ida B., 223
We Shall Never Forget, memorial (Hanlon, Pennsauken, NJ), 41
Whitney Museum of American Art (NYC), 195–196, 196, 216
Who Owns the Dead?: The Science and Politics of Death at Ground Zero (Aronson), 100
Willis (Sears) Tower (Chicago), 152
Without Sanctuary: Lynching Photography in America, book/exhibit (Allen), 260
World Financial Center, 160

World Trade Center (1973–2001, WTC): 1 WTC (North Tower), 41, 57, 94, 98, 106, 107, 109, 129, 216; 2 WTC (South Tower), 98, 109; observation deck of, 131–132; 1993 bombing at, 53, 57, 82, 102; opening of, 133; twin towers' design of, 34, 54; twin towers' destruction of, 28, 84; twin towers' images in memorials of, 37; underground complex of, 84. *See also* Flight 11; One World Trade Center; steel

World Trade Center Complex: *See* Four World Trade Center; Oculus; One World Trade Center; Three World Trade Center; Two World Trade Center

World Trade Center Families for Proper Burial (WTCFPB), 277–78n41

World Trade Center Memorial Competition, 198–199

World Trade Center Transportation Hub. *See* Oculus

World War II, 2, 12

World War II Memorial, 243

World War I Memorial (National Mall), 13

Y2K, 3

Yamasaki, Minoru, 137, 138, 146

Yamnicky, John D., 47

Yang, K. Wayne, 260

Yang, Regina, 248

Yeazel, Chris, 217–218

Young, James, 33, 52, 56, 63

Zero Dark Thirty (film), 81

Ziegel, Ty and Renee, 214–216

ABOUT THE AUTHOR

MARITA STURKEN is Professor in the Department of Media, Culture, and Communication at New York University. She is the author of *Tangled Memories: The Vietnam War, the AIDS Epidemic, and the Politics of Remembering*; *Practices of Looking: An Introduction to Visual Culture* (with Lisa Cartwright); and *Tourists of History: Memory, Kitsch, and Consumerism from Oklahoma City to Ground Zero*.

www.ingramcontent.com/pod-product-compliance
Lightning Source LLC
Chambersburg PA
CBHW020353080526
44584CB00014B/1007